Walt Disney
UNCLE $CROOGE
and
Donald Duck

The Don Rosa Library

Volume Three

Treasure Under Glass

FANTAGRAPHICS BOOKS

Fantagraphics Books
7563 Lake City Way NE
Seattle, Washington 98115

Editor: David Gerstein
Supervising Editor: Gary Groth
Color Restoration: Travis Seitler and Digikore Studios
Series Designer: Tony Ong
Designers: David Gerstein and Keeli McCarthy
Production: Paul Baresh and Preston White
Associate Publisher: Eric Reynolds
Publisher: Gary Groth

The editor would like to thank: John Clark, Stein Hjelmerud, Thomas Jensen, Nancy Dejgaard Lynnerup, Dan Shane, Ken Shue, Anders Christian Sivebæk, Svein Erik Søland, David Terzopoulos, and Solveig Thime.

First Fantagraphics Books edition: June 2015

Library of Congress Control Number: 2014960294

ISBN 978-1-60699-836-6

Printed in Singapore

Table of Contents

All stories and text features written and drawn by Don Rosa except where noted.

Preface

By Don Rosa

In this volume we present the Donald and Scrooge stories I wrote and drew roughly (and I *do* draw rather roughly!) from mid-1990 to late 1991. This was the start of my work for Egmont, the major Denmark-based European publisher of Duck comics; and in the back of this book you'll find out how I got together with them for the first time!

Featured are two long adventures that share a number of things in common—"Return to Xanadu" and "War of the Wendigo" were the two first sequels to Carl Barks classics that I did for Egmont. They also seem to be structured so the reader will not *know* they are Barks sequels until about ten pages in! I think this was only a coincidence—I wasn't trying to slip something past anyone's radar. But both stories just seemed to involve plot elements with definite similarities to existing legends. I thought it would be fun to tie the Barks concepts into these legends, and perhaps amuse the readers with a surprise halfway into my tale. Not like the usual "twist ending", but more like a "twist middle"...?

Furthermore, both "Xanadu" and "Wendigo"—even though created for the European comics market, for which I now worked—had direct links to famous English language poems. But I'll explain more of that oddball idea in our "Behind the Scenes" texts. A reader might get the idea I am a poetry buff, which isn't particularly true. But I've been called much worse things, so that's okay.

There are a few other shorter gag stories in this volume. "Super Snooper Strikes Again!" is a Barks sequel that is particularly dear to me, and one of the times that I think I might have done a pretty fair job. I took Barks' great 1949 "Super Snooper" comic book superhero parody (*Walt Disney's Comics and Stories* 107) and updated it to say something about the state of modern American comics. The great classic comic characters have been supplanted in this country by violent superhero comics to such an extent that—I think—some young comic readers may not even know any other kind of comic book ever existed! Surrounded by modern grim vigilante tales, I wanted to praise the superior imagination and characterization that is found in a Barks *Donald Duck* story!!!

In so doing, alas, I first encountered the *hazards* of working on the international scene. In certain European editions of my "Super Snooper" sequel, some local editors or translators decided to rewrite my script and remove all mention of my story *being* a sequel! Gone from the nephews' dialogue were memories of "when this had all happened before." As a result, it looked like I was shamelessly *swiping* Barks' whole "Super Snooper" idea instead of paying homage to the original! Some Barks fans complained about that, and I don't blame them. My original intent, of course, is on display here.

In fact, *all* of the stories in this book look more like I intended than in the past! The Fantagraphics editorial team has spruced up the colors for this edition, restoring almost all of my original intentions to this material for the first time so completely and totally. I'm not always proud of my needlessly detailed art; but I think our title story this time—"Treasure Under Glass"—might be one of the best-drawn, most visually interesting stories I ever did, and now it's colored so beautifully that I'm doubly proud.

Go to the Don Rosa and Fantagraphics Facebook pages for further interesting features. There's always more to say about this era!!! •

The Stories

THE MASTER LANDSCAPIST
Non-Rosa cover by Bob Foster (layout) and Jukka Murtosaari (final art) from *Donald Duck Adventures* [series II] 22, March 1992. Color by Anthony Tollin and Digikore Studios.

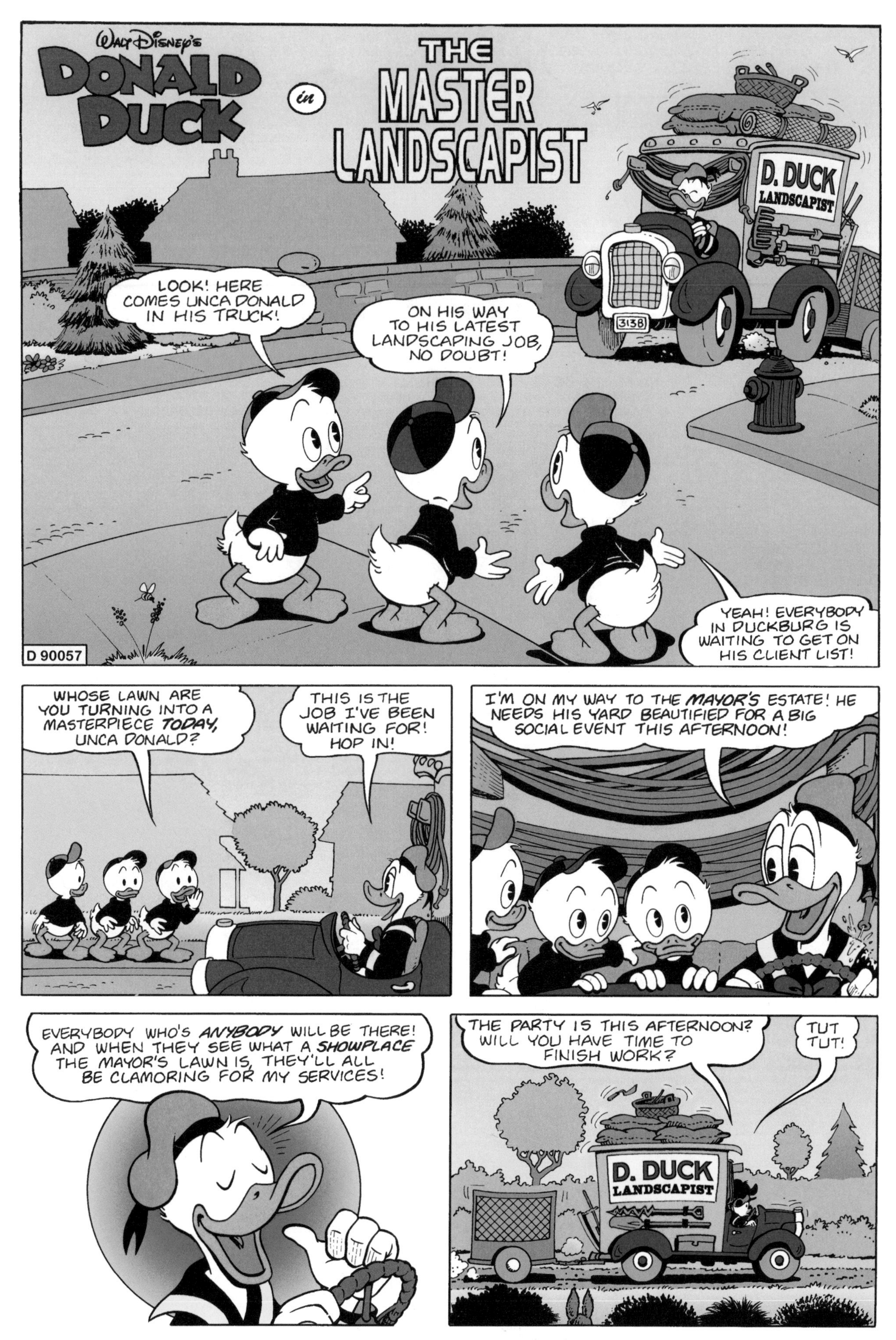
WALT DISNEY'S
DONALD DUCK
in
THE MASTER LANDSCAPIST
D. DUCK LANDSCAPIST
3138
LOOK! HERE COMES UNCA DONALD IN HIS TRUCK!
ON HIS WAY TO HIS LATEST LANDSCAPING JOB, NO DOUBT!
YEAH! EVERYBODY IN DUCKBURG IS WAITING TO GET ON HIS CLIENT LIST!
D 90057
WHOSE LAWN ARE YOU TURNING INTO A MASTERPIECE TODAY, UNCA DONALD?
THIS IS THE JOB I'VE BEEN WAITING FOR! HOP IN!
I'M ON MY WAY TO THE MAYOR'S ESTATE! HE NEEDS HIS YARD BEAUTIFIED FOR A BIG SOCIAL EVENT THIS AFTERNOON!
EVERYBODY WHO'S ANYBODY WILL BE THERE! AND WHEN THEY SEE WHAT A SHOWPLACE THE MAYOR'S LAWN IS, THEY'LL ALL BE CLAMORING FOR MY SERVICES!
THE PARTY IS THIS AFTERNOON? WILL YOU HAVE TIME TO FINISH WORK?
TUT TUT!
D. DUCK LANDSCAPIST

MY LANDSCAPING METHODS ARE THE QUICKEST BECAUSE THEY'RE THE NEWEST! AND I SHOULD KNOW...
I MADE THEM UP MYSELF, JUST LAST WEEK!
THERE'S THE MAYOR'S ESTATE NOW!
WOW! SOME SPREAD!
SHORTLY--
WE'RE SO PLEASED YOU COULD HELP US ON SUCH SHORT NOTICE, MR. DUCK!
YES, WE WANT OUR YARD TO BE PERFECT WHEN OUR GUESTS ARRIVE FOR OUR FOX HUNT!
A HIGH SOCIETY FOX HUNT? SO, THAT'S WHAT YOU'RE HOLDING!
YES! WE STAGE THE BEST FOX HUNTS AROUND!
IT'S EVEN A PLEASURE FOR THE FOX!
LET ME SHOW YOU WHAT NEEDS TO BE DONE!
THAT'S QUITE A CAT, MRS. MAYOR!
YES...
ZZZ!
BUT GRETCHEN IS GETTING OLD AND NEARSIGHTED! SHE WAS QUITE A MOUSER IN HER YOUTH!
GROWL!
ZZ PFT! Z...
THERE YOU HAVE IT, MR. DUCK!
Ah, YES! THE CANVAS FOR MY ARTISTRY! THE CLAY FOR MY GIFTED FINGERS!
D DUCK

OUT ON THE CROQUET LAWN THERE ARE TWO TREES NEEDING TRIMMING, AND A ROSE VINE THAT NEEDS TRAINING!
CHECK!
THE KOI POND IS A MESS, ALL CHOKED WITH ALGAE! AND THAT NEARBY BUSH NEEDS SHAPING UP!
...CHECK!
ALL THE GRASS NEEDS A PRECISION CUTTING BEING CAREFUL TO TRIM NEATLY AROUND THE STEPPING STONES TO THE KENNEL!
...CHECK!
D. DUCK LANDSCAPIST
AND THE GRASS NEAR THE STABLES NEEDS CUTTING AS WELL, BUT YOU CAN'T USE ANY LOUD MACHINERY LEST YOU UPSET THE HORSES SO CLOSE TO THE HUNT!
Z Z Z Z
...AND CHECK! I'LL GET RIGHT TO IT!
HOW'S THE JOB SOUND, UNCA DONALD?
MORE THAN A MERE MORTAL LANDSCAPIST COULD HANDLE! BUT FOR ME? A CINCH!
FIRST, I MUST CUT THE GRASS NEAR THE STABLES WITHOUT MAKING A SOUND!
JEEPERS! HOW CAN THAT BE DONE?
JUST LIKE WHEN I MOW THE LAWN AT THE DUCKBURG LIBRARY! I USE RABBIT POWER!
!
Z
THIS HORDE OF HUNGRY HARES IS TRAINED TO MUNCH GRASS DOWN TO EXACTLY 3 CENTI-METERS, AND THEY DON'T SO MUCH AS BELCH!
Z Z
MUNCH! MUNCH! MUNCH!

HOW ABOUT THIS MESS OF ROSE VINES ALONG THE CROQUET FIELD?
THAT CALLS FOR MY KNITTING NEEDLES!
LAST WEEK I KNITTED SOME IVY INTO A HAMMOCK... BUT THIS CALLS FOR EVEN MORE OF MY TALENTS!
HOW'S THAT? A CROQUET CROCHET!
ASTOUNDING!
REMARKABLE!
MAGNIFICENT!
THESE RATTY-LOOKING LITTLE TREES ARE NEXT!
STAND ASIDE, INFANT! MASTER LANDSCAPIST AT WORK!
SO, HOW YA DOIN' TODAY, PAL? YA THINK THE DUCKBURG GADWELLS HAVE A CHANCE AT THE PENNANT THIS YEAR?
DON'T FLINCH, SPORT, OR YOU MIGHT LOSE A TWIG!
I CAN ALMOST SMELL THE TALCUM POWDER AND COLOGNE!
THAT'S BUG DUST AND FERTILIZER!
NEXT!
NOW TO MANICURE THESE FLAGSTONES!
WOW! HE'S NOT CUTTING THE GRASS... HE'S FILING EACH BLADE WITH AN EMORY BOARD!

WHAT NEXT? THIS GHASTLY LOOKING BUSH BY THE POND?
YES... THIS HAS POSSIBILITIES!
SNIP SNIP SNIP
WAIT TILL THE MAYOR'S GUESTS SEE *THIS!* THEY'LL WANT TO *POT* IT AND HAUL IT AWAY TO THE MUSEUM!
BREATHTAKING!
I WOULD AGREE BUT I'M OUT OF BREATH!
UNCA DONALD... YOU'VE FINALLY FOUND THE CAREER YOU WERE *BORN* FOR!
NO TIME FOR AUTOGRAPHS! I MUST CLEAN THE KOI POND!
ANYONE ELSE WOULD SIMPLY CHANGE THE WATER!
PILE THOSE LILY PADS UP SO I CAN CLEAN THE ALGAE OFF THEM!
THIS OLD WASHING MACHINE IS IDEAL FOR THIS SORT OF THING!
HAS ANYONE SEEN THE BIG *BULLFROG* THAT WAS HERE?
OMIGOSH! I HOPE *THIS* ISN'T HIM!
DON'T WORRY, HERE HE IS! I WAS PRESOAKING HIM!
LOOK AT THE WONDERFUL JOB MR. DUCK IS DOING, GERTRUDE!
YES, BUT HE HASN'T CUT THE *GRASS* YET, AND IT'S *LATE!*

THE MAYOR SAID THAT THE GUESTS ARRIVE IN A HALF-HOUR, UNCA DONALD!
HOW WILL YOU GET THIS ENTIRE LAWN MOWED BY THEN?
FEAR NOT, MICROBES! I USE THE LATEST IN SELF-PROPELLED MOWERS!
BUT... TIME IS GETTING SHORT!
IF I OPERATE THESE TWO MONSTERS TOGETHER, I'LL CUT THE GRASS IN HALF MY NORMAL TIME!
WHY NOT LET US RUN ONE MOWER FOR YOU!
BAH! AN ARTIST NEVER ALLOWS PHILISTINES TO TOUCH A BRUSH TO HIS CANVAS! STAND BACK!
DISASTER LOOMS!
RRRR
FIRST I'LL DO THE TRIMMING! AROUND THE FISH POND...
RRRR
D. DUCK
RRRRRRR
...AND NOW THE CROQUET LAWN!
UNCA DONALD, WAIT!
THIS IS TOO IMPORTANT TO YOU! PLEASE LET US HELP BEFORE--
I TOLD YOU SHRIMPS TO BEGONE!
CRACK!
WAK!?!
RRR
RRR
ZOOM!
ZOOM!

MY FOOT IS CAUGHT!
THAT WAS THE THROTTLE LEVER HE BROKE! WE'LL NEVER CATCH HIM!
RRRR
HOW EMBARRASSING! I WONDER IF REMBRANDT EVER GOT HIS FOOT CAUGHT IN A PAINTBRUSH?!
RRRR
STOP, YOU GRASS-EATING JUGGERNAUT!
RIPP!
RRRR
RIP!
RIP!
RRRRRR
BRACE YOURSELF, UNCA DONALD!
WHY? WHAT'S GOING TO--
RRRRRRRRR
BOOM!
WHAT A STROKE OF LUCK! THE MOWERS COLLIDED BEFORE THEY DID TOO MUCH DAMAGE!
YEAH... I FEEL LIKE THE LUCKIEST DUCK ON EARTH! DO I LOOK IT!?
LET'S REPAIR THIS DAMAGE BEFORE THE MAYOR COMES OUT TO SEE WHAT ALL THE NOISE WAS!

I'M GOING OUT TO SEE WHAT ALL THE NOISE WAS!
Z
WHAT ON EARTH!!!
ZZ...?!
MEEE-YOW!!!
OH, GRETCHEN! EEEEK!!!
GERTRUDE! STOP! REMEMBER YOUR BAD HIP!
?
CRASH!
DUCK
DSCAPIST

!!!
CRASH!
AROOOOO!
AROOOOO!
!!
CRASH!
TALLY-HO!
CRASH!

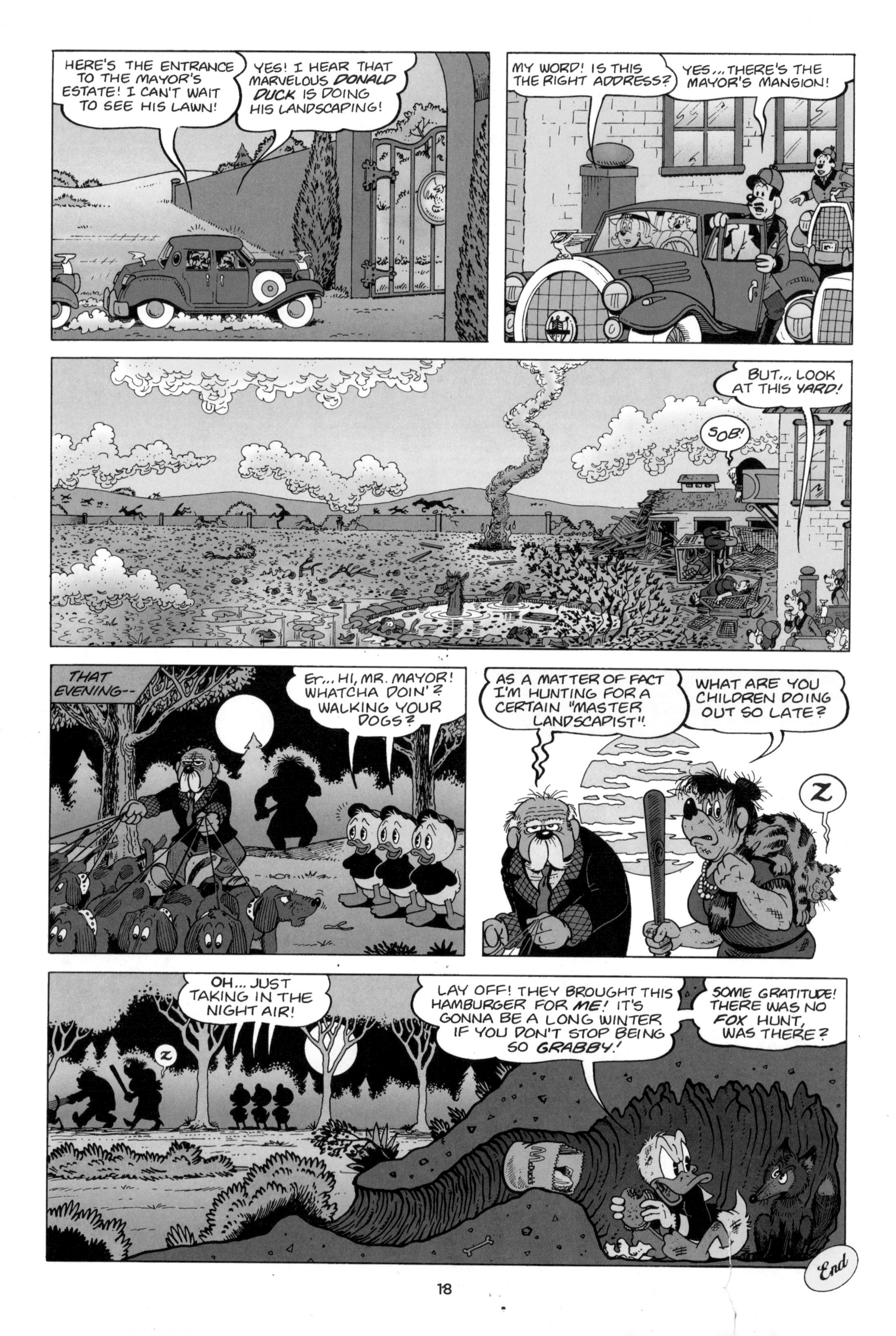

HERE'S THE ENTRANCE TO THE MAYOR'S ESTATE! I CAN'T WAIT TO SEE HIS LAWN!
YES! I HEAR THAT MARVELOUS DONALD DUCK IS DOING HIS LANDSCAPING!
MY WORD! IS THIS THE RIGHT ADDRESS?
YES... THERE'S THE MAYOR'S MANSION!
BUT... LOOK AT THIS YARD!
SOB!
THAT EVENING--
Er... HI, MR. MAYOR! WHATCHA DOIN'? WALKING YOUR DOGS?
AS A MATTER OF FACT I'M HUNTING FOR A CERTAIN "MASTER LANDSCAPIST".
WHAT ARE YOU CHILDREN DOING OUT SO LATE?
Z
OH... JUST TAKING IN THE NIGHT AIR!
Z
LAY OFF! THEY BROUGHT THIS HAMBURGER FOR ME! IT'S GONNA BE A LONG WINTER IF YOU DON'T STOP BEING SO GRABBY!
SOME GRATITUDE! THERE WAS NO FOX HUNT, WAS THERE?
End

Walt Disney's
UNCLE $CROOGE
ON STOLEN TIME
WOTTA JOB! UNCLE SCROOGE WANTS ME TO INVENTORY ALL THE LARGE BILLS IN THE BIN! THERE'S NOT ENOUGH TIME IN THE WORLD FOR THIS JOB!
DEPTH GAUGE
$1,000 BILLS
$100 BILLS
D 90147
WHEW! I OUGHTA...
?
CLIK!
$10,000 BILLS
!
CLIK!
UNCLE SCROOGE! COME QUICK! THOSE TERRIBLE BEAGLE BOYS JUST STOLE A HUGE PILE OF CASH FROM INSIDE YOUR BIN!
IMPOSSIBLE! HOW COULD THEY GET IN WITHOUT US SEEING THEM? THIS IS THE ONLY DOOR!

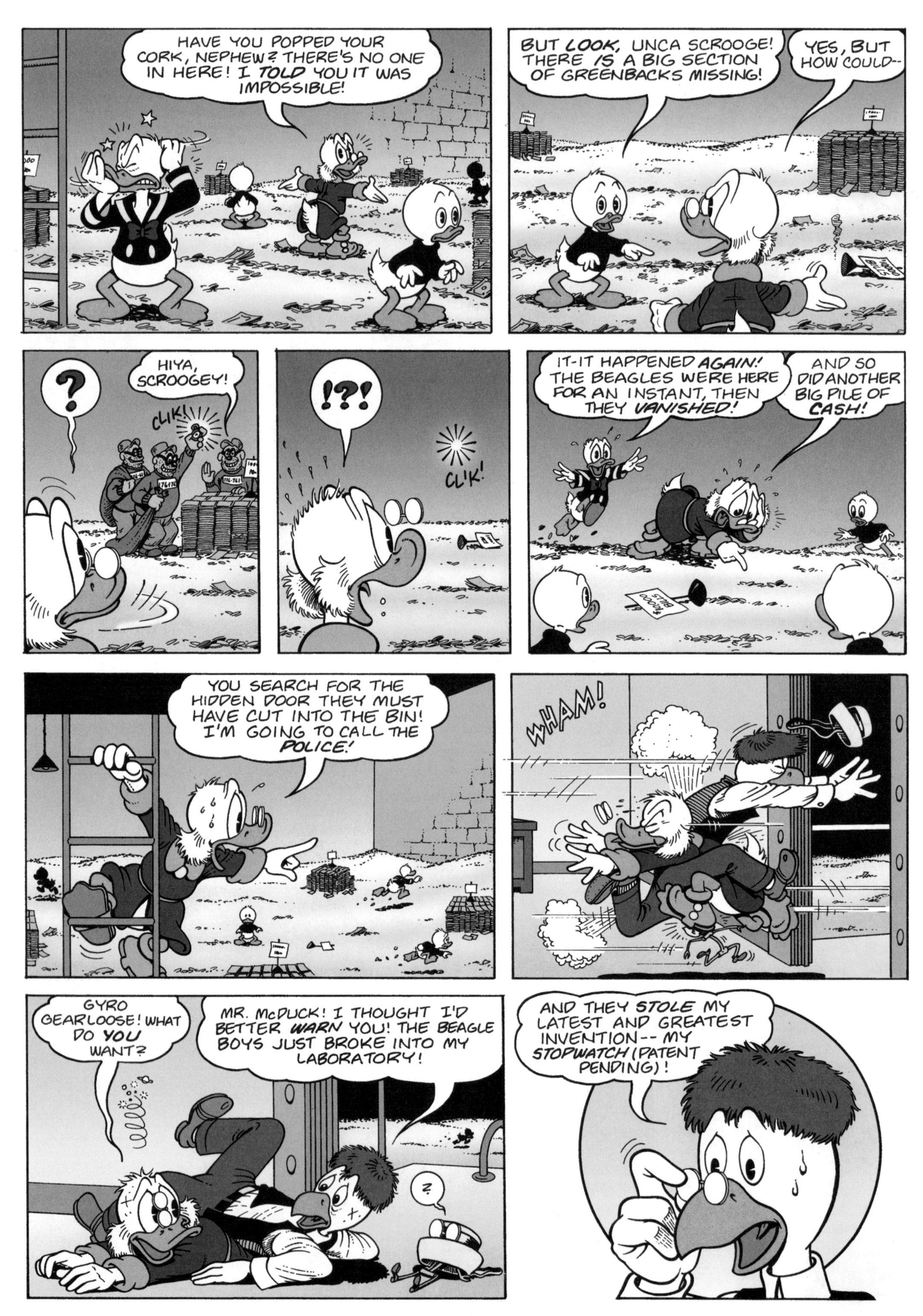
HAVE YOU POPPED YOUR CORK, NEPHEW? THERE'S NO ONE IN HERE! I TOLD YOU IT WAS IMPOSSIBLE!
BUT LOOK, UNCA SCROOGE! THERE IS A BIG SECTION OF GREENBACKS MISSING!
YES, BUT HOW COULD--
?
HIYA, SCROOGEY!
CLIK!
!?!
CLIK!
IT-IT HAPPENED AGAIN! THE BEAGLES WERE HERE FOR AN INSTANT, THEN THEY VANISHED!
AND SO DID ANOTHER BIG PILE OF CASH!
YOU SEARCH FOR THE HIDDEN DOOR THEY MUST HAVE CUT INTO THE BIN! I'M GOING TO CALL THE POLICE!
WHAM!
GYRO GEARLOOSE! WHAT DO YOU WANT?
MR. McDUCK! I THOUGHT I'D BETTER WARN YOU! THE BEAGLE BOYS JUST BROKE INTO MY LABORATORY!
AND THEY STOLE MY LATEST AND GREATEST INVENTION-- MY STOPWATCH (PATENT PENDING)!

I'M...UM...SORRY TO BREAK THIS TO YOU GYRO, BUT STOPWATCHES HAVE BEEN AROUND FOR *YEARS!*
NOT LIKE THIS ONE!
CALLS 5¢
WHOEVER USES *MY* STOPWATCH CAN *STOP TIME!* TIME WOULD STAND *STILL* FOR THEM... THE BEAGLES COULD ROB YOU BLIND IN AN *INSTANT!*
CRUNCH!
SUFFERIN' CATFISH! THAT'S WHAT'S HAPPENING! THEY'RE RAIDING THE BIN WITH YOUR TIME-STOPPER!
THERE'S ONE *CATCH* TO HOW IT WORKS...
WHEN THEY STOP TIME, EVERYTHING IS *FROZEN SOLID!*
THE BEAGLE BOYS CAN'T EVEN MOVE A FEATHER OR A DUST SPECK TILL THEY TURN TIME BACK ON!
CLIK!
$100 BILLS
176
THEN *HOW* ARE THEY STEALING MY MONEY?
THEY'D NEED TO TURN THE WATCH OFF THEN *BACK ON* AGAIN ONCE THEY WERE NEAR YOUR MONEY!
CLIK!
$100 BILLS
ANYTHING WITHIN 10 METERS OF THE STOPWATCH WOULD BE UNAFFECTED!
WHAT IF WE SIMPLY *BLOCKED* THE DOORWAY?
YOU'RE RIGHT, MR. McDUCK! IN FROZEN TIME, THE BEAGLE BOYS WON'T BE ABLE TO
CLIK!
HA HA! LOOK! OL' SCROOGE IS TRYING TO BLOCK THE DOOR!
THAT GEARLOOSE GUY MUST HAVE TIPPED HIM ABOUT THE STOPWATCH!

NO SWEAT! WE'LL JUST CLIMB OVER THEM!
EASY FOR YOU! YOU LOST 5 POUNDS DURING YOUR LAST STRETCH IN THE PEN!
OKAY... TURN OFF THE STOPWATCH SO WE CAN GRAB MORE OF THIS DOUGH THAT SCROOGE WAS NICE ENOUGH TO HAVE STACKED FOR US!!
176-176
176-671
HEY! IT'S THEM AGAIN! GRAB--
CLIK!
176-176
CLIK!
176-176
NOW WE CAN SNATCH ALL THE CASH THAT WAS WITHIN TEN METERS OF US WHEN I STOPPED TIME!
OTHERWISE IT'D BE AS IMMOVABLE AS THE ROCK OF GILBRALTAR!
176-176
176-761
WOTTA DEAL! STEALING SCROOGE'S MONEY RIGHT OUT FROM UNDER HIS BEAK!
AND WE HAVE ALL THE TIME IN THE WORLD TO DO IT!
176-671
CHUCKLE! I'M GONNA LEAVE SOME OF OUR CALLING CARDS FOR SCROOGEY!
C'MON -- WE'LL TURN TIME BACK ON WHEN WE GET BACK TO OUR HIDEOUT!
176-761
CLIK!
--GET PAST US IF WE STAND HERE IN THE DOORWAY!
Uh... I THINK THEY'VE ALREADY BEEN HERE AND GONE, GYRO!
HOW DO YOU KNOW?
JUST A HUNCH!

UNCLE SCROOGE! THE BEAGLES JUST--
I KNOW, NEPHEW! THEY'RE STEALING ME BLIND USING GYRO'S TIME-STOPPING GIZMO!
COFF! COFF!
TIME-STOPPING INVENTION? THAT EXPLAINS EVERYTHING!
HOW CAN WE FIGHT THAT?
SIMPLY CLOSE THE VAULT DOOR, MR. McDUCK!
THEY CAN'T OPEN OR BREAK THROUGH THE DOOR IN THE TIME-FREEZE STATE!
BUT I CAN'T LEAVE THE VAULT SHUT FOREVER!
I ASSUME THEY SWIPE THE MONEY BY ENVELOPING IT IN THE POWER OF THE STOPWATCH?
RIGHT-- ANYTHING WITHIN 10 METERS WILL BE OUTSIDE THE TIMEFREEZE!
MUMBLE!
MUMBLE!
THAT'S IT! WE HAVE A PLAN! WE'LL TRICK THE BEAGLE BOYS THE NEXT TIME THEY COME IN HERE TO SWIPE YOUR MONEY!
CLIK! CLIK!
TOO LATE!
NEVER MIND! JUST HURRY!
HAVING STASHED THEIR BOOTY, THE BEAGLE BOYS SOON RETURN FOR MORE--
KEEP OUT!
THIS IS CLOSE ENOUGH! PUNCH THE STOPWATCH AND FREEZE EVERYTHING!
RIGHT!
CLIK!
SCRAM!
GO AWAY!
LOOK--THAT GEARLOOSE GUY IS LEAVING!
HOW NICE OF HIM TO BE HOLDING THE DOOR OPEN FOR US! APRÉS VOUS!

POOR SCROOGE! LOOKS LIKE HE KNOWS WE'VE FINALLY LICKED HIM!
HA! HE CAN'T STOP US! WE'RE INVINCIBLE!
WHERE ARE THE OTHER DUCKS?
SCROOGE PROBABLY SENT 'EM HOME! HE'S NOT ONE TO WASTE PAYCHECKS IN A DOOMED BUSINESS! HAR!
DEPTH GAUGE
$10000 BILLS
THIS IS SO EASY I'M ALMOST ASHAMED OF MYSELF! BUT NOT QUITE! PUSH THE BUTTON AND UNFREEZE TIME SO WE CAN GLOM THIS LOVELY DOUGH!
RIGHT!
CLIK!
176·176
$10000 BILLS
HAH! SURPRISE!
I'VE A GOOD MIND TO REPORT YOU TO THE SOCIETY TO PREVENT CRUELTY TO BURGLARS!
I'LL FREEZE 'EM! TAKE THIS, DUCKS!
CLIK!
176·176
176·761
YOU FORGET! WE'RE TOO CLOSE! YOU'VE FROZEN TIME, BUT WE'RE INSIDE THE STOPWATCH'S AURA WITH YOU!
FOUL! FOUL!
RUN! WE'VE GOT TO GET AWAY FROM THOSE DUCKS OR THEY'LL FOLLOW US BACK TO THE HIDEOUT!
IF THEY GET MORE THAN TEN METERS AWAY FROM US, THEY CAN PUT US INTO THE TIME-FREEZE, TOO!
AFTER THEM!
176·761

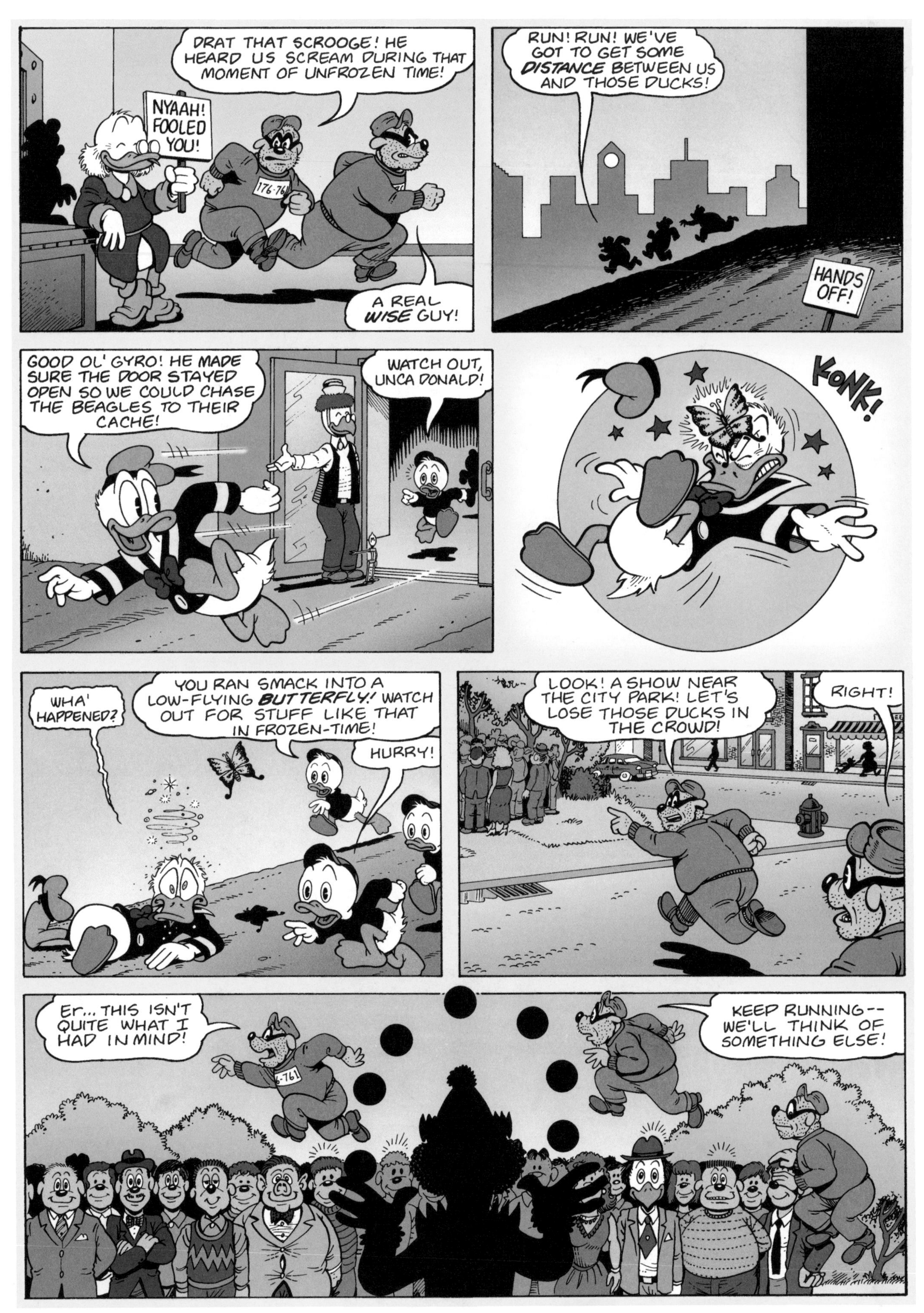
DRAT THAT SCROOGE! HE HEARD US SCREAM DURING THAT MOMENT OF UNFROZEN TIME!
NYAAH! FOOLED YOU!
176-761
A REAL WISE GUY!
RUN! RUN! WE'VE GOT TO GET SOME DISTANCE BETWEEN US AND THOSE DUCKS!
HANDS OFF!
GOOD OL' GYRO! HE MADE SURE THE DOOR STAYED OPEN SO WE COULD CHASE THE BEAGLES TO THEIR CACHE!
WATCH OUT, UNCA DONALD!
KONK!
WHA' HAPPENED?
YOU RAN SMACK INTO A LOW-FLYING BUTTERFLY! WATCH OUT FOR STUFF LIKE THAT IN FROZEN-TIME!
HURRY!
LOOK! A SHOW NEAR THE CITY PARK! LET'S LOSE THOSE DUCKS IN THE CROWD!
RIGHT!
Er... THIS ISN'T QUITE WHAT I HAD IN MIND!
KEEP RUNNING-- WE'LL THINK OF SOMETHING ELSE!

WE'LL CUT THROUGH THE PARK! THERE'S PLENTY OF ROOM TO RUN LIKE ANTELOPES!
BIG FAT OVER-WEIGHT ANTELOPES!
WHAT WILL THESE POOR PEOPLE THINK WHEN TIME UN-FREEZES AND THEY FIND FOOTPRINTS ALL OVER THEIR KISSERS!
LOOK! THE BEAGLES ARE HALFWAY AROUND THE PARK POND! THAT'S OVER 10 METERS AWAY!
WE'LL HAFTA TAKE A SHORTCUT!
THE DUCKS ARE NOWHERE IN SIGHT!
PUSH THE WATCH STEM TWICE AND THEY'LL BE FROZEN IN TIME!
NO, WAIT! IT'S TOO LATE!
THAT'S RIGHT! IN THE TIME-FREEZE, RUNNING ON THIS POND IS LIKE RUNNING ON BEDROCK!
GET UP, UNCA DONALD! HURRY!
THESE DARN KIDS AND THEIR TOY SAILBOATS!
WHAT'S THAT AHEAD?
A PARK EMPLOYEE IS CLEANING UP LITTER WITH A TRASH BLOWER!

OH, BROTHER! WE SHOULDA' GONE AROUND THIS MESS!
WATCH THOSE CANDY WRAPPERS -- THEY'RE AS SHARP AS KNIVES!
RIP!
176-671
THOSE DUCKS ARE RIGHT ON OUR TAIL!
WHAT'LL WE DO NOW?
RIP!
THERE'S OUR ANSWER! THAT FLOCK OF PIGEONS!
SO WHAT? WHO ARE YOU -- THE BIRD MAN OF ALCATRAZ?
NO, BUT FOLLOW ME! THIS IS OUR STAIRCASE TO FREEDOM!
YOW!
MY PAROLE OFFICER IS NEVER GONNA BELIEVE THIS!
WE'RE TOO SHORT TO CLIMB THIS BIRD-LADDER!
THEY'RE GETTING AWAY!
HA! THAT DID IT! WE'RE WAY OVER TEN METERS FROM THOSE PESTS!
PRESS THE WATCH STEM AND UN-FREEZE TIME!
NO! ARE YOU NUTS? IF YOU UN-FREEZE THESE PIGEONS, WE'LL FALL AND BREAK ALL SIX OF OUR HIPS!
DRAT! HE'S RIGHT! KEEP CLIMBING!

THEY'RE CLIMBING THE PIGEONS OVER THAT WALL!
SPLIT UP! MAYBE ONE OF US CAN CATCH UP TO THEM ON THE OTHER SIDE!
WE'RE BACK ON SOLID GROUND! PUSH THAT BUTTON!
TOO LATE! HERE COME THOSE THREE SQUIRTS HOT ON OUR TRAIL!
176-671
I... PANT! ...I CAN'T RUN ANOTHER STEP! LET'S GIVE UP!
WAIT! I HAVE AN IDEA THAT CAN'T FAIL! FOLLOW ME!
176-671
THEY RAN ACROSS THIS GRASSY AREA THEN STOPPED!
MAYBE THEY'RE GIVING UP! C'MON!
YOUCH!!
?
OOOOW! MY POOR LITTLE WEBBED TOES!
DON'T RUN ONTO THAT GRASS! WITH TIME FROZEN IT'S LIKE A FIELD OF RAZORS!
AND THE BEAGLES HAD ON SHOES!
WE NEED SOME SHOES! FAST!
SHOES FOR THESE FEET? DREAM ON!
BESIDES... EVERYTHING IS FROZEN! WE'RE LICKED!
IT WORKED! THOSE LITTLE RUNTS CAN'T CROSS THE GRASS!
PUSH THE STOPWATCH BUTTON TWICE AND THEY'LL BE FROZEN IN TIME!
176-761
176-671
6-176
RIGHT!

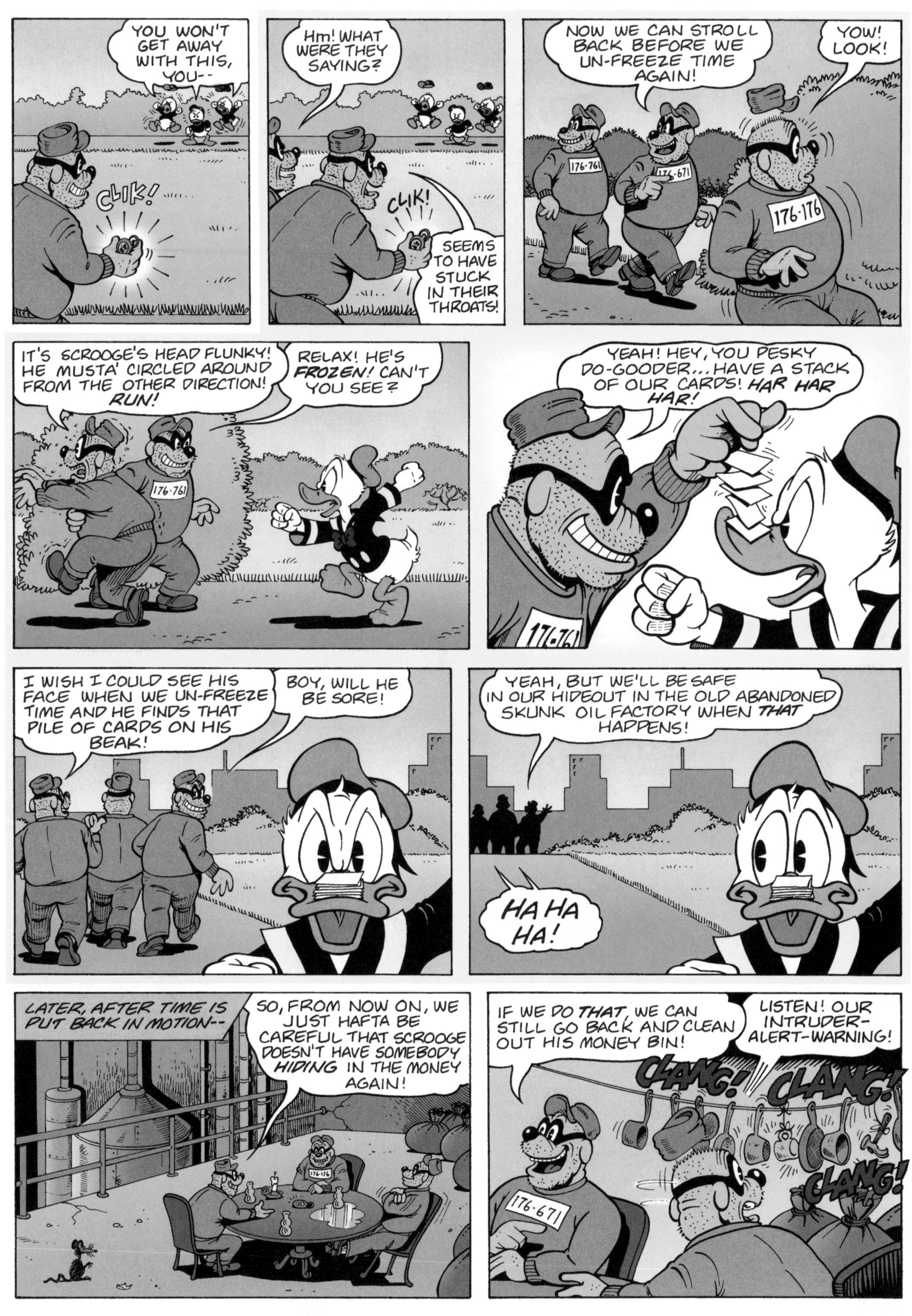
YOU WON'T GET AWAY WITH THIS, YOU--
CLIK!
Hm! WHAT WERE THEY SAYING?
CLIK!
SEEMS TO HAVE STUCK IN THEIR THROATS!
NOW WE CAN STROLL BACK BEFORE WE UN-FREEZE TIME AGAIN!
YOW! LOOK!
176-761
176-671
176-176
IT'S SCROOGE'S HEAD FLUNKY! HE MUSTA' CIRCLED AROUND FROM THE OTHER DIRECTION! RUN!
RELAX! HE'S FROZEN! CAN'T YOU SEE?
176-761
YEAH! HEY, YOU PESKY DO-GOODER... HAVE A STACK OF OUR CARDS! HAR HAR HAR!
176-761
I WISH I COULD SEE HIS FACE WHEN WE UN-FREEZE TIME AND HE FINDS THAT PILE OF CARDS ON HIS BEAK!
BOY, WILL HE BE SORE!
YEAH, BUT WE'LL BE SAFE IN OUR HIDEOUT IN THE OLD ABANDONED SKUNK OIL FACTORY WHEN THAT HAPPENS!
HA HA HA!
LATER, AFTER TIME IS PUT BACK IN MOTION--
SO, FROM NOW ON, WE JUST HAFTA BE CAREFUL THAT SCROOGE DOESN'T HAVE SOMEBODY HIDING IN THE MONEY AGAIN!
176-176
IF WE DO THAT, WE CAN STILL GO BACK AND CLEAN OUT HIS MONEY BIN!
LISTEN! OUR INTRUDER-ALERT-WARNING!
CLANG! CLANG!
CLANG!
176-671

YOW! IT'S SCROOGE!!!
HAH! I HAVE YOU NOW, VILLAINS! YOUR LITTLE STEALING SPREE IS OVER!
QUICK! FREEZE TIME!
RIGHT! WE MADE SURE NOBODY COULD SNEAK UP TO WITHIN 10 METERS OF US!
CLIK!
176-671
176-761
176-176
IT WORKED... BUT HOW DID HE FIND US?
WHO KNOWS! WE'LL HAVE TO PACK UP AND MOVE OUR BASE OF OPERATION!
MOVE OUR BOOTY DOWN TO THE TRUCK AND WE'LL MAKE A CLEAN GETAWAY!
THOUGHT YOU HAD US, eh? YOU OLD TURNIP SQUEEZER!
HEY! THE TRUCK IS LOCKED!
NO, IT'S IN TIME-FREEZE, REMEMBER! ONCE WE LOAD IT WITH CASH, WE'LL UNFREEZE TIME, HOP IN, AND TAKE OFF LIKE DEMONS!
BEAGLE BOYS INC.
BEAGLE
WE'LL BE OUT OF SIGHT BY THE TIME SCROOGE REALIZES WHAT HAPPENED!
HA HA!
BEAGLE BOYS INC.
KEEP IT COMING!
SAY... I DON'T RECALL THIS ROAD BEING LITTLE COBBLESTONES!
176-671
BEAGLE B
THIS IS THE LAST LOAD! AND I EVEN LEFT SCROOGE ANOTHER LOAD OF CALLING CARDS!
Wuh-oh!
176-671
MARBLES

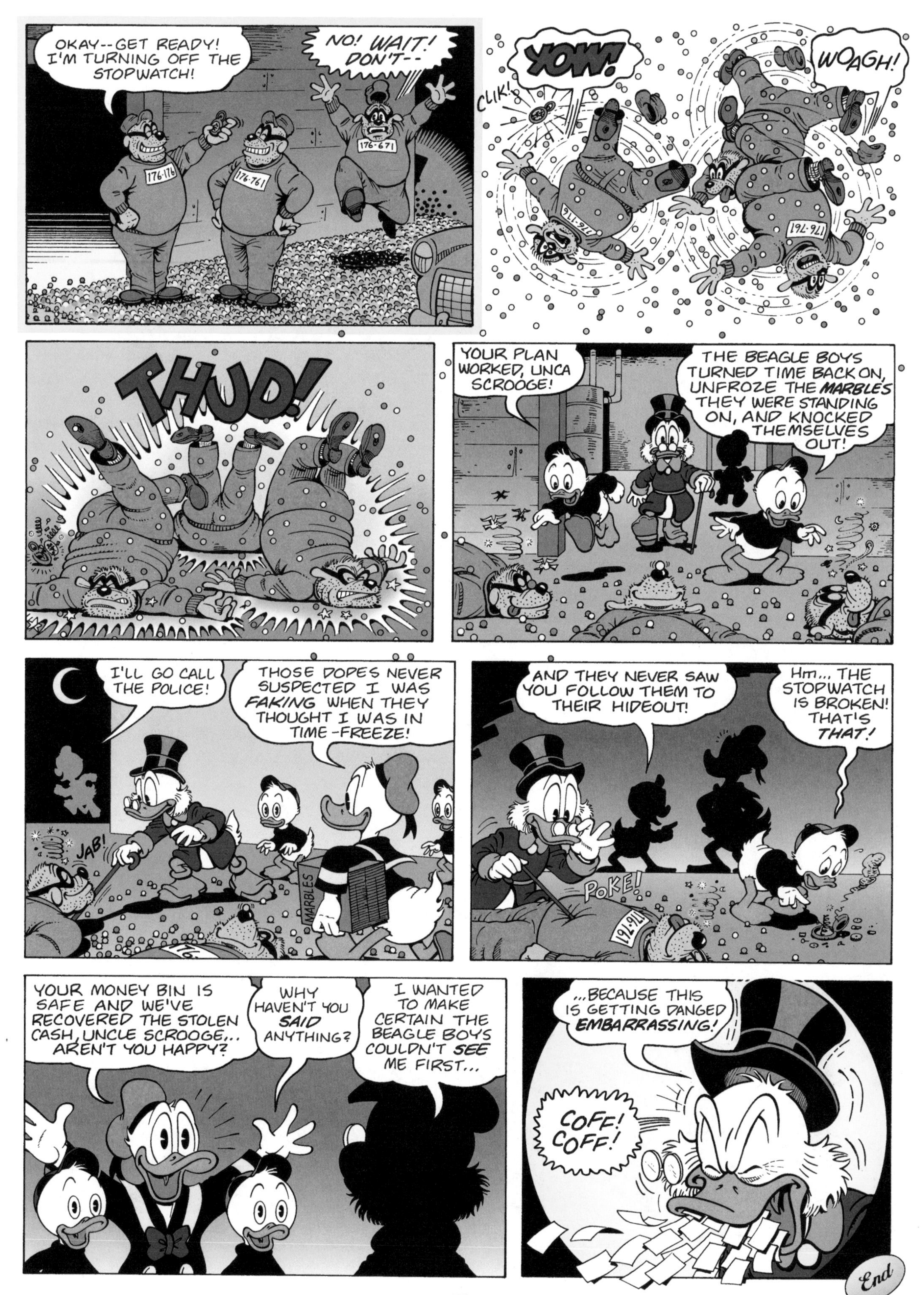

OKAY--GET READY! I'M TURNING OFF THE STOPWATCH!
NO! WAIT! DON'T--
176-176
176-761
176-671
YOW!
CLIK!
WOAGH!
THUD!
YOUR PLAN WORKED, UNCA SCROOGE!
THE BEAGLE BOYS TURNED TIME BACK ON, UNFROZE THE MARBLES THEY WERE STANDING ON, AND KNOCKED THEMSELVES OUT!
I'LL GO CALL THE POLICE!
THOSE DOPES NEVER SUSPECTED I WAS FAKING WHEN THEY THOUGHT I WAS IN TIME-FREEZE!
JAB!
MARBLES
AND THEY NEVER SAW YOU FOLLOW THEM TO THEIR HIDEOUT!
Hm... THE STOPWATCH IS BROKEN! THAT'S THAT!
POKE!
YOUR MONEY BIN IS SAFE AND WE'VE RECOVERED THE STOLEN CASH, UNCLE SCROOGE... AREN'T YOU HAPPY?
WHY HAVEN'T YOU SAID ANYTHING?
I WANTED TO MAKE CERTAIN THE BEAGLE BOYS COULDN'T SEE ME FIRST...
...BECAUSE THIS IS GETTING DANGED EMBARRASSING!
COFF! COFF!
End

TREASURE UNDER GLASS
Danish *Anders And Ekstra* 1991-02, January 1991; first American printing on *Uncle Scrooge* 263, February 1992. Color by Egmont and David Gerstein.

Walt Disney's
Uncle $crooge
in
Treasure under Glass
The Florida Keys-- the chain of islands off the southern tip of Florida, was once part of the Spanish Main, the ancient route of the treasure galleons from the New World!
Gulf of Mexico
Miami
Florida
The Everglades
Atlantic Ocean
♪ Yo ho, blow the man down...♪
But, nowadays, most ships plying these waters are on a mission for pleasure, not treasure!
D 90227
Yes, travellers now seek only a carefree vacation amid surf and sun...
♪ Yo ho ho, blow the man down...♪
...Unless, perhaps, the ship's port of registry is Duckburg, USA!
HEY!!
I didn't hire a barbershop quartet! You're supposed to be searching for sunken ships, not perfect pitch!
Give us a break, Unca Scrooge! We've been looking for salvage for weeks!
Every shipwreck not hidden below the sand has been searched a dozen times by other treasure hunters!
CLICK!

SALVAGERS HAVE BARELY FOUND A FRACTION OF THE BILLIONS IN LOST TREASURE BELOW THESE WATERS!
OH, HOW WOULD YOU KNOW?!
BECAUSE I SPENT MONTHS IN SPAIN AT THE ARCHIVO GENERAL de INDIAS IN SEVILLA! I STUDIED TONS OF WORMEATEN LOGBOOKS FROM TREASURE GALLEONS AND TREASURE SALVERS OF THE 1600S!
WHAT? THEY HAD TREASURE HUNTERS BACK THEN?
CERTAINLY! YOU DON'T SUPPOSE THAT WHEN A SHIP PACKED WITH GOLD SANK THEY JUST FORGOT ABOUT IT?
"SPAIN HAD A FLEET OF TREASURE SALVAGE SHIPS! THE CAPTAIN OF THE FLAGSHIP, FRANCISCO MELIAN, HAD A CONTRACT WITH KING PHILIP IV TO SALVAGE THE LOST TREASURE ARMADA OF 1622!"
"IN THOSE DAYS, THEY KNEW EXACTLY WHERE THE TREASURE SHIPS SANK! THEY COULD EVEN SEE THEM IN THE SHALLOW WATERS!"
IF THAT'S TRUE, HOW COME THERE'S ANY TREASURE LEFT TO FIND NOW?
WHY DIDN'T THEY RETRIEVE IT ALL OVER 300 YEARS AGO?
THEY WOULD HAVE...
"...BUT THEY HAD NO MODERN DIVING GEAR... ONLY LUNG POWER! ACTUALLY, CAPTAIN MELIAN DID INVENT ONE OF THE FIRST DIVING BELLS..."
"...BUT THE MEN COULDN'T LEAVE THE BELL WITHOUT BREATHING EQUIPMENT! ALL THEY COULD DO WAS TAKE A QUICK LOOK BEFORE THEIR AIR WENT STALE."

WELL, WE HAVE DIVING GEAR! DIDN'T THEY MAKE ANY MAPS OF WRECK SITES?
EXCELLENT MAPS! BUT THEY WERE ALL LOST IN 1655!
WITH THOSE CHARTS I COULD HAVE FOUND EVERY LOST DOUBLOON IN THE WEST INDIES!
SIGH!
HERE'S ANOTHER OLD SHIPWRECK NOW! SHOULD WE CHECK IT?
MIGHT AS WELL-- THERE'S STILL A BIT OF AIR IN TODAY'S TANKS!
THERE'S ANOTHER BOAT OFF PORT, UNCLE SCROOGE! OTHER DIVERS?
I'D BETTER CHECK! SOME OF THE LOCAL TREASURE HUNTERS ARE MIGHTY COMPETITIVE!
OOPS!
LOOK, CAP'N KUDA! SOME WEEKEND TREASURE HUNTERS ARE DIVING BY THE EDGE OF THE REEF!
LEMMEE SEE, CONCHY!
THEY MUST BE TOURISTS NOT TO KNOW THIS IS YOUR TERRITORY!
I'LL TEACH 'EM THAT BARRY KUDA IS THE ONLY TREASURE HUNTER IN THIS PIECE A' OCEAN!

WHY BOTHER? THE WRECK THEY'RE DIVING TO IS AN EMPTY HULK!
I DON'T CARE! I DON'T LIKE BEING CROWDED!
CAP'N, WE SCUTTLE EVERY TREASURE HUNTER'S SHIP THAT COMES NEAR HERE! IS IT WORTH IT? WE'VE HARDLY FOUND ANYTHING BUT OLD ANCHORS AND CANNONS!
I KNOW THERE'S DOZENS OF TREASURE GALLEONS HIDDEN BENEATH THE CORAL AND SAND HEREABOUTS! AND I'M GONNA BE THE SWAB THAT FIGURES OUT HOW TO FIND 'EM!
WHAT'S THIS STUFF, CAP'N?
MEAT SCRAPS FROM THE GALLEY! REMEMBER HOW SHARKS GATHER BY THAT REEF OVER THERE?
VROOM!
THIS APPETIZER WILL STIR THOSE SHARKS UP GOOD!
HEY! WHAT'S THE IDEA, YOU MANIAC?! I HAVE DIVERS DOWN!!!
VROOM!
THERE'S NO LAW SAYS WE CAN'T FEED THE FISHIES, YOU OLD COOT!
VROOM!
OH, ME! OH, MY! THIS IS BAD!
MEANWHILE, SEVERAL FATHOMS BELOW...
IT'S JUST ANOTHER EMPTY BARQUE!
RADIO
MAYBE IT WAS ONE THAT CUT CORAL FOR BUILDING FORTS ON THE KEYS WHERE THEY HAD NO STONE!
YEAH... I'VE HEARD OF CORAL BARQUES!
WHAT THE... DID SOMEBODY ORDER OUT FOR LUNCH?

YIPE! SOME NUT IN A SPEEDBOAT IS DUMPING MEAT!
LOOK OUT! SHARKS ARE COMING OUT OF THE REEF!
SWIM FOR COVER!!!
YOU HOODLUMS! STOP! I'LL CALL THE COAST GUARD!
WE'D BETTER SKEEDADDLE, CAP'N!
VROOM!
DON'T WORRY, CONCHY! THIS SOUPED-UP SKIFF IS THE FASTEST THING IN THE KEYS! NOBODY COULD CATCH US UNLESS THEY CHASED US TO THE EDGE OF THE WORLD!
VROOM!
MY POOR NEPHEWS! THEY'RE TRAPPED DOWN THERE, AND I'M POWERLESS TO HELP!
=COFF COFF= MY AIR IS RUNNING OUT! THIS LOOKS LIKE CURTAINS!
WHAT'S THAT? LOOKS LIKE A WINDOW IN THE HUNK OF CORAL!
IT IS A WINDOW! THIS ISN'T ALL CORAL-- IT'S SOMETHING OFF THAT SHIPWRECK!
LOOKS LIKE AIR IN THERE! IS THAT POSSIBLE?!
IT BETTER BE POSSIBLE! =COFF= IT'S OUR ONLY CHANCE!
HERE'S A WAY IN!
GASP!
GASP!

WHAT IS THIS WE'RE IN? IT EVEN HAS SEATS!
MAYBE IT'S DAVEY JONES' LOCKERROOM! WHO CARES? THERE'S AIR IN HERE!
NOT MUCH AIR FOR FOUR PANTING DUCKS! WE'RE STILL IN A PICKLE!
MAYBE UNCA SCROOGE CAN SEE US!
HE CAN!
WHAT HAVE THEY CRAWLED INTO? IT'S COVERED WITH CORAL GROWTHS, BUT... WHAT'S THAT ON TOP?
A CHAIN! WHATEVER IT IS, IT'S GOT A CHAIN ATTACHED TO IT! MAYBE I CAN SNAG IT WITH THE ANCHOR!
LOOK! HE'S GOT AHOLD OF THAT CHAIN!
ATTA BOY, UNCA SCROOGE! WOTTA GUY!
?
BROTHER, IS IT HEAVY! BUT IT'S COMING UP, RELATIVES AND ALL!
CREEEAAAK
HOORAY FOR UNCA SCROOGE!
NO DUCK DESSERT FOR THE SHARKS TODAY!
WELL, SWOGGLE MY SCUPPERS! A DIVING BELL FROM THAT 17TH CENTURY SHIPWRECK!

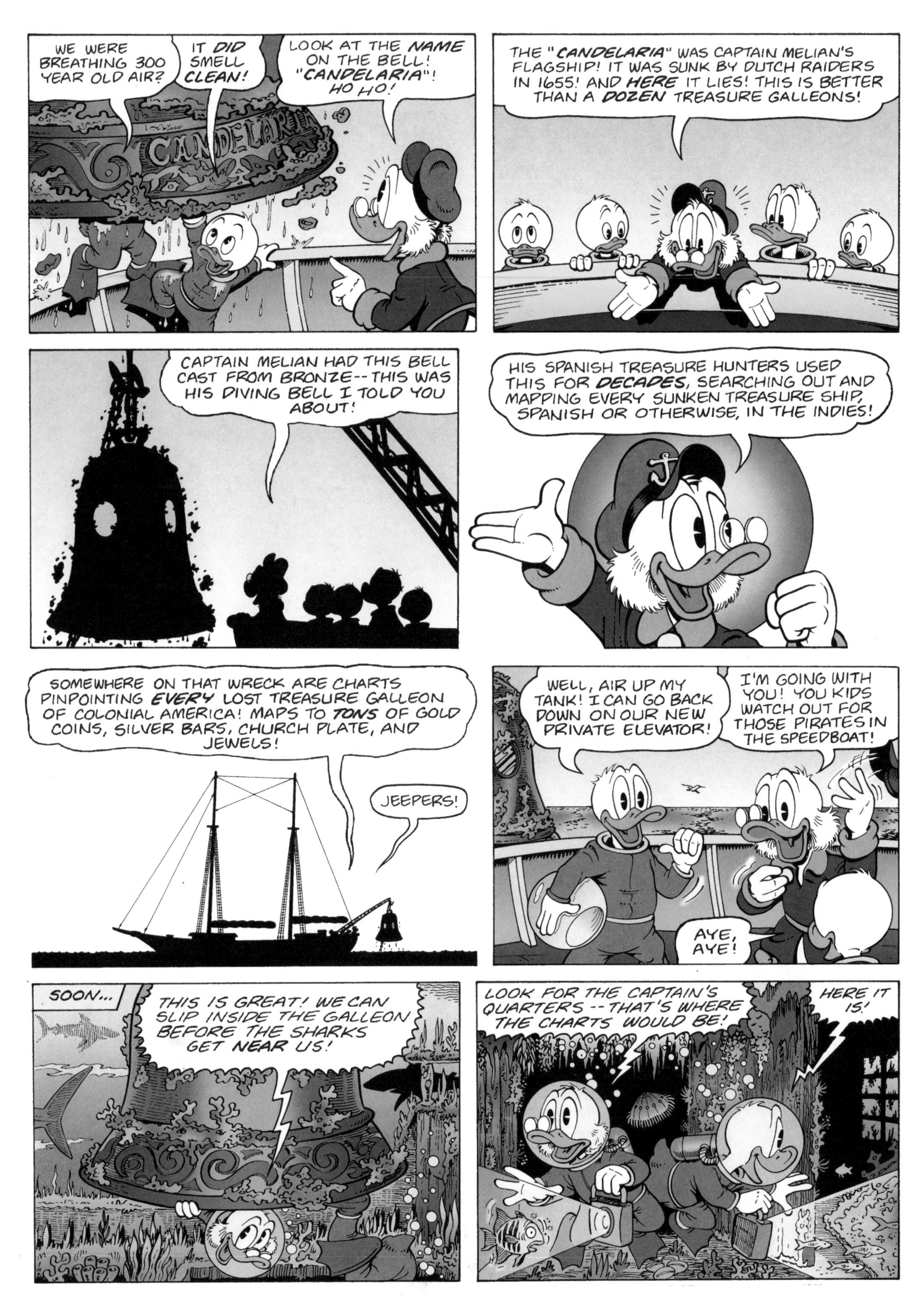
WE WERE BREATHING 300 YEAR OLD AIR?
IT DID SMELL CLEAN!
LOOK AT THE NAME ON THE BELL! "CANDELARIA"! HO HO!
CANDELARIA
THE "CANDELARIA" WAS CAPTAIN MELIAN'S FLAGSHIP! IT WAS SUNK BY DUTCH RAIDERS IN 1655! AND HERE IT LIES! THIS IS BETTER THAN A DOZEN TREASURE GALLEONS!
CAPTAIN MELIAN HAD THIS BELL CAST FROM BRONZE-- THIS WAS HIS DIVING BELL I TOLD YOU ABOUT!
HIS SPANISH TREASURE HUNTERS USED THIS FOR DECADES, SEARCHING OUT AND MAPPING EVERY SUNKEN TREASURE SHIP, SPANISH OR OTHERWISE, IN THE INDIES!
SOMEWHERE ON THAT WRECK ARE CHARTS PINPOINTING EVERY LOST TREASURE GALLEON OF COLONIAL AMERICA! MAPS TO TONS OF GOLD COINS, SILVER BARS, CHURCH PLATE, AND JEWELS!
JEEPERS!
WELL, AIR UP MY TANK! I CAN GO BACK DOWN ON OUR NEW PRIVATE ELEVATOR!
I'M GOING WITH YOU! YOU KIDS WATCH OUT FOR THOSE PIRATES IN THE SPEEDBOAT!
AYE, AYE!
SOON...
THIS IS GREAT! WE CAN SLIP INSIDE THE GALLEON BEFORE THE SHARKS GET NEAR US!
LOOK FOR THE CAPTAIN'S QUARTERS -- THAT'S WHERE THE CHARTS WOULD BE!
HERE IT IS!

I SHOULD HAVE KNOWN! ANY CHARTS DOWN HERE WOULD HAVE DISSOLVED HUNDREDS OF YEARS AGO!
WHAT'S THAT ON THE WALL?
SOMETHING PAINTED AND CARVED INTO THE WOOD! WHAT'S THAT INSCRIPTION SAY?
"MAPA DE LOS BARCOS HUNDIDOS"!... MAP OF SUNKEN SHIPS!
THAT'S IT!!!
I CAN'T MAKE IT OUT! THERE'S TOO MUCH STUFF GROWING ALL OVER IT!
DON'T TOUCH IT! IT'LL CRUMBLE TO MUSH!
YOW! THIS ROTTING HULK IS NO PROTECTION FROM THOSE MONSTERS!
HEAD FOR THE BELL!
SUFFERIN' SAWFISH! THOSE TOOTHY TERRORS ARE AFTER OUR CAP'N AND FIRST MATE!
BOS'N HUEY! ACTIVATE THE WENCH!
HALP!
YIPES!
BEAT IT, YOU BIG SARDINES! OUR UNCLES ARE NOT ON YOUR MENU!
WHAP!

SHORTLY...
THERE IT WAS, RIGHT BEFORE MY EYES! KING PHILIP'S LOST SALVAGE CHART! THE LOCATION OF EVERY SUNKEN TREASURE GALLEON ON THE SPANISH MAIN!
FAT LOTTA GOOD IT IS! WE CAN'T READ IT UNDERWATER, AND IT'S TOO ROTTEN TO MOVE! NOT TO MENTION THE LITTLE MATTER OF THE DUCK-EATING FISH!
I WON'T GIVE UP! I MUST HAVE THE DATA ON THAT CHART! THERE MUST BE A WAY TO EXAMINE IT!
IF WE DRIED THE CHART WE COULD GENTLY BRUSH OFF THE GROWTHS!
BUT IT CAN'T BE BROUGHT UP TO DRY!
AND IT CAN'T BE CLEANED UNDERWATER!
THE ONLY ANSWER IS TO DRAIN THE OCEAN! THERE'S A CRAZY IDEA!
YEAH, AND IT'S SO CRAZY IT MIGHT JUST WORK! UNCLE SCROOGE, WHAT IF I SOLVED THIS PROBLEM?
I'D DO ANYTHING! EVEN GIVE YOU A 10 CENT PER HOUR RAISE!
Z
THAT WOULD BE A TRIUMPH, IF NOT FINANCIALLY! LET'S GET ON THE RADIO TO SOME FACTORIES YOU OWN IN MIAMI!
WHAT'S YOUR ANGLE?
?
?
FROM A NEARBY BOAT, SINISTER EYES CONTINUE TO OBSERVE THE ACTIVITY ABOARD THE GOLDEN GOOSE II...
CONCHY, I RECOGNIZE THAT OLD DUCK NOW! THAT'S SCROOGE McDUCK, THE WORLD'S RICHEST TYCOON!
WHAT'S HE ONTO OVER THERE?
ANYTHING HE'S AFTER HAS GOT TO BE BIG! WE'LL JUST LET HIM DO THE WORK, THEN MOVE IN WHEN THE TIME'S RIGHT!

SEVERAL DAYS LATER...
LOOK, UNCA SCROOGE! THE HELICOPTERS ARE COMING!
RIGHT ON SCHEDULE!
WAKE UP, CAP'N! I HEAR WEIRD NOISES!
ZZZZZ-- Hah? Wha?
CHOPCHOPCHOPCHOPCHOPCH
YIPES! WHAT'S THAT?!
LEAPIN' WINDJAMMERS! I THINK I JUST SPLIT MY MAINS'L!
CHOPCHOPCHOPCHOPCHOPCHOPCHO
I'LL MANEUVER THEM SO WE CAN SINK THE GLASS DOME JUST RIGHT!
HALF THE GLASS-BLOWERS IN FLORIDA PASSED OUT MAKING THAT THING!
WE'RE DONE, UNCA DONALD! ALL THE STAKES ARE SET IN THE CORAL AROUND THE "CANDELARIA"!
GREAT!
ONCE OUR DOME IS IN PLACE, WE'LL SECURE IT TO THE STAKES WITH STEEL CABLES!
NEPHEWS, THIS IS THE WILDEST IDEA YOU EVER HAD!
GOLDEN GOOSE
GLASS DOME
CANDELARIA
AIR HOSE
STAKED CABLES
BUT IT'LL WORK! YOU WATCH!
THE PUMP AND AIR HOSE ARE IN PLACE AND READY TO START!
I'M RESISTING PREMONITIONS OF DISASTER! I REALLY AM!

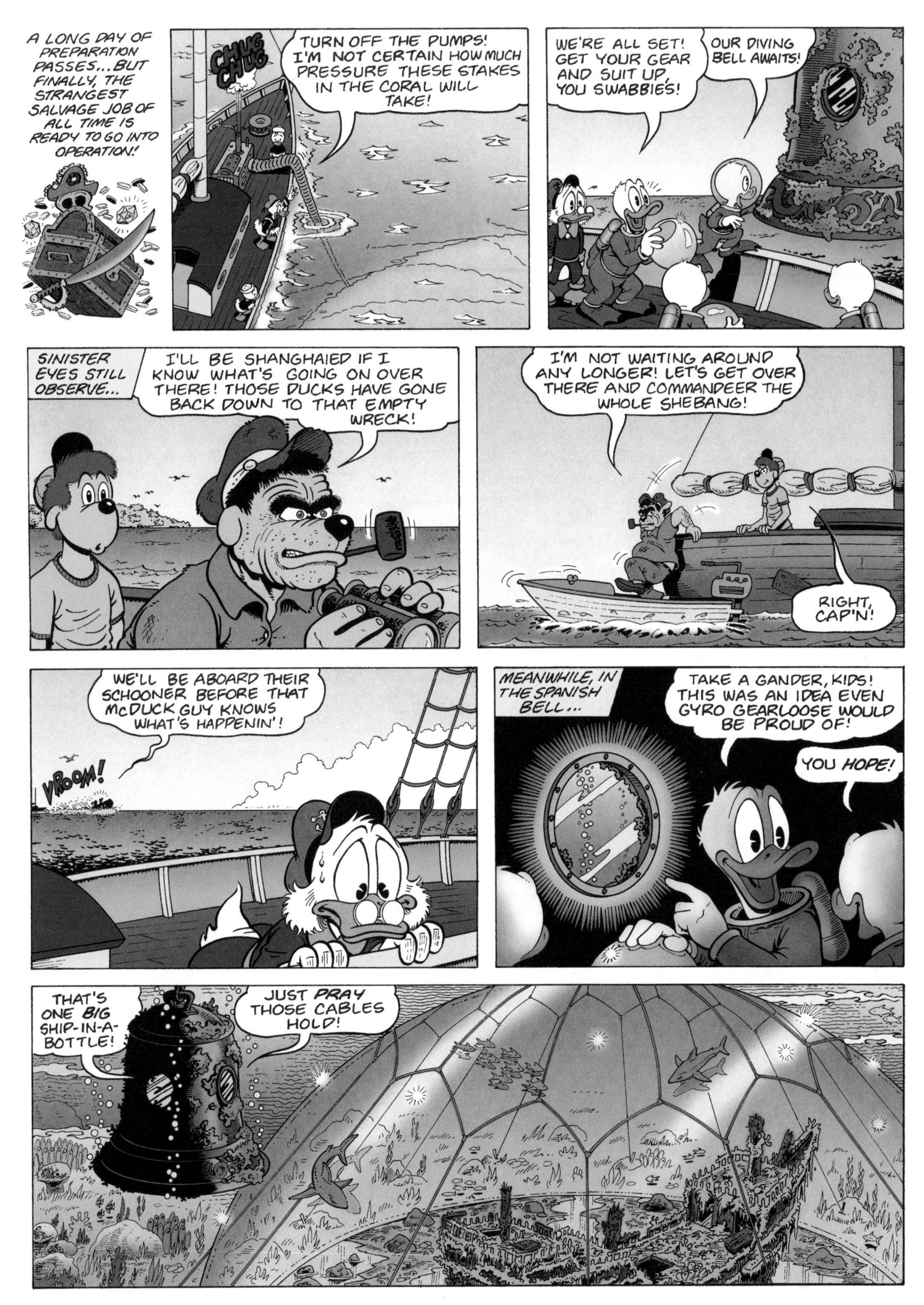

A LONG DAY OF PREPARATION PASSES... BUT FINALLY, THE STRANGEST SALVAGE JOB OF ALL TIME IS READY TO GO INTO OPERATION!
CHUG CHUG
TURN OFF THE PUMPS! I'M NOT CERTAIN HOW MUCH PRESSURE THESE STAKES IN THE CORAL WILL TAKE!
WE'RE ALL SET! GET YOUR GEAR AND SUIT UP, YOU SWABBIES!
OUR DIVING BELL AWAITS!
SINISTER EYES STILL OBSERVE...
I'LL BE SHANGHAIED IF I KNOW WHAT'S GOING ON OVER THERE! THOSE DUCKS HAVE GONE BACK DOWN TO THAT EMPTY WRECK!
I'M NOT WAITING AROUND ANY LONGER! LET'S GET OVER THERE AND COMMANDEER THE WHOLE SHEBANG!
RIGHT, CAP'N!
WE'LL BE ABOARD THEIR SCHOONER BEFORE THAT McDUCK GUY KNOWS WHAT'S HAPPENIN'!
VROOM!
MEANWHILE, IN THE SPANISH BELL...
TAKE A GANDER, KIDS! THIS WAS AN IDEA EVEN GYRO GEARLOOSE WOULD BE PROUD OF!
YOU HOPE!
THAT'S ONE BIG SHIP-IN-A-BOTTLE!
JUST PRAY THOSE CABLES HOLD!

IS THE CAMERA READY?
WATERTIGHT AND FULL OF FILM!
WE'RE ON THE BOTTOM!
THERE'S A SPACE BETWEEN THE CORAL TO SQUEEZE UNDER THE DOME!
THIS IS JUST LIKE WHEN YOU HOLD A DRINKING GLASS UPSIDE DOWN IN A SINK OF WATER!
SURE! THE AIR CAN'T GET OUT OR THE WATER IN!
AND NEITHER CAN THE SHARKS! LOOK!
NO, THANKS! THAT'S THE SAME EXPRESSION I HAVE LOOKING IN A CANDY STORE WINDOW!
GET A LOAD OF THIS! DON'T THAT TAKE THE WHOLE BISCUIT!
THE GLITTERDOME BENEATH THE SEA!
TREASURE UNDER GLASS!

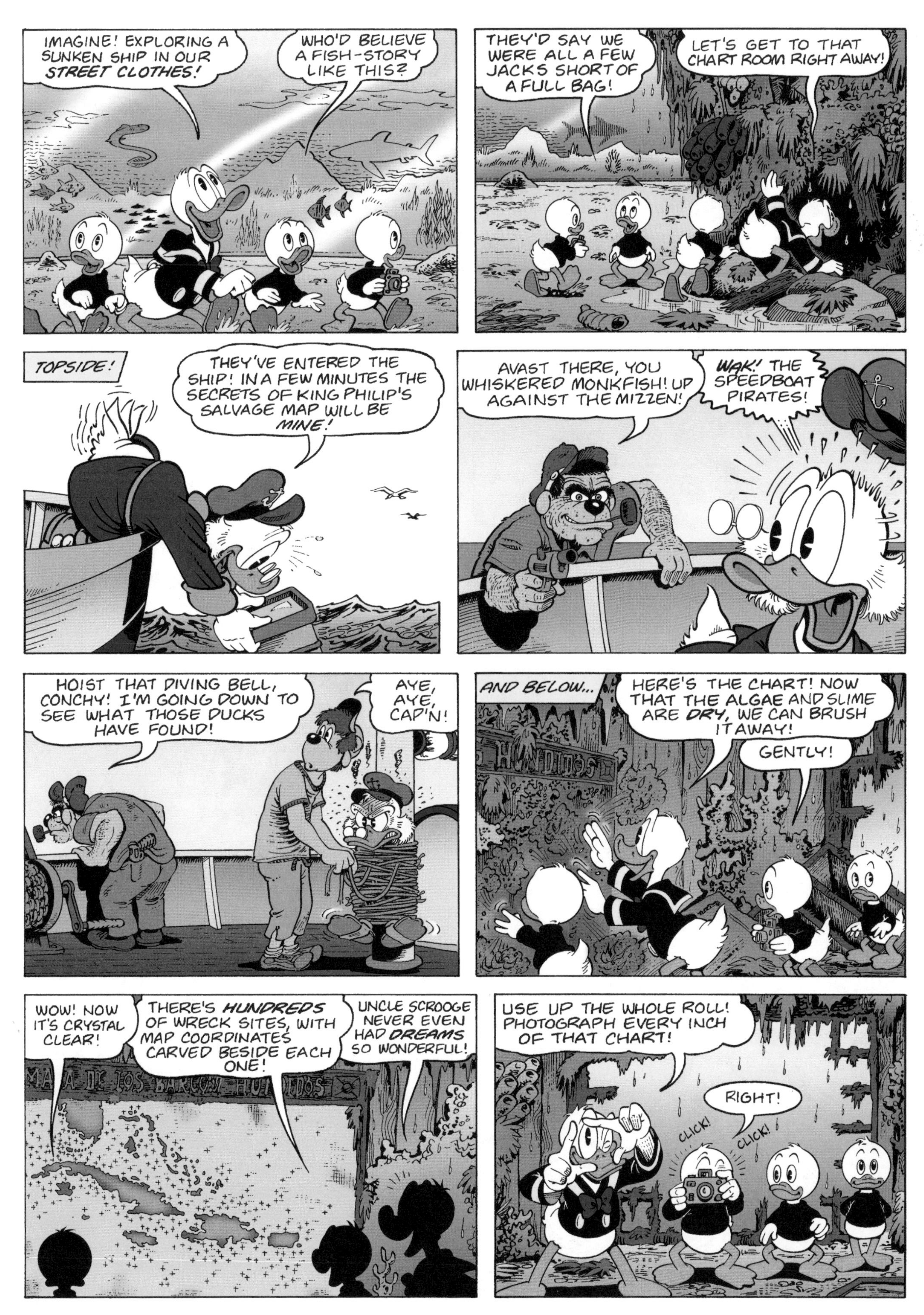

IMAGINE! EXPLORING A SUNKEN SHIP IN OUR STREET CLOTHES!
WHO'D BELIEVE A FISH-STORY LIKE THIS?
THEY'D SAY WE WERE ALL A FEW JACKS SHORT OF A FULL BAG!
LET'S GET TO THAT CHART ROOM RIGHT AWAY!
TOPSIDE!
THEY'VE ENTERED THE SHIP! IN A FEW MINUTES THE SECRETS OF KING PHILIP'S SALVAGE MAP WILL BE MINE!
AVAST THERE, YOU WHISKERED MONKFISH! UP AGAINST THE MIZZEN!
WAK! THE SPEEDBOAT PIRATES!
HOIST THAT DIVING BELL, CONCHY! I'M GOING DOWN TO SEE WHAT THOSE DUCKS HAVE FOUND!
AYE, AYE, CAP'N!
AND BELOW...
HERE'S THE CHART! NOW THAT THE ALGAE AND SLIME ARE DRY, WE CAN BRUSH IT AWAY!
GENTLY!
WOW! NOW IT'S CRYSTAL CLEAR!
THERE'S HUNDREDS OF WRECK SITES, WITH MAP COORDINATES CARVED BESIDE EACH ONE!
UNCLE SCROOGE NEVER EVEN HAD DREAMS SO WONDERFUL!
USE UP THE WHOLE ROLL! PHOTOGRAPH EVERY INCH OF THAT CHART!
RIGHT!
CLICK!
CLICK!

FINISHED! LET'S HEAD BACK!
THIS CAMERA HOLDS DIRECTIONS TO EVERY BIT OF TREASURE IN THE WEST INDIES!
WELL, MATEY, THAT SOUNDS LIKE SOME PHOTOS THAT BELONG IN MY SOUVENIR ALBUM!
WAK!
YOU CAN'T DO THIS! THAT'S OUR CAMERAMPDH!
BELAY THAT, YOU SEA MONKEY! YOU SHOULDA KEPT CLEAR OF MY SHOAL!
SEE YOU TOPSIDE, IF YOU WANNA RISK THE SWIM!
HSSSS
HSSSS
THERE GOES THE BELL!
SHOULD WE TRY SWIMMING TO THE SURFACE?
THROUGH THOSE SHARKS? I'M TOO YOUNG TO BE EATEN!
WHERE ARE MY NEPHEWS? YOU DIDN'T LEAVE THEM DOWN THERE...?
CONCHY, IF WHAT THOSE LANDLUBBERS SAID IS TRUE, THE FILM IN THIS CAMERA WILL LEAD US TO BILLIONS IN TREASURE!
SO LONG, McDUCK! DON'T TAKE ANY WOODEN PEGLEGS!
COME BACK HERE, YOU SEA SLUGS!
VROOM!

THERE THEY GO IN THEIR SPEEDBOAT!
I HOPE UNCA SCROOGE IS OKAY!
IT'S A CINCH HE'S BETTER OFF THAN WE ARE!
MAYBE, IF WE ALL SWIM IN FOUR DIFFERENT DIRECTIONS...?
WE'LL EACH BE GOING IN AT LEAST FOUR DIFFERENT DIRECTIONS ONCE WE TANGLE WITH THOSE SHARKS!
WHAT'S THAT VIBRATION?
AWK! I WAS AFRAID OF THIS! THE PINIONS ARE PULLING OUT OF THE CORAL!
?
ALL THE STAKES ARE PULLING FREE!
THIS DOME WILL SHOOT UP LIKE A ROCKET!
THE SEA WILL IMPLODE ON US LIKE A CIRCULAR TIDAL WAVE!
WE'LL BE SQUISHED LIKE BUGS!
WE HAVE TO CHANCE SWIMMING TO THE SURFACE! WE HAVE NO CHOICE!
THERE GOES THE "CANDELARIA"... TREASURE CHART AND ALL! SMASHED TO SMITHEREENS!

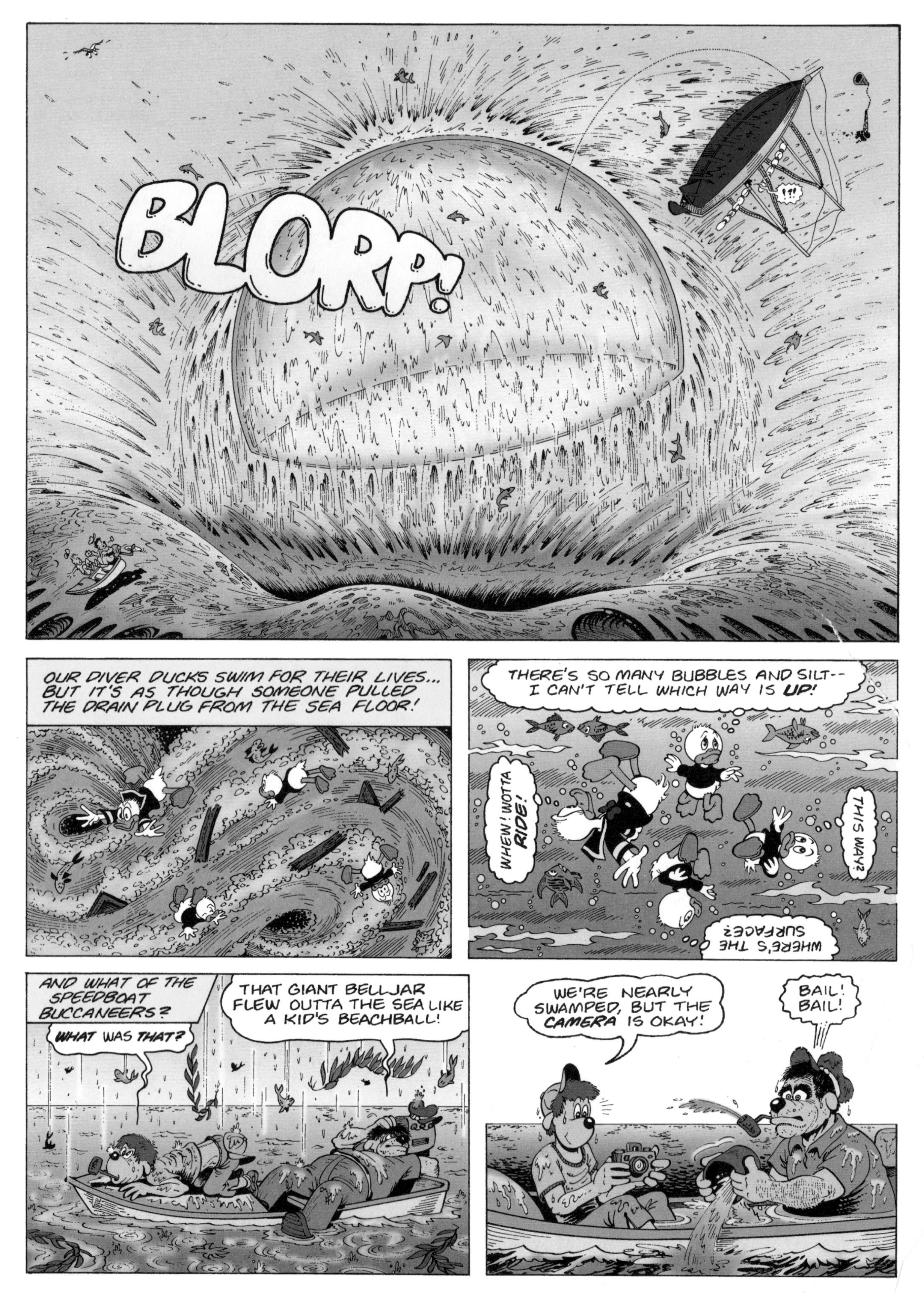
BLORP!
!?!
OUR DIVER DUCKS SWIM FOR THEIR LIVES... BUT IT'S AS THOUGH SOMEONE PULLED THE DRAIN PLUG FROM THE SEA FLOOR!
THERE'S SO MANY BUBBLES AND SILT-- I CAN'T TELL WHICH WAY IS UP!
WHEW! WOTTA RIDE!
THIS WAY?
WHERE'S THE SURFACE?
AND WHAT OF THE SPEEDBOAT BUCCANEERS?
WHAT WAS THAT?
THAT GIANT BELLJAR FLEW OUTTA THE SEA LIKE A KID'S BEACHBALL!
WE'RE NEARLY SWAMPED, BUT THE CAMERA IS OKAY!
BAIL! BAIL!

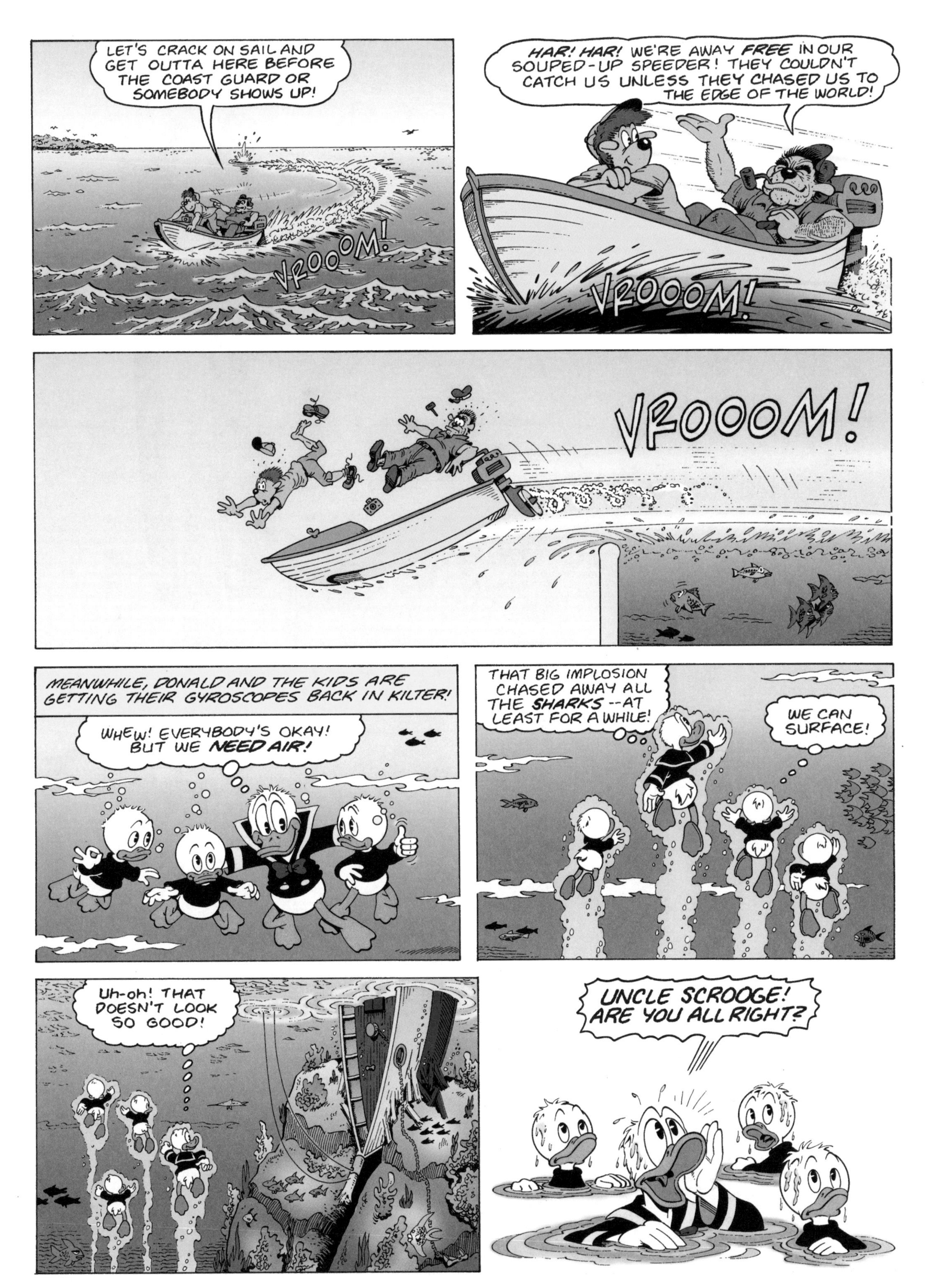
LET'S CRACK ON SAIL AND GET OUTTA HERE BEFORE THE COAST GUARD OR SOMEBODY SHOWS UP!
VROOOM!
HAR! HAR! WE'RE AWAY FREE IN OUR SOUPED-UP SPEEDER! THEY COULDN'T CATCH US UNLESS THEY CHASED US TO THE EDGE OF THE WORLD!
VROOOM!
VROOOM!
MEANWHILE, DONALD AND THE KIDS ARE GETTING THEIR GYROSCOPES BACK IN KILTER!
WHEW! EVERYBODY'S OKAY! BUT WE NEED AIR!
THAT BIG IMPLOSION CHASED AWAY ALL THE SHARKS --AT LEAST FOR A WHILE!
WE CAN SURFACE!
Uh-oh! THAT DOESN'T LOOK SO GOOD!
UNCLE SCROOGE! ARE YOU ALL RIGHT?

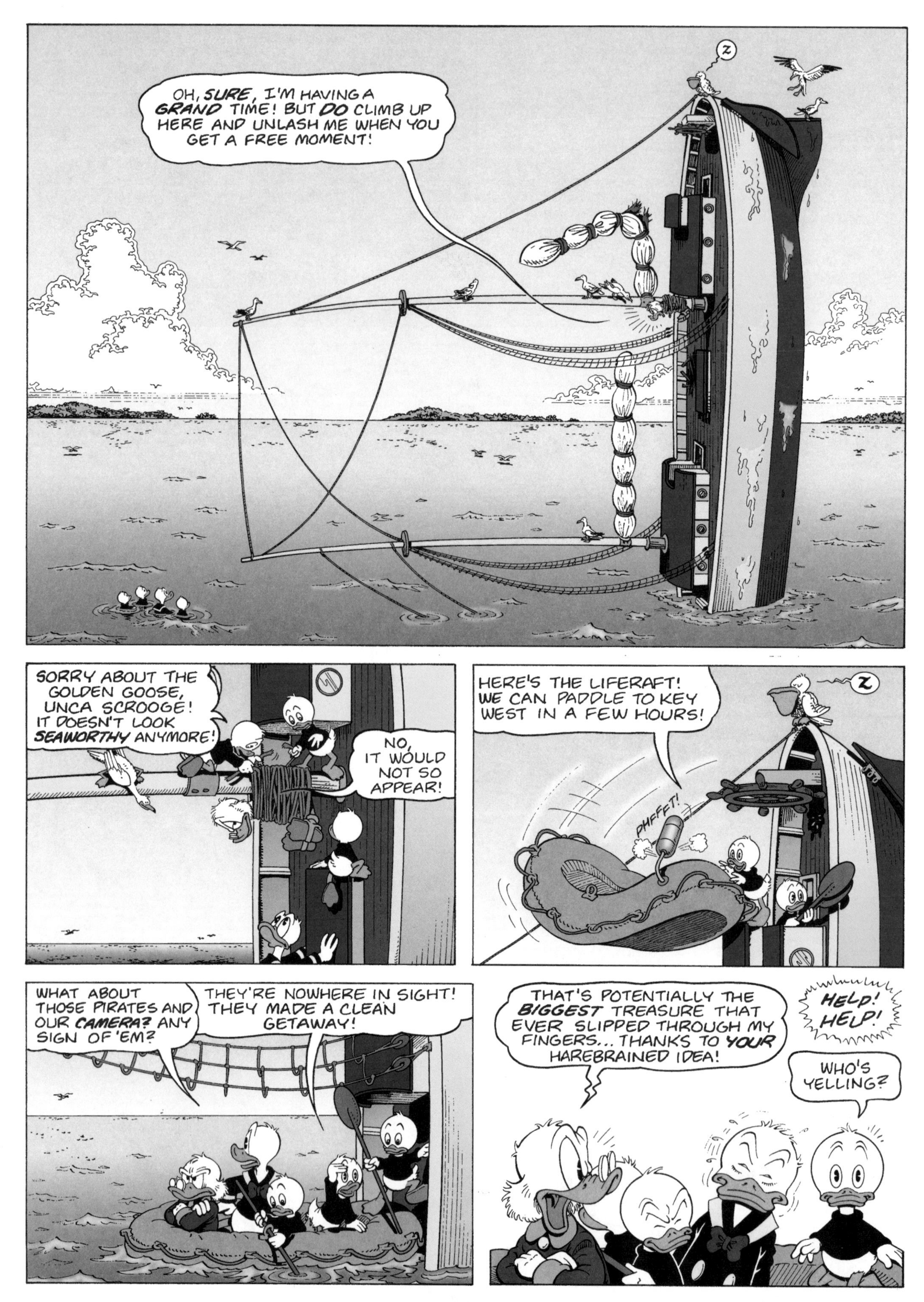
Z
OH, SURE, I'M HAVING A GRAND TIME! BUT DO CLIMB UP HERE AND UNLASH ME WHEN YOU GET A FREE MOMENT!
SORRY ABOUT THE GOLDEN GOOSE, UNCA SCROOGE! IT DOESN'T LOOK SEAWORTHY ANYMORE!
NO, IT WOULD NOT SO APPEAR!
HERE'S THE LIFERAFT! WE CAN PADDLE TO KEY WEST IN A FEW HOURS!
Z
PHFFFT!
WHAT ABOUT THOSE PIRATES AND OUR CAMERA? ANY SIGN OF 'EM?
THEY'RE NOWHERE IN SIGHT! THEY MADE A CLEAN GETAWAY!
THAT'S POTENTIALLY THE BIGGEST TREASURE THAT EVER SLIPPED THROUGH MY FINGERS... THANKS TO YOUR HAREBRAINED IDEA!
HELP! HELP!
WHO'S YELLING?

HELP! HELP!
THE CRIES ARE COMING FROM THAT HOLE IN THE OCEAN!
..."HOLE IN THE OCEAN"?
HEY! THAT'S OUR GLASS DOME...FLOATING UPSIDE-DOWN!
WELL, WELL AND WELL! WATCHA' KNOW ABOUT THAT!
YOU BOYS TOSS UP OUR CAMERA, AND MAYBE WE'LL DROP A LINE DOWN TO YOU!
@#%

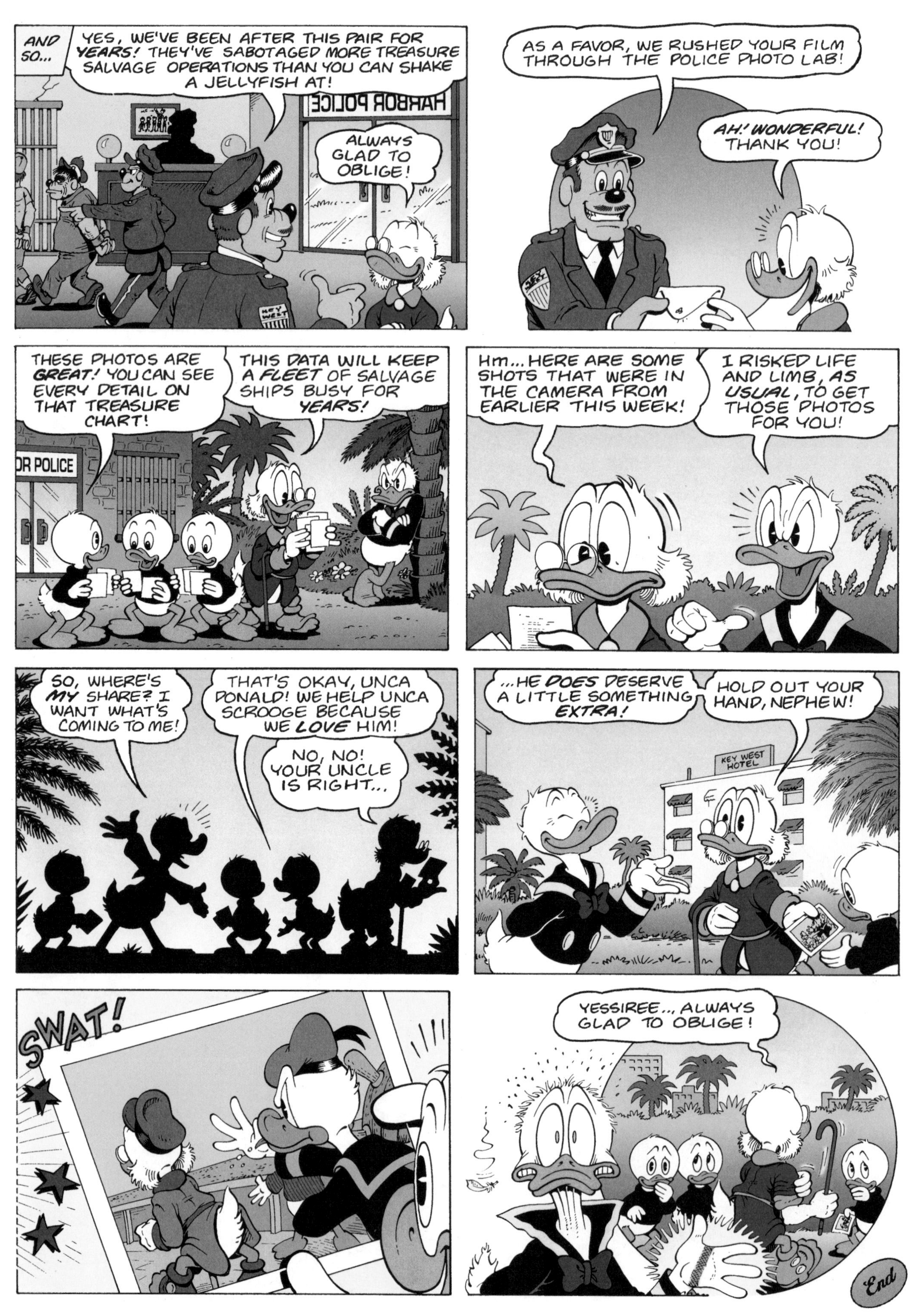
AND SO...
YES, WE'VE BEEN AFTER THIS PAIR FOR YEARS! THEY'VE SABOTAGED MORE TREASURE SALVAGE OPERATIONS THAN YOU CAN SHAKE A JELLYFISH AT!
HARBOR POLICE
ALWAYS GLAD TO OBLIGE!
AS A FAVOR, WE RUSHED YOUR FILM THROUGH THE POLICE PHOTO LAB!
AH! WONDERFUL! THANK YOU!
THESE PHOTOS ARE GREAT! YOU CAN SEE EVERY DETAIL ON THAT TREASURE CHART!
THIS DATA WILL KEEP A FLEET OF SALVAGE SHIPS BUSY FOR YEARS!
OR POLICE
Hm... HERE ARE SOME SHOTS THAT WERE IN THE CAMERA FROM EARLIER THIS WEEK!
I RISKED LIFE AND LIMB, AS USUAL, TO GET THOSE PHOTOS FOR YOU!
SO, WHERE'S MY SHARE? I WANT WHAT'S COMING TO ME!
THAT'S OKAY, UNCA DONALD! WE HELP UNCA SCROOGE BECAUSE WE LOVE HIM!
NO, NO! YOUR UNCLE IS RIGHT...
...HE DOES DESERVE A LITTLE SOMETHING EXTRA!
HOLD OUT YOUR HAND, NEPHEW!
KEY WEST HOTEL
SWAT!
YESSIREE... ALWAYS GLAD TO OBLIGE!
End

WALT DISNEY'S
UNCLE $CROOGE
in
RETURN TO XANADU
PEN RENTAL 5¢
NO BILL COLLECTORS
YES, BOYS, I'M RATHER PROUD OF THIS COLLECTION OF TROPHIES FROM MY MANY ADVENTURES!
OUR MANY ADVENTURES, YOU MEAN!
1916
D 90314
LIKE THIS CROWN OF GENGHIS KHAN! WE HELPED YOU RECOVER IT AFTER A YETI STOLE IT!
YOU WERE PAID, NEPHEW... AND QUITE HANDSOMELY!
A QUARTER AND A NICKEL PER HOUR IS "HANDSOME" ONLY IF YOU THINK WASHINGTON AND JEFFERSON ARE CUTE!
UNCA SCROOGE, YOU NEVER TOLD US HOW YOUR AGENTS FOUND THE CROWN!
DIDN'T I? WELL, IT ALL BEGAN WHEN THE SHERPAS AT MY YAK FARM IN LADAKH HEARD TELL OF A GOAT-HERDER WHO'D FOUND SOME SORT OF FANCY TOPPER!
I FIGURED IT WAS SOME TREASURE FROM THE MONGOL EMPIRE! ONCE WE FOUND THE GOAT MAN, I SIMPLY TRADED HIM MY YAK FARM FOR THE CROWN!
SCRAM!

THE CROWN WAS LOST FROM MY CARAVAN IN THE HINDU KUSH, BUT I RECOVERED IT!
SEE IF THERE'S ANYTHING ABOUT THAT CROWN IN OUR JUNIOR WOODCHUCKS MANUAL!
WE! WE!
KISS
IT SAYS HERE THAT MARCO POLO SAW THE CROWN DURING HIS SEARCH FOR THE REALM OF PRESTOR JOHN IN CHINA!
THAT'S THE FABLED LAND THAT TRAVELERS SOUGHT THROUGHOUT THE MIDDLE AGES!
MARCO POLO CLAIMED TO HAVE FOUND PRESTOR JOHN'S LAND AND TOLD KUBLAI KHAN OF IT WHEN HE REACHED CATHAY! KUBLAI INVADED TIBET AND MOVED INTO THE KINGDOM!
KUBLAI EVEN MOVED THE TREASURE OF THE MONGOL EMPIRE THERE FOR SAFE-KEEPING, SINCE THE PLACE WAS SO INACCESSIBLE!
THE ENTIRE TREASURE OF THE BIGGEST EMPIRE IN HISTORY??
INCLUDING HIS GRANDFATHER'S CROWN! WHEREVER THIS CROWN WAS, SO SHOULD BE THE REST OF THAT TREASURE!
I'VE HAD THE CROWN FOR YEARS WITHOUT KNOWING IT'S A KEY TO A MUCH VASTER TROVE!
YOU KIDS ARE FANTASTIC! MISS QUACKFASTER--DOUBLE MY ANNUAL DONATION TO THE "JUNIOR WOODCHUCKS OF THE WORLD"!
YESSIR! THAT WILL STILL BE THE SAME AMOUNT, SIR!
KISS
DONALD! KIDS! PACK YOUR BAGS! WE'RE OFF TO THE HIMALAYAS IN SEARCH OF THE TREASURE OF GENGHIS KHAN!
NOT ME!
IT'LL BE A COLD DAY BEFORE I EVER GO ON ANOTHER OF YOUR SCREWBALL TREASURE HUNTS FOR ONLY 30 CENTS AN HOUR!
BRRRRR...

WHERE ARE WE NOW, UNCA SCROOGE?
BOYS, WE'RE IN THE FOOTHILLS BETWEEN THE HIMALAYAS AND THE KUNLUN MOUNTAINS... WHERE I ONCE TRADED YAKS MANY YEARS AGO!
AH, THIS IS LIKE OLD TIMES!
THERE'S MY OLD YAK COMPANY! AND THAT MUST BE THE GOATHERDER WHO FOUND THE CROWN!
McDuck's Yaks
(UNDER NEW OWNERSHIP)
WE SELL YAK WITH NO YAKKETY-YAK!
JOOLAY! JOOLAY!
I'LL SHOW HIM THE CROWN! THAT SHOULD JOG HIS MEMORY!
HAH, SO! SHO MEECDOCK SCROOTCH!
PLEASE TELL ME HE'S POINTING SOUTH! TELL ME HE'S SAYING HE FOUND IT UNDER A PALM TREE!
HE'S POINTING NORTH TOWARDS THAT BIG MOUNTAIN!
SUCCESS! HE FOUND THE CROWN IN AN ICE CAPE AT THE BASE OF MOUNT KARAKAL!
DID HE SAY "KARAKAL," OR WAS THAT THE SOUND OF MY BEAK FREEZING OFF?
AS THE DAYS WEAR ON, DONALD PONDERS WHAT THE FORMER GOATHERDER'S INFORMATION COST UNCLE SCROOGE...
ALL I CAN SAY IS THAT GUY'S A SHARPER YAK TRADER THAN YOU EVER WERE!
GRIPE, GRIPE, GRIPE! HIKING IS HEALTHY!

BESIDES, WE'RE ALMOST THERE! WATCH FOR A CAVE IN THE MOUNTAINSIDE!
I CAN BARELY SEE WHERE I'M GOING IN THIS BLIZZARD!
EUREKA! THERE'S THE CAVE, BETWEEN THOSE ICE PILLARS! C'MON!
THESE AREN'T ICE PILLARS, UNCA SCROOGE! THEY'RE ANCIENT TIBETAN CHORTENS!
SAY WHAT?
TRAIL MARKERS, CENTURIES OLD! THIS IS MORE THAN JUST A CAVE!
I KNOW IT! IT'S THE ENTRANCE TO KUBLAI KHAN'S MONGOLIAN MONEY BIN! HOO HAH!
IT'S A DEAD END!
NO, WAIT! WHAT'S THIS IN THE ICE?
THE REMAINS OF AN ANCIENT TEAKWOOD BOX! AND SEE? THERE'S WHERE THE GOATHERDER PULLED THE CROWN FROM THE ICE!
THE MONGOL TREASURY MUST BE NEARBY!
WELL, I HOPE THERE'S A THRONE TO GO WITH THE CROWN! I NEED TO SIT AND REST!
YOW!
CRUNCH!

HE BROKE THROUGH THE ICE INTO A LARGER CAVE!
I'LL BET IT'S THE TREASURE VAULT OF CATHAY IN ALL ITS SPLENDOR!
SPLENDOR? LOOKS LIKE THE DUCKBURG SEWER TO ME!
IT'S AN UNDERGROUND RIVER!
A WALKWAY CARVED INTO THE ROCK! WHAT DOES THAT CHORTEN SAY, UNCA SCROOGE?
IT'S IN ANCIENT CATHAYIC... "WHOSOEVER WALKS THIS TRAIL, BESIDE MY SACRED RIVER ALPH..."
"...BEWARE THE WRATH OF KUBLAI KHAN!"
THE RIVER ALPH? DID YOU SAY ALPH??
"IT WAS A MIRACLE OF RARE DEVICE, A SUNNY PLEASURE DOME WITH CAVES OF ICE!"
WHAT? WHERE'S IT SAY THAT?
NO, UNCA SCROOGE! THAT'S FROM THE POEM OF THE LEGEND OF KUBLAI KHAN'S PALACE IN THE LOST VALLEY OF XANADU!
XANADU? I'VE HEARD OF THAT PLACE!
ALPH WAS THE RIVER IN THE LEGEND! UNCA SCROOGE, THIS IS THE ROAD TO XANADU!
YOU'VE HIT THE JACKPOT! THE MOST WONDROUS VALLEY ON EARTH! THE LAND OF MILK AND HONEY!
MILK AND HONEY AND TREASURE! LEAD ON!
WELL, I'LL TELL YOU WHO'LL GET THE TREASURE...
...AND WHO'LL END UP WITH THE COW JUICE AND BEE GRAVY!

ONLY A TIMEPIECE CAN DETERMINE WHEN NIGHT FALLS ON THE MOUNTAINS FAR ABOVE, BUT ONCE IT DOES...
WHAT WAS THAT POEM YOU MENTIONED, HUEY? WHAT DOES IT TELL OF XANADU?
WELL, IN 1798 SAMUEL TAYLOR COLERIDGE WROTE A POEM CALLED "KUBLA KHAN" BASED ON WHAT HE READ IN BOOKS THAT WERE ANCIENT EVEN THEN!
IN THE 15TH CENTURY, SAMUEL PURCHAS WROTE OF XANADU IN HIS TRAVEL DIARIES, BOOKS THAT FASCINATED COLERIDGE!
SO YOU WIN THE MERIT BADGE IN POETRY! SO I'M IMPRESSED!
IS THE POEM IN OUR JUNIOR WOOD-CHUCK MANUAL?
WHAT DO YOU THINK?
"IN XANADU DID KUBLA KHAN A STATELY PLEASURE DOME DECREE...
"...WHERE ALPH, THE SACRED RIVER, RAN THROUGH CAVERNS MEASURELESS TO MAN DOWN TO A SUNLESS SEA."
"SO TWICE FIVE MILES OF FERTILE GROUND WITH WALLS AND TOWERS WERE GIRDLED ROUND."
"AND THERE WERE GARDENS BRIGHT WITH SINUOUS RILLS, WHERE BLOSSOMED MANY AN INCENSE-BEARING TREE."
"AND HERE WERE FORESTS ANCIENT AS THE HILLS, ENFOLDING SUNNY SPOTS OF GREENERY."
GOSH, THAT DOES SOUND NICE...
...AND, Y'KNOW...THAT PLACE SOUNDS SORTA FAMILIAR, TOO!
SURE! I GUESS YOU'VE BEEN TO XANADU AND JUST FORGOT ABOUT IT! GO TO SLEEP! TOMORROW'S ANOTHER DAY!

TOMORROW WAS ANOTHER DAY... AND ANOTHER, UNTIL...
UNCLE SCROOGE, OUR FOOD IS RUNNING LOW! WE'D BETTER TURN BACK!
HEY!
THERE'S SOMETHING UP AHEAD! I THINK THE TUNNEL ENDS!
DO YOU SEE HUGE PILES OF GOLD AND JEWELS??
NOT REALLY!
ROAR!
WELL...I'LL BE DOUBLE-JABBERED! WHAT DO YOU MAKE OF ALL THIS?
LOOKS LIKE THERE WAS A WOODEN BRIDGE OVER TO THOSE IRON DOORS, BUT IT ROTTED AWAY CENTURIES AGO!
WHAT'S THAT UP AHEAD?
IT'S SOME SORT OF SLUICE GATE FOR THE RIVER WATER!
THAT'S KUBLAI KHAN'S WORK, ALL RIGHT! HE BUILT CHINA'S GRAND CANAL!
ROAR!
WHAT'S BEYOND THE GATE?
HERE--WE CAN LEAN OUT AND PEEK THROUGH THE OPENING!
ROAR!
WOW!

SWOGGLE MY EYE-BULBS! IT'S THE "SUNLESS SEA" FROM THAT POEM!
LOOK AT THE WATERFALL! YOU CAN SEE DAYLIGHT SHOWING THROUGH FROM UP ABOVE!
ROAR!
"THROUGH WOOD AND DALE THE SACRED RIVER RAN, THEN REACHED THE CAVERNS MEASURELESS TO MAN, AND SANK IN TUMULT TO A LIFELESS OCEAN."
POETRY BOY AGAIN!
THERE'S THE FINAL PROOF, UNCA SCROOGE! XANADU IS DIRECTLY ABOVE US!
YES... SNIFF... I CAN ACTUALLY SMELL THE GOLD AND GEMS NEARBY!
AND THERE'S THE DOORWAY TO MY VALLEY OF TREASURE!
BUT HOW DO WE CROSS THIS RUSHING RIVER?
CLOSE THE SLUICE GATE! THE WATER WILL STOP FLOWING AND WE'LL JUST WALK ACROSS!
YES!

GRUNT!
GASP!
UNGH!
MORE! MORE!
GROAN!
SQUEAAK!
CREAAK!
THERE! IT'S SHUT!
WHAT ARE WE WAITING FOR? LET'S GO!
LOOK AT THE BAR ON THE DOORS! KUBLAI SURE DIDN'T WANT ANYONE GETTING AT HIS TREASURE!
BUT...THE BAR IS ON THE OUTSIDE...
...LIKE KUBLAI WAS TRYING TO KEEP SOMEONE FROM GETTING OUT, NOT IN!
GULP! I'LL TAKE A CHANCE-- OPEN IT!
CREEAAK!
THIS DEFINITELY LEADS OUT! FEEL THE BREEZE?
HEY! WATCH THE DOORS!
CREEEAAKK...
SLAM!
CLUNK!
THOSE DOORS WERE HUNG AT AN ANGLE TO CLOSE EASILY! WE'RE STUCK HERE NOW!
WE'LL WORRY ABOUT THAT LATER!
I SURE HOPE THIS PLACE IS ALL IT'S CRACKED UP TO BE! IF IT ISN'T...OH, WHAT A JAM WE'RE IN!
OH, HUSH! THAT'S WHAT YOU SAID LAST TIME!

LAST TIME? WHAT LAST TIME?
I...I DON'T KNOW! BUT THERE'S SOMETHING FAMILIAR ABOUT ALL THIS!
LOOK-- SOME SORT OF BOX!
BUT HOW COULD IT BE FAMILIAR? I'VE NEVER BEEN HERE BEFORE!
YOW! DON'T BE SO SURE, UNCA SCROOGE!
READ THIS LABEL: "NERVE TONIC-- PROPERTY OF SCROOGE McDUCK"!
HA! YOU HAVE BEEN HERE BEFORE! WE ALL HAVE!
OH, MY SOCKS AND SHOES! YOU DON'T MEAN...
WELCOME BACK, UNCA SCROOGE!
WELCOME BACK TO XANADU!
WELCOME BACK TO TRALLA LA!!

THE LOST VALLEY OF TRALLA LA! WHO? WHAT? WHERE?
THIS MATCHES THE POEM OF XANADU PERFECTLY!
TRALLA LA IS "TWICE FIVE" MILES OF FERTILE GROUND, SURROUNDED BY ROCK WALLS AND TOWERING MOUNTAINS, WITH GARDENS BRIGHT WITH STREAMS!
EVEN THE WHIRLPOOL IS IN THE POEM!
THE RIVER SINKS IN TUMULT TO A SUNLESS SEA AND CAVES OF ICE!
SO, THIS IS XANADU, WHERE THE TREASURE OF KUBLAI KHAN IS KEPT! AND THESE TRALLA LALLIANS CLAIMED TO BE SO POOR AND SIMPLE!
HAH!
AREN'T YOU WORRIED, UNCLE SCROOGE? WHEN YOU LAST LEFT TRALLA LA, THE NATIVES WERE TRYING TO LYNCH YOU!
ULP! YOU'RE RIGHT!
LET'S GET OUTTA HERE!
WE CAN'T! THAT ANCIENT DOOR LOCKED AND TRAPPED US HERE!
SOMEONE'S COMING!
WE'LL NEED THE HELP OF THE TRALLA LALLIANS TO CLIMB OUT OF HERE!
...ER...HELLO, THERE! ...UH...REMEMBER ME?
?
MISTER McDUCK SCROOGE! YOU HAVE RETURNED TO OUR HAPPY VALLEY! WELCOME! WELCOME!
YOU'RE...NOT STILL SORE AT ME?

US? CERTAINLY NOT! EVERYTHING IS BACK TO NORMAL NOW! FRIENDSHIP IS STILL WHAT WE VALUE MOST!
TO WHAT DO WE OWE THE JOY OF YOUR RETURN?
WELL, I SEEK THE TREASURE THAT GOES WITH THIS OLD CROWN! HAVE YOU EVER SEEN--
AAAIIIEEE! THE SIGN OF THE GOLDEN HORDE!
THE CROWN OF THE EVIL MONGOL INVADERS!
SEIZE THEM!
HE'S DONE IT AGAIN! BROUGHT ANOTHER PLAGUE TO OUR HAPPY LAND!
FIRST PLAIN AWFUL AND NOW HERE! UNCLE SCROOGE, WE CAN'T TAKE YOU ANYWHERE!
THE DUCKS ARE TAKEN TO THE CHOSCHAMBO... THE HIGH LAMA'S TOP AIDE!
MISTER SCROOGE! YOU HAVE RETURNED! I AM LAH DEEDAH!
YEAH, YEAH, I REMEMBER YOU!
AND RETURNING WITH YOU IS THE CROWN OF THE KHAN KUBLAI, THAT WHICH WE RID OURSELVES OF OVER SIX CENTURIES AGO! WHAT IS THE MEANING?
THAT CROWN IS THE KEY TO THE ENTIRE TREASURE OF THE MONGOL EMPIRE--AND IT LEAD ME STRAIGHT HERE! WHY DO YOU FIB ABOUT THERE BEING NO WEALTH HERE IN TRALLA LA?!
YOU KNOW WE HAVE NO USE FOR SUCH WORLDLY THINGS! WE BELIEVE IN THE RICHES OF HEART AND MIND!
YOU'RE NOT ANSWERING THE QUESTION!

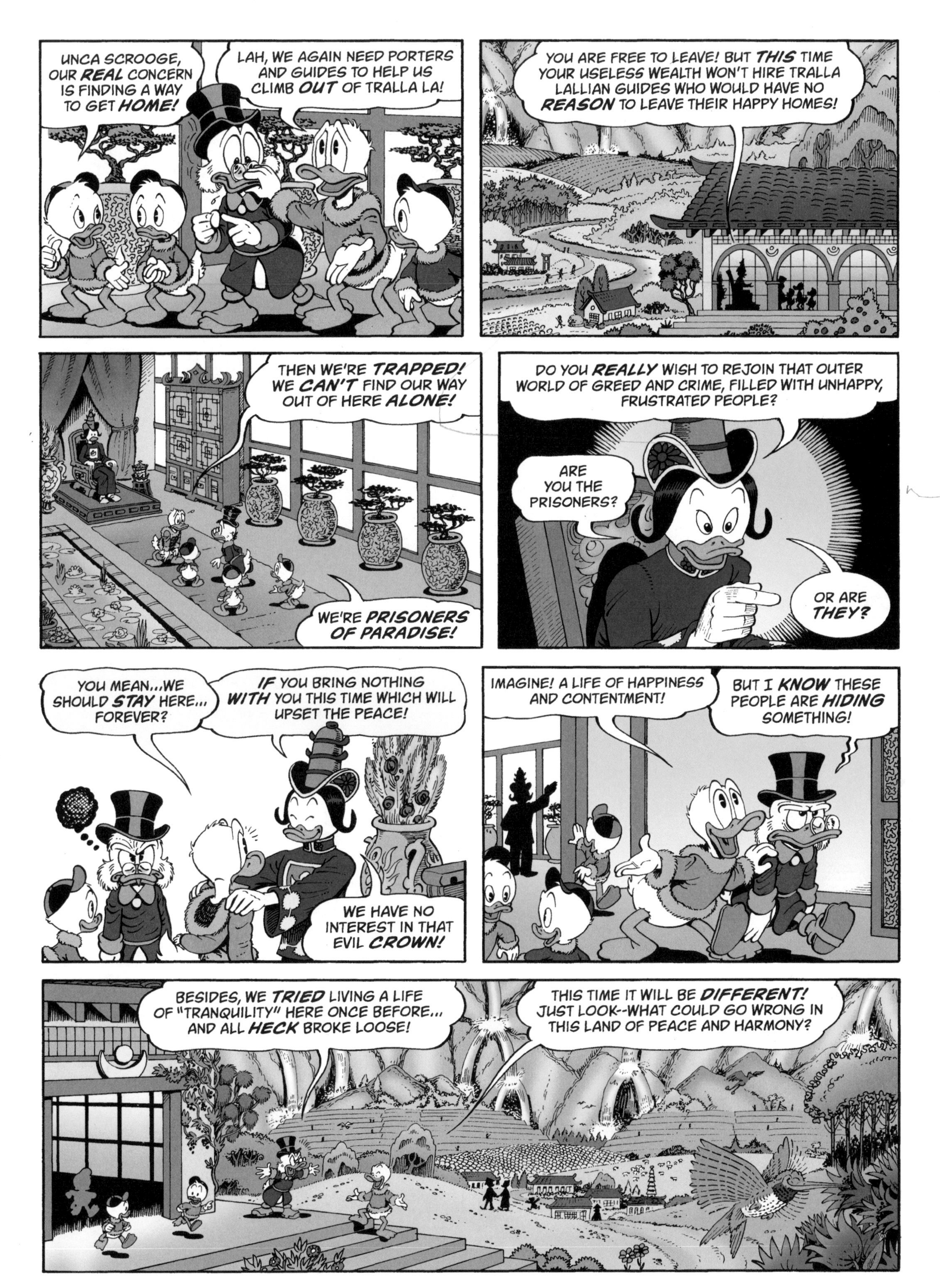
UNCA SCROOGE, OUR REAL CONCERN IS FINDING A WAY TO GET HOME!
LAH, WE AGAIN NEED PORTERS AND GUIDES TO HELP US CLIMB OUT OF TRALLA LA!
YOU ARE FREE TO LEAVE! BUT THIS TIME YOUR USELESS WEALTH WON'T HIRE TRALLA LALLIAN GUIDES WHO WOULD HAVE NO REASON TO LEAVE THEIR HAPPY HOMES!
THEN WE'RE TRAPPED! WE CAN'T FIND OUR WAY OUT OF HERE ALONE!
WE'RE PRISONERS OF PARADISE!
DO YOU REALLY WISH TO REJOIN THAT OUTER WORLD OF GREED AND CRIME, FILLED WITH UNHAPPY, FRUSTRATED PEOPLE?
ARE YOU THE PRISONERS?
OR ARE THEY?
YOU MEAN...WE SHOULD STAY HERE... FOREVER?
IF YOU BRING NOTHING WITH YOU THIS TIME WHICH WILL UPSET THE PEACE!
WE HAVE NO INTEREST IN THAT EVIL CROWN!
IMAGINE! A LIFE OF HAPPINESS AND CONTENTMENT!
BUT I KNOW THESE PEOPLE ARE HIDING SOMETHING!
BESIDES, WE TRIED LIVING A LIFE OF "TRANQUILITY" HERE ONCE BEFORE... AND ALL HECK BROKE LOOSE!
THIS TIME IT WILL BE DIFFERENT! JUST LOOK--WHAT COULD GO WRONG IN THIS LAND OF PEACE AND HARMONY?

WHAT SENTIMENTAL DRIVEL! WE BELONG IN CIVILIZATION! LOOK AT THIS BACKWARD PLACE--ALL FARMS AND FLOWERS AND NATURE PRESERVES!
OH, IT MIGHT SEEM NICE, LIVING SOMEWHERE THAT'S POLLUTION-FREE, AND WHERE ANIMALS DON'T FEAR BEING SHOT ON SIGHT...BUT...
AND LOOK! WORK! IF YOU LIVE HERE, IT'LL MEAN BACK-BREAKING LABOR--BUILDING YOUR OWN HOME, GROWING YOUR OWN FOOD!
OH, SURE, I RECALL FROM MY DAYS IN THE KLONDIKE HOW SATISFYING A GOOD DAY'S WORK CAN FEEL, ESPECIALLY IN SUCH IDYLLIC SURROUNDINGS...BUT...
DONALD?
HUEY?
LOUIE?
DEWEY?
HMMPH! IT DIDN'T TAKE LONG FOR THEM TO BE SWEPT UP IN TRALLA LA'S JOYOUS LIFE OF...I MEAN WRETCHED LIFE OF MISERY AND--
MASTER SCROOGE?
MY MOTHER TOLD ME OF YOU! SHE REMEMBERS YOU AS A MAN OF GREATNESS!
YES, CHILD! I'M THE WORLD'S RICHEST DUCK! YOUR MOTHER WAS IMPRESSED BY ALL MY MONEY!
NO...MOTHER SAID YOU WERE GOOD AT FIXING DOLLIES! MINE BROKE HER LITTLE ARM!
!

HM! I DO RECALL HELPING KIDS FIX BROKEN DOLLS ON MY LAST VISIT! I USED TO FIX MY TWO SISTERS' DOLLS BACK HOME IN SCOTLAND WHEN I WAS YOUR AGE!
THAT WAS LONG AGO...
...LONG, LONG AGO! LIFE WAS DIFFERENT THEN...WHEN I WAS YOUR AGE...BACK IN SCOTLAND...
I DON'T KNOW WHAT "MAH-NEE" IS, MASTER SCROOGE, BUT I'M SURE HAVING IT DOESN'T MAKE YOU A BAD MAN!
NO...NOT SO BAD, I GUESS...
WELL, WHERE WAS I? I CAN'T RECALL...
Y'KNOW, THIS PLACE KIND OF REMINDS ME OF THE SCOTTISH COUNTRYSIDE!
I WONDER IF THE FISHING HERE IS AS GOOD AS SCOTLAND!
A WEEK IN TRALLA LA IS ENOUGH TO MELT THE FROSTIEST OF HEARTS... EVEN THAT OF THE WORLD'S RICHEST DUCK!
THIS IS THE LIFE!
WHY, IT'S BEEN DAYS SINCE I EVEN THOUGHT ABOUT THAT TREASURE OF...UH... WHOEVER IT WAS!
I DON'T KNOW WHAT IT IS ABOUT THIS VALLEY, BUT I HAVEN'T FELT SO STRONG AND HEALTHY SINCE MY YOUTH!
DONALD! HOW ARE YOU THIS WONDERFUL MORNING? HELPING TO BUILD A HOUSE, I SEE!
I SURE AM, UNCLE SCROOGE!
AND I'M GOOD AT IT, TOO! I DON'T SEEM TO CONSTANTLY MESS THINGS UP, NOW THAT I'M FREE FROM ALL THE PRESSURES AND RESPONSI-BILITIES OF DUCKBURG!

BUT WHERE ARE THE KIDS? SHOULDN'T YOU BE WATCHING THEM?
OH, GET OFF MY BACK! THEY'RE ENTERTAINING THEMSELVES AT THAT BIG LIBRARY THERE!
SPLOCK!
MEANWHILE, SURE ENOUGH...
TRALLA LA MUST HAVE BEEN A CENTER OF CULTURE IN THE DAYS OF MARCO POLO!
LOTS OF THESE ANCIENT BOOKS AND MANUSCRIPTS WERE THOUGHT LOST SINCE THE LIBRARY OF ALEXANDRIA BURNED!
LOOK AT THIS, MEN! IN THIS MANUSCRIPT WRITTEN BY PLINY THE ELDER IN 73 A.D.!
IN VOLUME XIII, ON PAGE MCVI, IN THE LAST PARAGRAPH...
...A FACT NOT IN THE JUNIOR WOODCHUCKS MANUAL AND RESERVOIR OF INEXHAUSTIBLE KNOWLEDGE!
WOW!
LAH DEEDAH INVITES THE DUCKS TO TEA TO ASK HOW THEY ARE ADJUSTING TO HAPPINESS...
SO, YOU SAY WHEN KUBLAI KHAN LEARNED OF TRALLA LA, HE MOVED IN?
SADLY, YES-- IT WAS A DARK TIME IN OUR HISTORY!
KUBLAI LOVED NATURE AND SCIENCE, AND HE AND HIS WARLORDS MADE TRALLA LA THEIR SECRET RETREAT! BUT THEY MADE SLAVES OF ALL OUR PEACEFUL PEOPLE!
JEEPERS! WHAT FINALLY HAPPENED?
ONE DAY HE LEFT AND NEVER RETURNED! HE AND HIS GENERALS TOOK THE SECRET OF TRALLA LA TO THEIR GRAVES!
YEARS PASSED, AND WE ULTIMATELY GOT RID OF ALL EVIDENCE OF KUBLAI KHAN'S EVIL OCCUPATION!
THAT'S HOW THE CROWN GOT OUTSIDE OF THE VALLEY! IT FLOATED DOWN THE RIVER IN ITS TEAKWOOD BOX!

HOW DID KUBLAI BULLY HIS WAY IN HERE? COULDN'T YOUR PEOPLE SIMPLY SEAL THE CAVE ENTRANCE?
ALAS, NO! THEY LIVED UNDER A TERRIBLE THREAT!
KUBLAI SEALED THE ENTRANCE HIMSELF, AND BEYOND THAT AWFUL DOOR HE GUARDED A MECHANISM OF DESTRUCTION!
BRRR! WHAT WAS IT?
IT WAS A DEVICE HE SAID WOULD STOP THE FLOW OF OUR SACRED WHIRLPOOL AND FLOOD TRALLA LA TO THE MOUNTAINTOPS!
WHUH-OH! THE SLUICE GATE WE CLOSED SO WE COULD CROSS THE RIVER! DID WE REOPEN IT!?!
NO!! WE LEFT IT SHUT!
UK-WUK!
WHEN THAT HUGE CAVERN FINALLY FILLS WITH WATER, THINGS WILL START TO GET DAMP AROUND HERE!
WE GOTTA GO BACK AND OPEN THAT SLUICE!
AND FAST!
MASTER LAH, WE HAVE LEISURE STUFF AND RELAXING JUNK TO ATTEND TO...IN A HURRY! IF YOU'LL EXCUSE US...?
OF COURSE! AND I MUST SEE WHAT THE COMMOTION IS OUTSIDE!
BY THE POWERS OF MAKALU! THE WHIRLPOOL... IT HAS STOPPED!!

OH, MY ACHING DUCKFEATHERS! WE'VE DONE IT AGAIN!
IF WE DON'T DESTROY THIS VALLEY ONE WAY, WE'LL DO IT ANOTHER!
HIGHTAIL IT BACK TO THE CAVE FAST! THE WATER IS ALREADY RISING!
THAT WHIRLPOOL CARRIED A LOT OF GLACIAL RUNOFF!
OH, KHUMBILA!
WHAT IS ALL THIS WATER??
HEY, CHANG! YOUR TUB OVERFLOWS AGAIN!
NO! THE SACRED RIVER ALPH OVERFLOWS ITS BANKS!
OUR WHIRLPOOL HAS CEASED!!
HONORABLE SCROOGE! DO YOU KNOW ANY-THING ABOUT THIS?
SO SOLLY! NO SPEAKEE YOUR LINGO!
AS FAST AS TEN WEBBED FEET CAN CARRY HALF AS MANY DUCKS, OUR HEROES HURRY BACK DOWN THE CAVE TO THE UNDER-GROUND RIVER!
OOF! GRUNT! THAT 700-YEAR-OLD BAR DIDN'T HAPPEN TO RUST AWAY IN THE PAST WEEK!
WHAT CAN YOU SEE THROUGH THAT MIDDLE SPACE?
THE SLUICE GATE IS SHUT, OKAY! AS IF THERE WAS SOME DOUBT!
WE'LL CLIMB OVER THE MOUNTAINS AND COME BACK UP THE TUNNEL!
THERE'S NO TIME!

BY TOMORROW THEY'LL CALL THIS VALLEY TRALLA LAKE! ANYONE WHO CAN TALK UNDERWATER, THAT IS!
THE ONLY ANSWER IS TO CUT THROUGH THAT BAR WITH A METAL SAW!
BUT...THERE IS NO METAL IN TRALLA LA!
LET'S TELL LAH DEEDAH THE TRUTH! MAYBE HE CAN THINK OF SOMETHING!
BUT LAH DEEDAH CAN ONLY SUGGEST THEY CONSULT THE LEADER OF TRALLA LA...THE HIGH LAMA!
WE NEVER SAW HIM LAST TIME!
HE SPEAKS ONLY THROUGH ME--EXCEPT IN THE WORST EMERGENCIES!
TRALLA LA! LAH DEEDAH! SO, WHAT'S THE LAMA'S NAME? LAMA DAMA DINGDONG?
NO! IT IS TSAMJAH PHEE! WHAT A STRANGE PERSON YOU ARE!
THE HIGH LAMA RESIDES IN THE GOMPA OVERLOOKING THE VALLEY! KUBLAI KHAN BUILT THIS AS HIS PALACE WHEN HE INVADED!
YES...JUST LIKE IN THE POEM...
..."IN XANADU DID KUBLA KHAN A STATELY PLEASURE DOME DECREE"!
HURRY!

SOON THEY ARE IN THE DUKHANG--THE MEETING HALL OF THE LAMASERY--STANDING BEFORE A WIZENED AND ANCIENT FIGURE... THE HIGH LAMA OF TRALLA LA!
MY TRUSTED AIDE TELLS ME OF THE PERIL THREATENING THE VALLEY! THE KHAN'S DEVICE OF DOOM IS IN MOTION!
YOU GOT IT, HIGH! AND UNLESS YOU CAN COUGH UP SOME METAL, WE HAVE NO WAY TO STOP THE SUBMERSION OF TRALLA LA!
I CAN'T BE BLUFFED! I CAN TELL BY THE WAY THE PEOPLE HERE ACTED WHEN I SHOWED THEM THE KHAN'S CROWN THAT THERE ARE SECRETS BEING KEPT IN THIS VALLEY!
THERE'D BE METAL IN THE TREASURE OF THE MONGOL EMPIRE! YOU'D BETTER SPILL THE BEANS!
"BEANS," MY SON? I THOUGHT IT WAS METAL YOU SOUGHT!
WHAT OUR UNCLES MEAN, SIR, IS THAT THIS IS NO TIME FOR SECRETS!
YOU ARE WISE, LITTLE ONE! YOU MUST EXCUSE OUR MYSTERIOUS WAYS!
BUT LIVING IN THIS WONDROUS LAND OF PLENTY AMID A WORLD OF GREED, WE HAVE LEARNED TO KEEP SECRETS! TRALLA LA, LIKE ALL OTHER BEAUTY, LIES AT THE MERCY OF THOSE WHO KNOW NOT HOW TO VALUE IT!
BROTHER! HE'S GOT THAT RIGHT!
BUT YOU MUST HELP US STOP THE FLOOD!!
YOU ARE CORRECT, MY CHILD! I MUST TELL YOU THE TRUTH...
...THERE IS METAL IN TRALLA LA!
!

THERE IS A GREAT DEAL OF METAL, BROUGHT HERE BY OUTSIDERS YEARS AGO! IT IS KEPT HIDDEN IN A SUBTERRANEAN VAULT!
YOU HEAR THAT?!
THE TREASURY OF KUBLAI KHAN! I KNEW IT WAS HERE! I COULD SMELL THE GOLD NEARBY!
EASY, UNCLE SCROOGE!
I THOUGHT YOU'D FORGOTTEN ABOUT THE TREASURE!
BAH! I WAS LULLED INTO A STUPOR BY THIS BORING PLACE!
YOUR LAMANESS, WE NEED THAT METAL!
I WILL TAKE YOU TO THE VAULT! WALK THIS WAY!
HEE HEE! I'D RATHER WALK THIS WAY! TREASURE, TREASURE! TRALLA LA! LA LA! DEE LA!
YOU SEE WHAT THE EVIL METAL DOES TO PEOPLE? IT BRINGS ON THE BRAIN FEVER!
THERE IS THE VAULT OF THE "GOLD" AS YOU CALL IT! IF IT WILL HELP SAVE OUR VALLEY, PLEASE TAKE ALL YOU WISH!
GOLD--GOLD--WONDERFUL GOLD!
THE TREASURE OF KUBLAI KHAN! AND HE'S BEGGING ME TO TAKE IT! BE STILL, MY HEART!
GRUNT!
CREEEAAK

GASP! LOOK! THIS IS MORE FANTASTIC THAN WE EVER DREAMED!
ONE SIDE! LEMME SEE! LEMME SEE!
WAK!!
OH, NO! HOW DO YOU FIGURE THIS IS BETTER THAN YOU'D HOPED?
GOLD WOULD HAVE BEEN TOO SOFT FOR MAKING TOOLS! WE NEED STEEL! AND NOW WE HAVE PLENTY...
?
...OF STEEL BOTTLE CAPS!
YES! THE SAME BOTTLE CAPS THAT NEARLY DESTROYED TRALLA LA YEARS EARLIER NOW MAY HELP TO SAVE THE LEGENDARY VALLEY!
KEEP PUMPING! THE FIRE MUST BE BLAST-FURNACE HOT TO MELT THESE CAPS!
OKAY, IT'S MOLTEN!
START POURING IT INTO THESE CLAY MOULDS! WE'LL NEED SEVERAL BLADES TO SAW THROUGH THE IRON BARS ON THOSE DOORS!
THERE! NOW WE'LL USE ONE BLADE TO FILE TEETH INTO THE OTHERS, AND WE'LL HAVE HACKSAWS!
I CARVED A HOLDER WITH A HANDLE!
WE'RE IN BUSINESS!
LAH DEEDAH HAS SOMETHING FOR US OUTSIDE!

THE HIGH LAMA HAD THIS REED BOAT CONSTRUCTED FOR YOU! HE FORESAW THAT YOU WOULD NEED SUCH A CRAFT!
THIS REED CANOE IS PERFECT! IT'LL FLOAT EVEN IF IT GETS SWAMPED!
FASTER, UNCA DONALD! WE NEED TO HURRY TO THAT CAVE!
HEY! DON'T GO WITHOUT ME! HERE--CATCH!
WE HARDLY NEED GENGHIS KHAN'S CROWN ON THIS MISSION, UNCA SCROOGE!
YEAH, BUT I'M LOOKING AHEAD!
IF WE GET THE DOORS OPEN BUT CAN'T RAISE THE SLUICE GATE, WE'LL HAFTA FLEE DOWN THE UNDER-GROUND RIVERBED, AND I'M NOT LEAVING MY CROWN BEHIND!
WE WOULD NEVER ABANDON THE TRALLA LALLIANS LIKE THAT!
OH, NO! WE WERE AFRAID OF THIS! LOOK!
THE CAVE IS NEARLY SUBMERGED!
GREAT ROCKETBALLS! NOW WHAT?
MAYBE THE INNER CAVES STILL HAVE AIR POCKETS! HURRY, UNCA DONALD
ME?! WHY ME?!
YOU'RE THE BIGGEST AND STRONGEST! WE KIDS COULD NEVER RAISE THAT HEAVY SLUICE GATE!

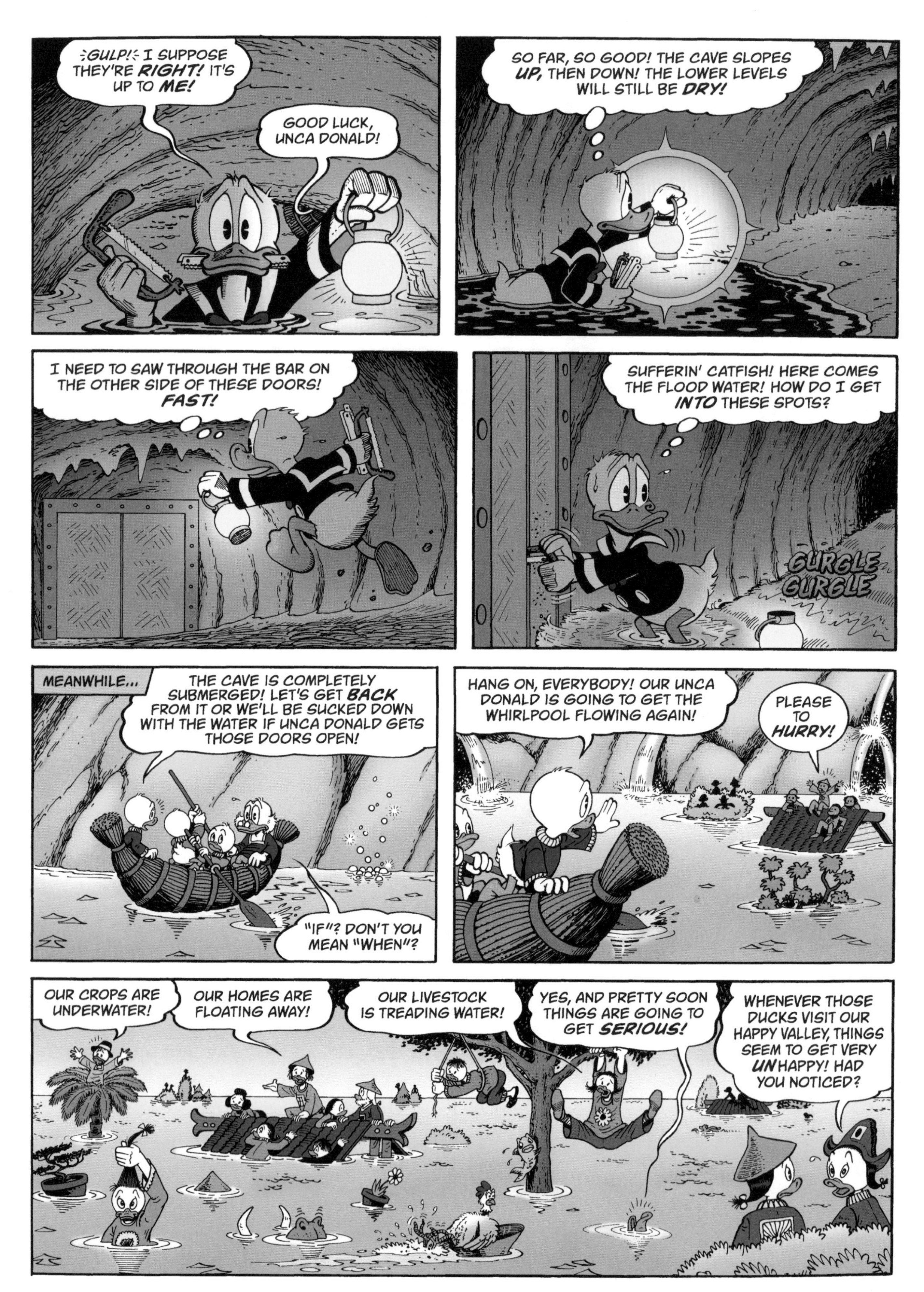

GULP! I SUPPOSE THEY'RE RIGHT! IT'S UP TO ME!
GOOD LUCK, UNCA DONALD!
SO FAR, SO GOOD! THE CAVE SLOPES UP, THEN DOWN! THE LOWER LEVELS WILL STILL BE DRY!
I NEED TO SAW THROUGH THE BAR ON THE OTHER SIDE OF THESE DOORS! FAST!
SUFFERIN' CATFISH! HERE COMES THE FLOOD WATER! HOW DO I GET INTO THESE SPOTS?
GURGLE GURGLE
MEANWHILE...
THE CAVE IS COMPLETELY SUBMERGED! LET'S GET BACK FROM IT OR WE'LL BE SUCKED DOWN WITH THE WATER IF UNCA DONALD GETS THOSE DOORS OPEN!
"IF"? DON'T YOU MEAN "WHEN"?
HANG ON, EVERYBODY! OUR UNCA DONALD IS GOING TO GET THE WHIRLPOOL FLOWING AGAIN!
PLEASE TO HURRY!
OUR CROPS ARE UNDERWATER!
OUR HOMES ARE FLOATING AWAY!
OUR LIVESTOCK IS TREADING WATER!
YES, AND PRETTY SOON THINGS ARE GOING TO GET SERIOUS!
WHENEVER THOSE DUCKS VISIT OUR HAPPY VALLEY, THINGS SEEM TO GET VERY UNHAPPY! HAD YOU NOTICED?

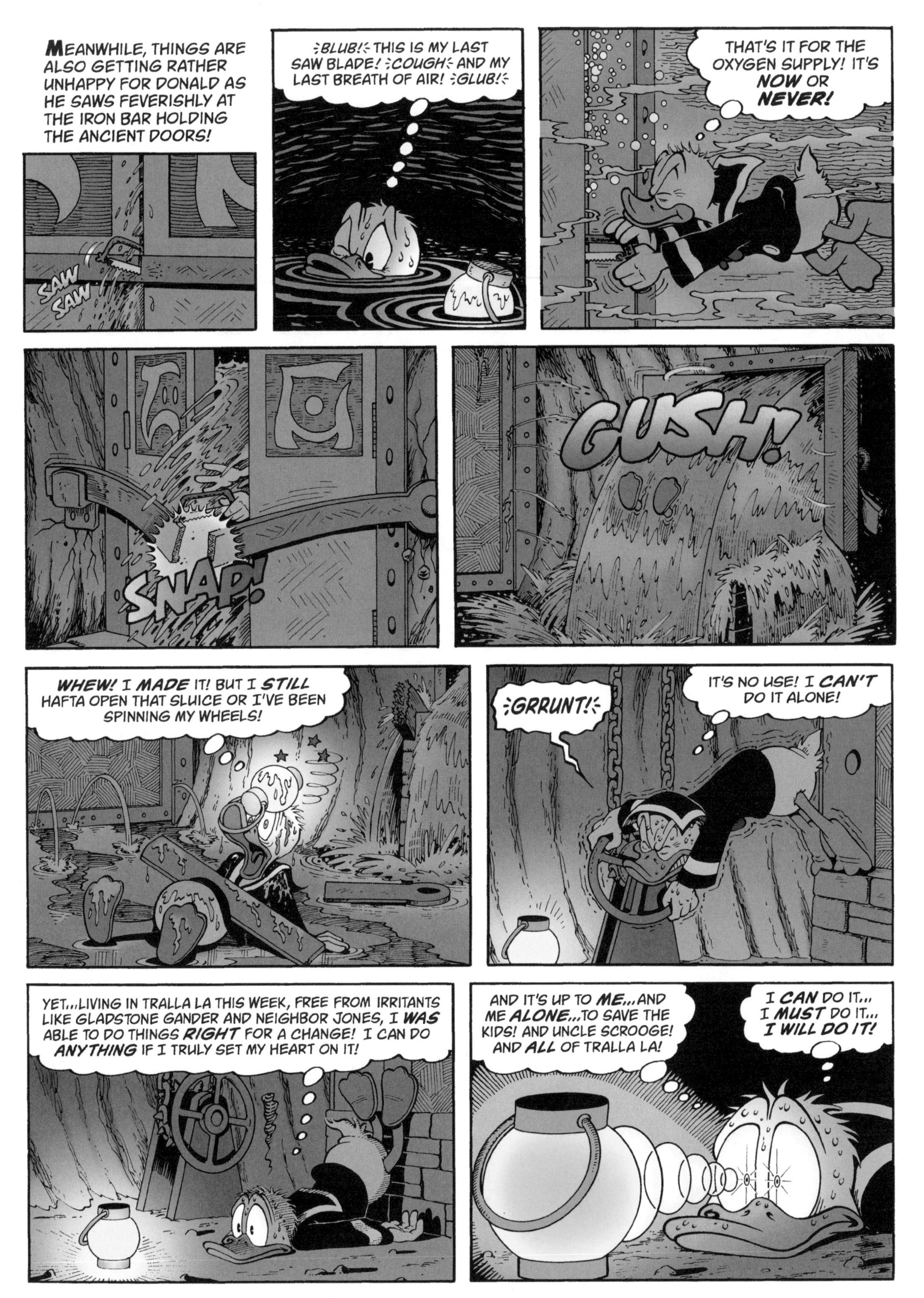
MEANWHILE, THINGS ARE ALSO GETTING RATHER UNHAPPY FOR DONALD AS HE SAWS FEVERISHLY AT THE IRON BAR HOLDING THE ANCIENT DOORS!
SAW SAW
:BLUB!: THIS IS MY LAST SAW BLADE! :COUGH: AND MY LAST BREATH OF AIR! :GLUB!:
THAT'S IT FOR THE OXYGEN SUPPLY! IT'S NOW OR NEVER!
SNAP!
GUSH!
WHEW! I MADE IT! BUT I STILL HAFTA OPEN THAT SLUICE OR I'VE BEEN SPINNING MY WHEELS!
:GRRUNT!:
IT'S NO USE! I CAN'T DO IT ALONE!
YET...LIVING IN TRALLA LA THIS WEEK, FREE FROM IRRITANTS LIKE GLADSTONE GANDER AND NEIGHBOR JONES, I WAS ABLE TO DO THINGS RIGHT FOR A CHANGE! I CAN DO ANYTHING IF I TRULY SET MY HEART ON IT!
AND IT'S UP TO ME...AND ME ALONE...TO SAVE THE KIDS! AND UNCLE SCROOGE! AND ALL OF TRALLA LA!
I CAN DO IT... I MUST DO IT... I WILL DO IT!

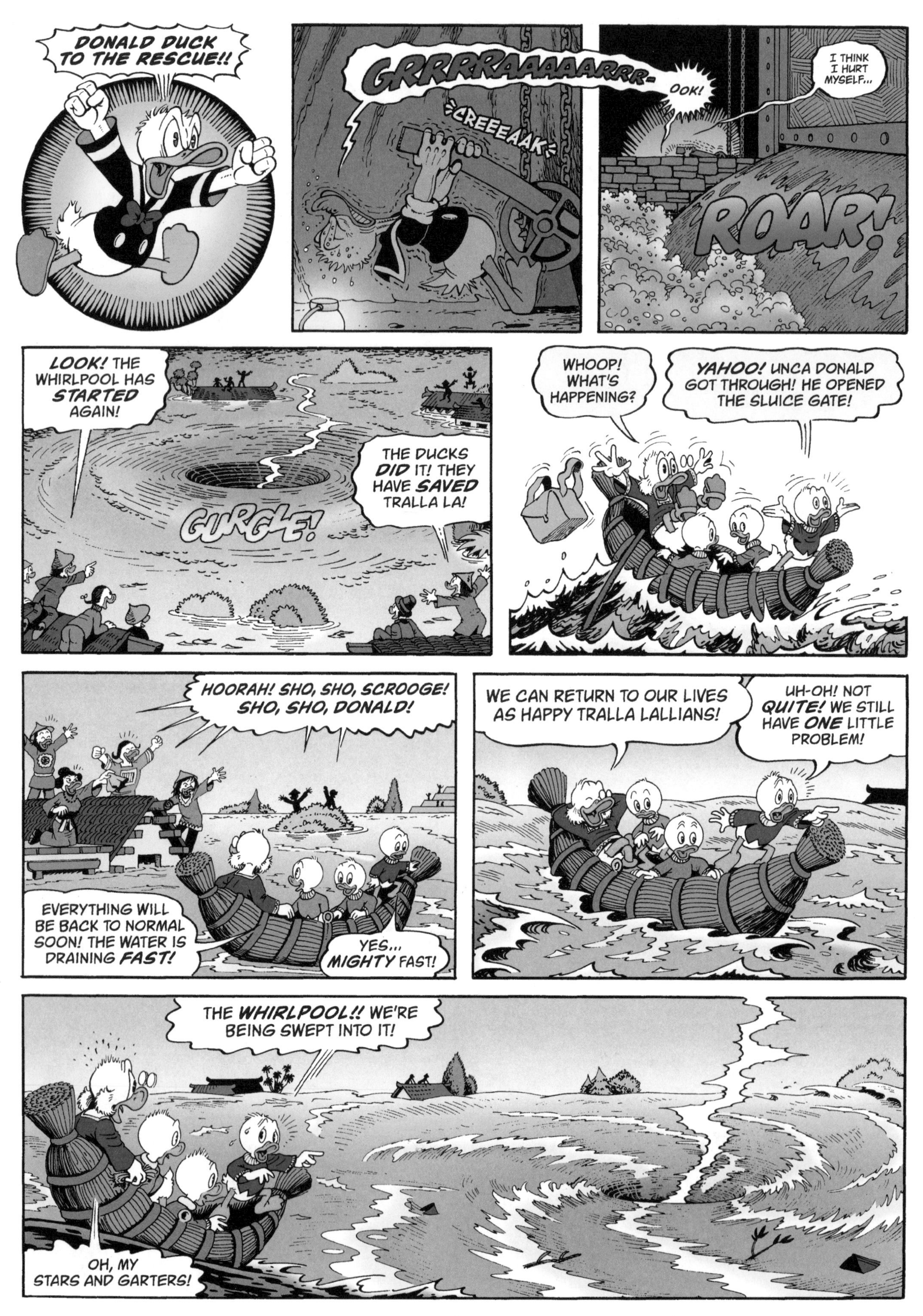
DONALD DUCK TO THE RESCUE!!
GRRRRAAAAAARRR-
CREEEAAK
OOK!
I THINK I HURT MYSELF...
ROAR!
LOOK! THE WHIRLPOOL HAS STARTED AGAIN!
THE DUCKS DID IT! THEY HAVE SAVED TRALLA LA!
GURGLE!
WHOOP! WHAT'S HAPPENING?
YAHOO! UNCA DONALD GOT THROUGH! HE OPENED THE SLUICE GATE!
HOORAH! SHO, SHO, SCROOGE! SHO, SHO, DONALD!
EVERYTHING WILL BE BACK TO NORMAL SOON! THE WATER IS DRAINING FAST!
YES... MIGHTY FAST!
WE CAN RETURN TO OUR LIVES AS HAPPY TRALLA LALLIANS!
UH-OH! NOT QUITE! WE STILL HAVE ONE LITTLE PROBLEM!
THE WHIRLPOOL!! WE'RE BEING SWEPT INTO IT!
OH, MY STARS AND GARTERS!

THERE'S NO NET TO SAVE US THIS TIME!
HOLD ONTO YOUR PINFEATHERS!
HERE WE GOOOOOO...
WHOOOOOAAAAA!!
AUGH! I WISH I HADN'T EATEN SUCH A HEAVY BREAKFAST!
ROAR!
WE MADE IT! WE'RE STILL AFLOAT!
THAT WAS JUST THE BEGINNING OF THIS RIDE! HERE COMES THE SLUICE GATE!
ROAR!
BUT MEANWHILE...
THERE! NOBODY WILL EVER SHUT THAT SLUICE GATE AGAIN!
BUT HOW WILL I GET BACK ACROSS THE RIVER? I'VE MADE MYSELF AN EXILE FROM PARADISE!
MAYBE I CAN SWING ACROSS LIKE IN A "DUCKZAN" MOVIE!
NO...THIS CHAIN IS TOO SHORT!
ROAR!
THAT DOES IT! I'LL NEVER AGAIN SEE HUEY! OR DEWEY! OR LOUIE! OR UNCLE SCR--
--OOGE!!
WHUMP!

UNCA DONALD!!
WHAT THE--WHA' HAPPENED?
THIS IS ALL YOUR FAULT, NEPHEW! WHY DIDN'T YOU WAIT UNTIL WE WERE ASHORE BEFORE YOU PULLED THE DRAIN PLUG?!
HOLD TIGHT, EVERYONE! WE'RE ON A FAST BOAT TO CHINA!
ROAR!
THE DUCKS' TRIP DOWN-RIVER IS MUCH FASTER THAN THEIR JOURNEY UP RIVER! SEVERAL HOURS LATER...
LOOK! WE'RE APPROACHING THE CAVE WHERE WE ENTERED THIS ANCIENT AQUEDUCT ON OUR TREK IN!
GET READY TO JUMP OFF THIS WATERY ROLLERCOASTER! THAT CAVE IS OUR ONLY HOPE!
NO, WAIT! LOOK!
THE FIRST FLOOD SURGE COLLAPSED THE CAVE!
NO ONE WILL EVER ENTER OR LEAVE TRALLA LA THAT WAY AGAIN! NOW WHAT DO WE DO?
THE ONLY ANSWER IS TO HANG ON AND RIDE IT OUT, UNTIL...
WE'VE BEEN RUSHING THROUGH THIS TUNNEL FOR HOURS! WHEN WILL THIS RIVER COME OUT?
YOW! THERE'S YOUR ANSWER!
WE DON'T COME OUT! WE GO UNDER! THE RIVER IS POURING DOWN AN AIRLESS PASSAGE!
HOLY HANNAH!
GURGLE!
MY NET WORTH IS FLASHING BEFORE MY EYES!
CRASH!
LOOK OUT!

SWITCH TO A CERTAIN PUBLIC FOUNTAIN IN A VILLAGE IN THE KASHMIR HIGHLANDS OF INDIA...
MY FATHER--I'M THROWING A MANI STONE INTO THE SACRED SPRING!
MAKE A WISH, MY SON!
I'M WISHING I KNEW WHY MY STONE BOUNCES UPON THE WATERS! IS IT A BAD OMEN?
CHOMOLUNGMA!
PEOPLE! HELP THEM!
DOINK!
GASP!
KOFF! I COULDN'T HAVE HELD MY BREATH ANOTHER SECOND!
WHERE'S UNCA DONALD?!
I SAW HIM SWEPT INTO ANOTHER CHANNEL!
PLEASE TO BE GETTING OUT OF THE TROUGH, SAHIB! YOU ARE MAKING MY YAK NAUSEOUS!
WELL, TRALLA LA IS SAFE!
BUT FATE FLUSHED US OUT!
WE'D BETTER STAY OUT! WE AND THAT VALLEY CAUSE EACH OTHER BAD LUCK!
I'LL VOUCH FOR THAT...
MY PACK WITH THE CROWN OF GENGHIS KHAN--IT MUST HAVE FALLEN OVERBOARD!
LOST IN AN UNDERGROUND RIVER! THAT'S ABOUT AS LOST AS IT CAN GET!
THE TREASURE OF THE MONGOL EMPIRE WASN'T IN TRALLA LA AS I EXPECTED! AND NOW I'VE EVEN LOST MY CROWN! THIS HAS NOT BEEN A GOOD TRIP!
MAYBE...SOMETIMES GREED LOSES MORE THAN IT GAINS!

WHAT NOW, UNCA SCROOGE?
WHEW! I...I FEEL LIKE I COULD USE A VACATION AFTER ALL THAT!
A VACATION? YOU'VE NEVER TAKEN A VACATION IN YOUR LIFE!
I KNOW...BUT I HAVE THIS STRANGE YEN TO PAY A VISIT TO THE GREEN HILLS OF SCOTLAND!
BUT THE CROWN FELL OVERBOARD BEFORE THE DUCKS WERE SWEPT DOWN THE WHIRLPOOL! FOR EVEN NOW, BACK IN THE SUNNY, IF SOMEWHAT SOGGY, VALLEY OF TRALLA LA...
MASTER LAH! I FOUND THIS IN A PACK LYING IN MY RICE PADDY!
THE MONGOL CROWN! IT IS A MYSTERY HOW THOSE DUCKS HAD THIS EVIL THING! OUR ANCESTORS DISCARDED THIS AND ALL SUCH REMNANTS OF THE TERRIBLE KUBLAI KHAN!
AND NOW EVEN THE HERO DUCKS HAVE BEEN LOST DUE TO THE POWER OF THIS WICKED RELIC!
BACK INTO THE SACRED WHIRLPOOL WITH THIS CORRUPTING BAUBLE! MAY IT NEVER AGAIN RETURN!!
END

Walt Disney's
Donald Duck in
The Duck Who Fell to Earth
IT'S MIGHTY NICE OF YOU TO GIVE ME A JOB IN YOUR NEW COMPANY, UNCLE SCROOGE!
THIS BUSINESS WILL TAKE OFF LIKE A ROCKET! AND THERE'S NO OVERHEAD! THE SKY'S THE LIMIT!
BOB'S NEARLY NEW AUTO PARTS
D 90161
KEEP OUT
WHAT SORT OF BUSINESS IS IT?
HIGH-TECH SALVAGE! WE'LL RESELL EXPENSIVE ELECTRONIC HARDWARE THAT WE GET ABSOLUTELY FREE!
WE BUY JUNK
WE SELL Antiques
FREE? WHAT KIND OF HIGH-TECH HARDWARE COMES FREE?
OLD SATELLITES! THEY FALL FROM ORBIT EVERY DAY!
FOR SALE
FALLING SATELLITES? BUT THEY BURN UP IN THE ATMOSPHERE!
AH, BUT PROFESSOR MOLLICULE HAS FOUND A CHEAP WAY TO FLY UP AND GRAB THEM BEFORE THAT!
OH, SURE! I'D LIKE TO SEE A CHEAP SPACE SHIP!
FEAST YOUR EYES, NEPHEW! THERE IT IS!
McDUCK SALVAGE YARD

WAK! THAT'S AN OLD TURBOPROP AIRPLANE!
A 1949 AIRCARGO MAILPLANE, TO BE PRECISE! I BOUGHT IT FOR A SONG AT A GOVERNMENT AUCTION!
RIGHT! WHAT'S THE GAG?
NO GAG! IT'S SIMPLE! I INVENTED A CONCENTRATED FUEL THAT BURNS WITHOUT OXYGEN... AND ADDED AN OLD JET ENGINE TO THIS CRATE!
SAME AUCTION?
GARAGE SALE.
ROCKETS NEED TONS OF FUEL TO GAIN ENOUGH SPEED TO THROW THEMSELVES INTO ORBIT BEFORE THEY LEAVE THE ATMOSPHERE!
MY FUEL DOESN'T NEED OXYGEN TO BURN... SO WE JUST CHUG ALONG AT ABOUT 50 MILES PER HOUR UNTIL WE REACH THE EDGE OF SPACE! CHEAP SPACE FLIGHT!
BEST OF ALL, AT SLOW SPEEDS, WE DON'T RISK BREAKING INTO A SPACE/TIME WARP! THAT'S ALWAYS WORRIED ME!
?
YEAH? WELL, YOUR WHOLE IDEA WORRIES ME! I'M NOT GOING UP IN THAT CONTRAPTION FOR 30 CENTS PER HOUR!
I WANT FLIGHT PAY! AN EXTRA 10¢ PER HOUR!
ALWAYS TRYING TO BEAT YOUR POOR UNCLE OUT OF EXTRA PAY! ALL RIGHT, YOU WIN— JUST PUT ON THIS SPACE SUIT!
NOW? WE'RE GOING NOW?

YES! THERE'S A SATELLITE DUE TO DROP OUT OF ORBIT TODAY, RIGHT OVER DUCKBURG!
USED SPACE SUITS! SAME GARAGE SALE?
YARD SALE!
$3
SIT DOWN AND FASTEN YOUR SEAT BELT, NEPHEW!
READY, PROFESSOR?
READY, MR. McDUCK! CONTACT!
OFF WE GO INTO THE WILD BLUE SOON-TO-BE-BLACK-AND-STARRY YONDER!
HOLD ON— I'M GOING TO PUT HER INTO A STEEP CLIMB!
McDUCK SALVAGE YARD
ZOOM!
CRASH!
YAAAAAH!
CRASH!
OWTCH!
VRROOOMM!
SORRY, NEPHEW! USED SEATBELTS... SAME YARD SALE!
NO, THE SEATBELT WORKED FINE! I THINK IT WAS THE SEAT!
OH, YOU'RE NEVER SATISFIED!
SHORTLY!
WOW! WE'RE WAY ABOVE THE CLOUDS! BUT...
POP
SPUTTER
YIKES! THE ENGINES ARE FAILING!
YES, THERE'S NOT ENOUGH OXYGEN HERE TO OPERATE OUR NORMAL ENGINES! TIME FOR YOU TO LIGHT THE SPECIAL JET ENGINES, NEPHEW!
THIS WHOLE DEAL IS RIDICULOUS!

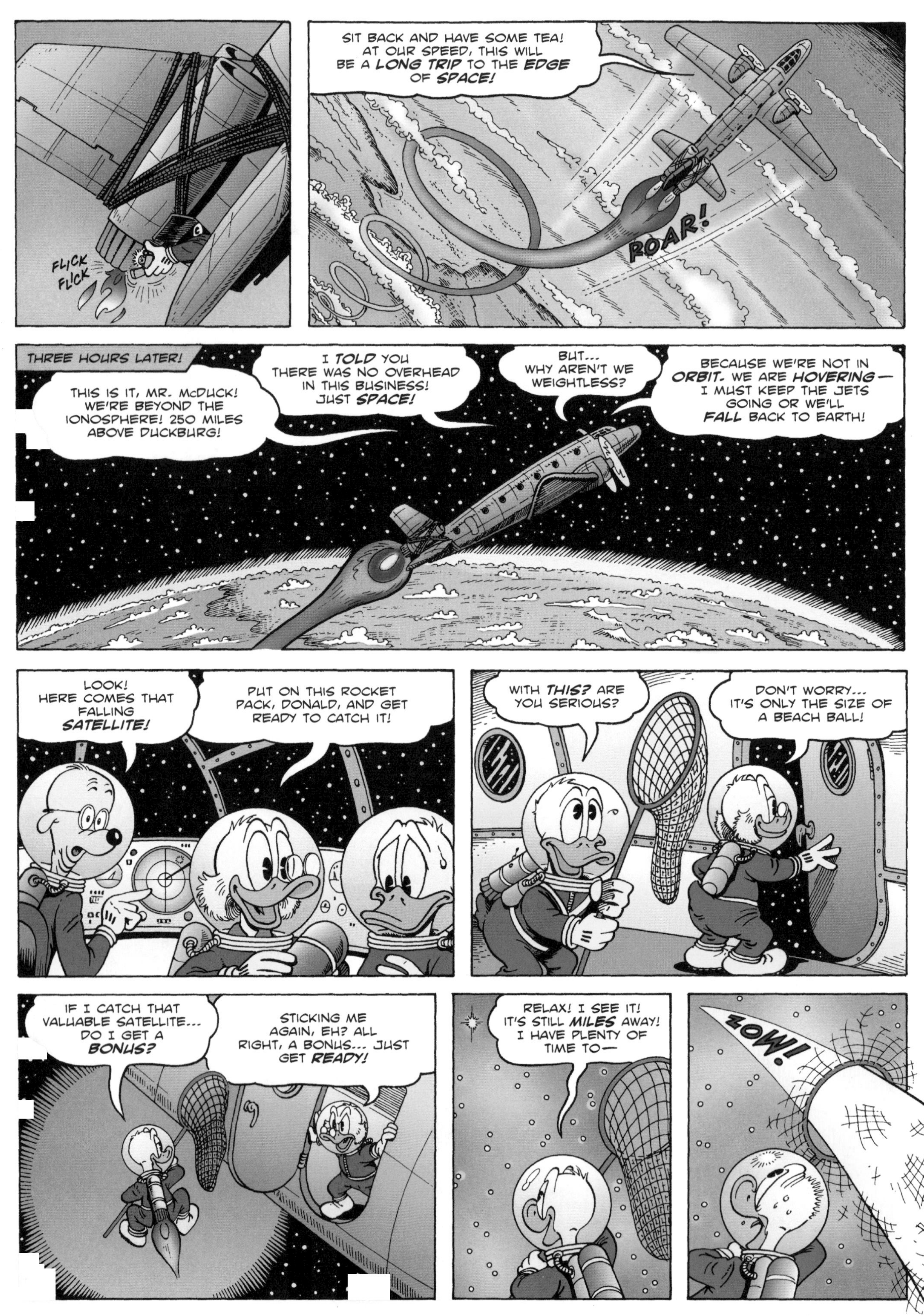
FLICK FLICK
SIT BACK AND HAVE SOME TEA! AT OUR SPEED, THIS WILL BE A LONG TRIP TO THE EDGE OF SPACE!
ROAR!
THREE HOURS LATER!
THIS IS IT, MR. McDUCK! WE'RE BEYOND THE IONOSPHERE! 250 MILES ABOVE DUCKBURG!
I TOLD YOU THERE WAS NO OVERHEAD IN THIS BUSINESS! JUST SPACE!
BUT... WHY AREN'T WE WEIGHTLESS?
BECAUSE WE'RE NOT IN ORBIT. WE ARE HOVERING — I MUST KEEP THE JETS GOING OR WE'LL FALL BACK TO EARTH!
LOOK! HERE COMES THAT FALLING SATELLITE!
PUT ON THIS ROCKET PACK, DONALD, AND GET READY TO CATCH IT!
WITH THIS? ARE YOU SERIOUS?
DON'T WORRY... IT'S ONLY THE SIZE OF A BEACH BALL!
IF I CATCH THAT VALUABLE SATELLITE... DO I GET A BONUS?
STICKING ME AGAIN, EH? ALL RIGHT, A BONUS... JUST GET READY!
RELAX! I SEE IT! IT'S STILL MILES AWAY! I HAVE PLENTY OF TIME TO—
ZOW!

GREAT HOWLING SPUTNIKS! HOW FAST WAS THAT LITTLE STINKER GOING?!
OH, I'D SAY ABOUT 6,000 MILES PER HOUR!
WE CAN'T CATCH SATELLITES MOVING AT SPEEDS LIKE THAT! WHY DIDN'T YOU TELL ME ABOUT THAT DETAIL?
YOU NEVER ASKED!
TO CATCH A FALLING SATELLITE, WE'D NEED TO MATCH ITS SPEED AS IT FLIES EARTHWARD... THEN WE'D HAVE TO SLOW DOWN AGAIN OR BURN UP IN THE EARTH'S ATMOSPHERE!
AND HOW WOULD WE HAUL ENOUGH FUEL FOR ALL THAT, PRAY TELL?
OH, I GUESS FIND A YARD SALE WITH A USED NASA MOON ROCKET TO CARRY THE FUEL!
YOU ONLY SAID YOU WANTED TO GET 300 MILES ABOVE DUCKBURG IN A 1949 CARGO PLANE! YOU DIDN'T TELL ME IT WAS TO CATCH SATELLITES! I INVENT WHAT I'M TOLD TO INVENT!
ALL RIGHT! FORGET IT!
LET'S GO HOME! SHUT OFF THE JET ENGINES!
NO! DON'T DO THAT!!!
CLIK
WHOAA! NOW WE ARE WEIGHTLESS!
WE'RE FALLING BACK TO EARTH! I INTENDED TO LOWER US DOWN WITH THE JETS!
BACK IN THE PLANE'S HOLD!
WHAT THE... EVERYTHING'S FLOATING AROUND! WHAT'S GOING ON?

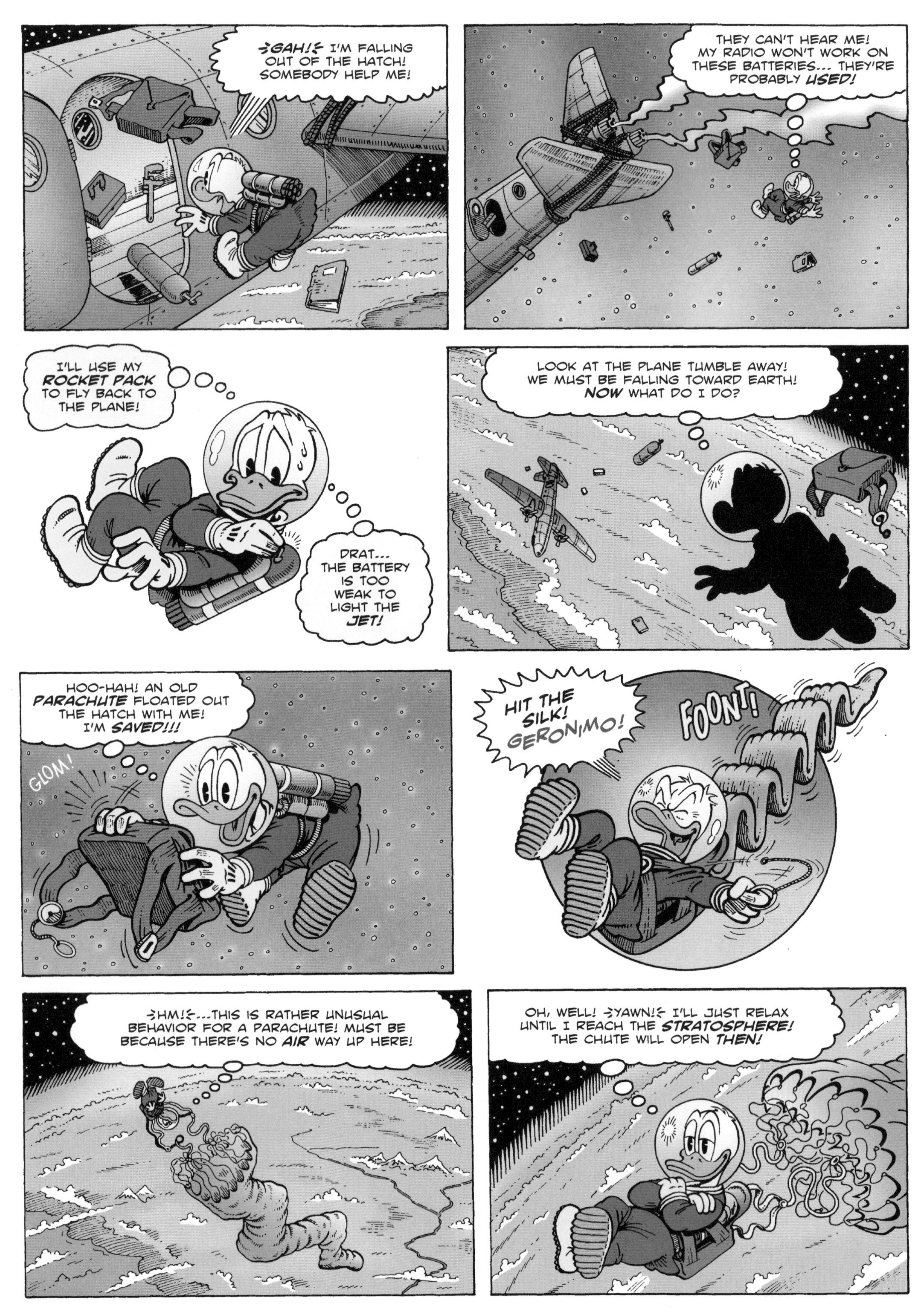
GAH! I'M FALLING OUT OF THE HATCH! SOMEBODY HELP ME!
THEY CAN'T HEAR ME! MY RADIO WON'T WORK ON THESE BATTERIES... THEY'RE PROBABLY USED!
I'LL USE MY ROCKET PACK TO FLY BACK TO THE PLANE!
DRAT... THE BATTERY IS TOO WEAK TO LIGHT THE JET!
LOOK AT THE PLANE TUMBLE AWAY! WE MUST BE FALLING TOWARD EARTH! NOW WHAT DO I DO?
HOO-HAH! AN OLD PARACHUTE FLOATED OUT THE HATCH WITH ME! I'M SAVED!!!
GLOM!
HIT THE SILK! GERONIMO!
FOONT!
HM!...THIS IS RATHER UNUSUAL BEHAVIOR FOR A PARACHUTE! MUST BE BECAUSE THERE'S NO AIR WAY UP HERE!
OH, WELL! YAWN! I'LL JUST RELAX UNTIL I REACH THE STRATOSPHERE! THE CHUTE WILL OPEN THEN!

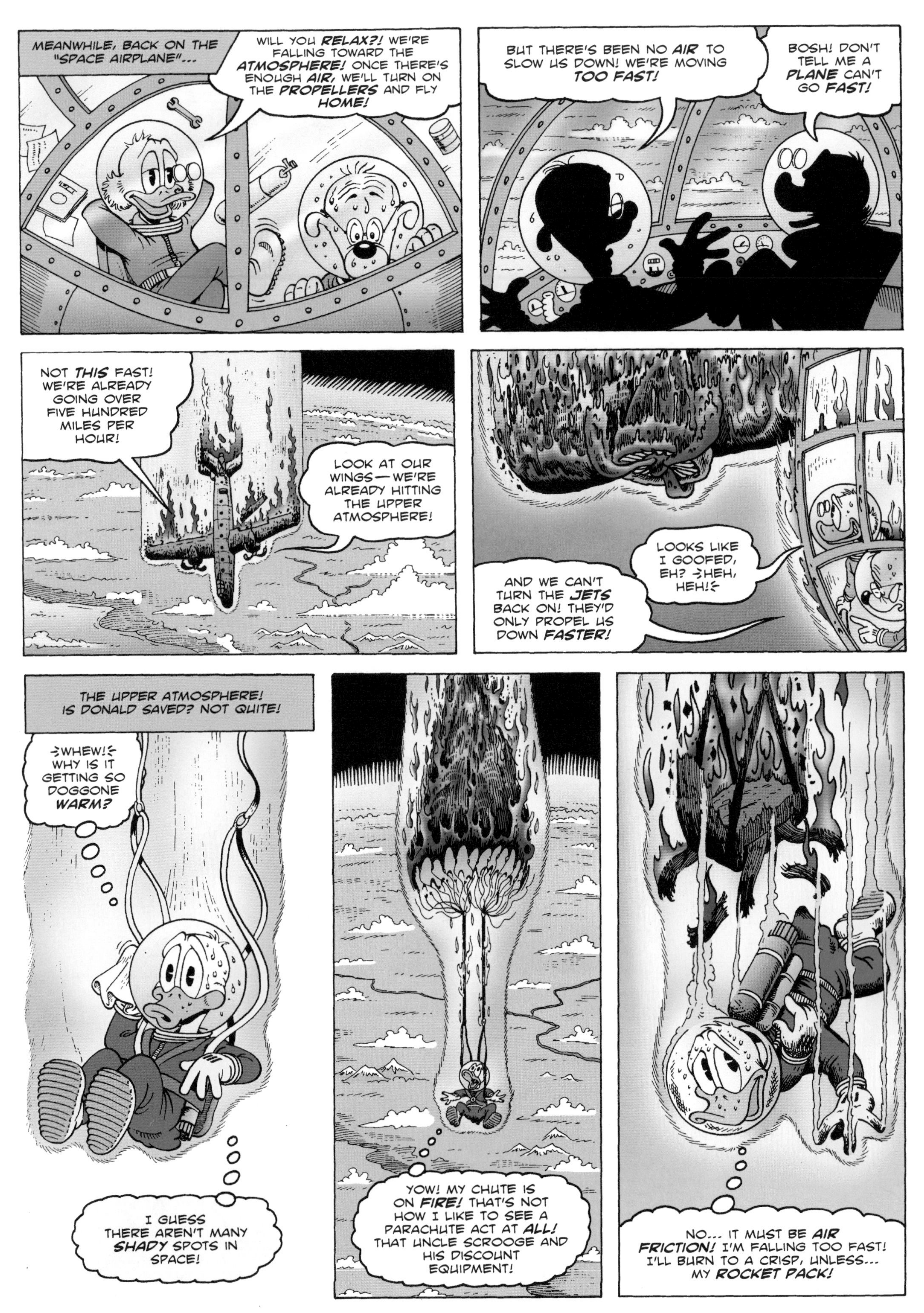
MEANWHILE, BACK ON THE "SPACE AIRPLANE"...
WILL YOU RELAX?! WE'RE FALLING TOWARD THE ATMOSPHERE! ONCE THERE'S ENOUGH AIR, WE'LL TURN ON THE PROPELLERS AND FLY HOME!
BUT THERE'S BEEN NO AIR TO SLOW US DOWN! WE'RE MOVING TOO FAST!
BOSH! DON'T TELL ME A PLANE CAN'T GO FAST!
NOT THIS FAST! WE'RE ALREADY GOING OVER FIVE HUNDRED MILES PER HOUR!
LOOK AT OUR WINGS—WE'RE ALREADY HITTING THE UPPER ATMOSPHERE!
LOOKS LIKE I GOOFED, EH? HEH, HEH!
AND WE CAN'T TURN THE JETS BACK ON! THEY'D ONLY PROPEL US DOWN FASTER!
THE UPPER ATMOSPHERE! IS DONALD SAVED? NOT QUITE!
WHEW! WHY IS IT GETTING SO DOGGONE WARM?
I GUESS THERE AREN'T MANY SHADY SPOTS IN SPACE!
YOW! MY CHUTE IS ON FIRE! THAT'S NOT HOW I LIKE TO SEE A PARACHUTE ACT AT ALL! THAT UNCLE SCROOGE AND HIS DISCOUNT EQUIPMENT!
NO... IT MUST BE AIR FRICTION! I'M FALLING TOO FAST! I'LL BURN TO A CRISP, UNLESS... MY ROCKET PACK!

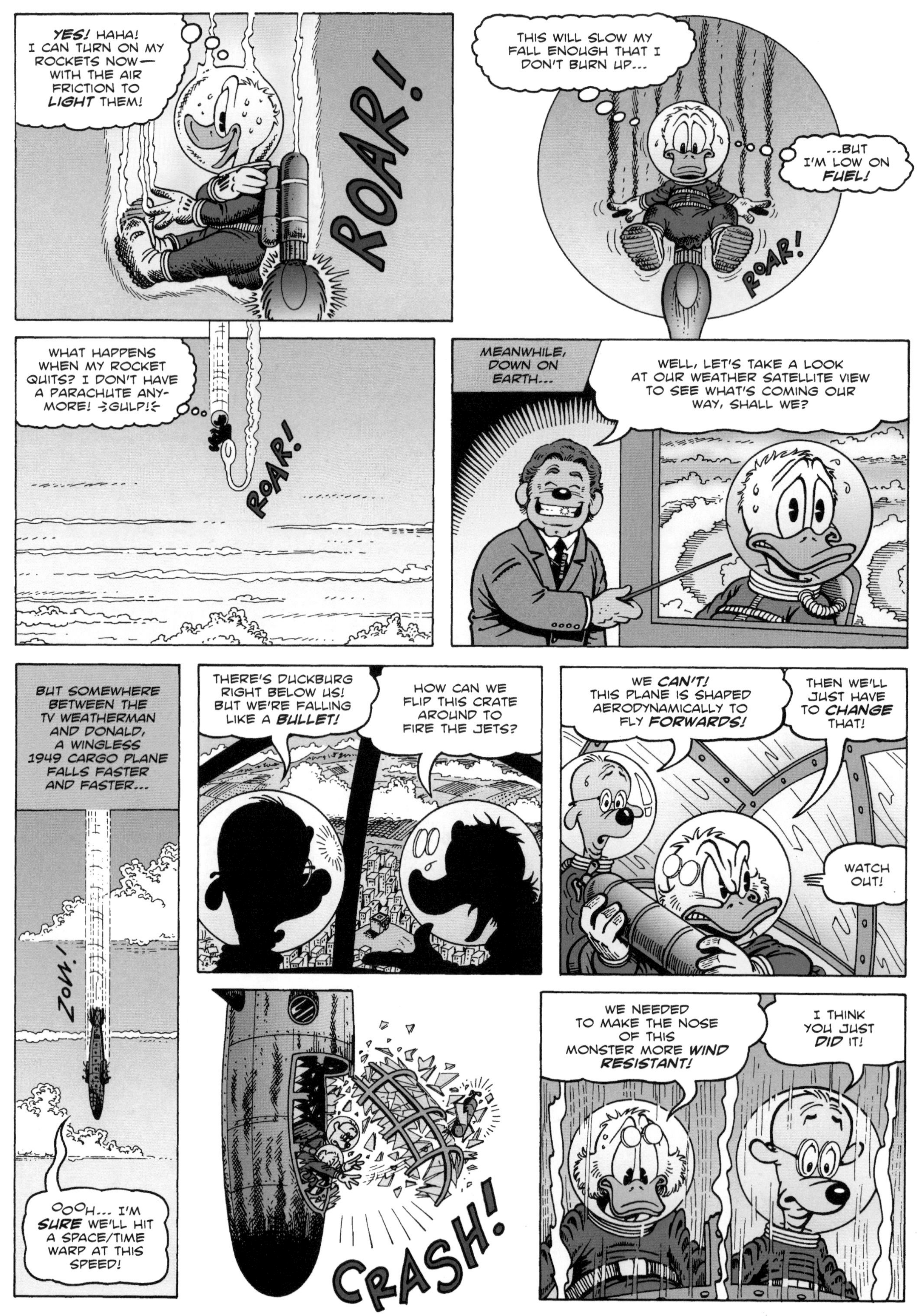
YES! HAHA! I CAN TURN ON MY ROCKETS NOW— WITH THE AIR FRICTION TO LIGHT THEM!
ROAR!
THIS WILL SLOW MY FALL ENOUGH THAT I DON'T BURN UP...
...BUT I'M LOW ON FUEL!
ROAR!
WHAT HAPPENS WHEN MY ROCKET QUITS? I DON'T HAVE A PARACHUTE ANY-MORE! ≯GULP!≮
ROAR!
MEANWHILE, DOWN ON EARTH...
WELL, LET'S TAKE A LOOK AT OUR WEATHER SATELLITE VIEW TO SEE WHAT'S COMING OUR WAY, SHALL WE?
BUT SOMEWHERE BETWEEN THE TV WEATHERMAN AND DONALD, A WINGLESS 1949 CARGO PLANE FALLS FASTER AND FASTER...
ZOW!
OOOH... I'M SURE WE'LL HIT A SPACE/TIME WARP AT THIS SPEED!
THERE'S DUCKBURG RIGHT BELOW US! BUT WE'RE FALLING LIKE A BULLET!
HOW CAN WE FLIP THIS CRATE AROUND TO FIRE THE JETS?
WE CAN'T! THIS PLANE IS SHAPED AERODYNAMICALLY TO FLY FORWARDS!
THEN WE'LL JUST HAVE TO CHANGE THAT!
WATCH OUT!
CRASH!
WE NEEDED TO MAKE THE NOSE OF THIS MONSTER MORE WIND RESISTANT!
I THINK YOU JUST DID IT!

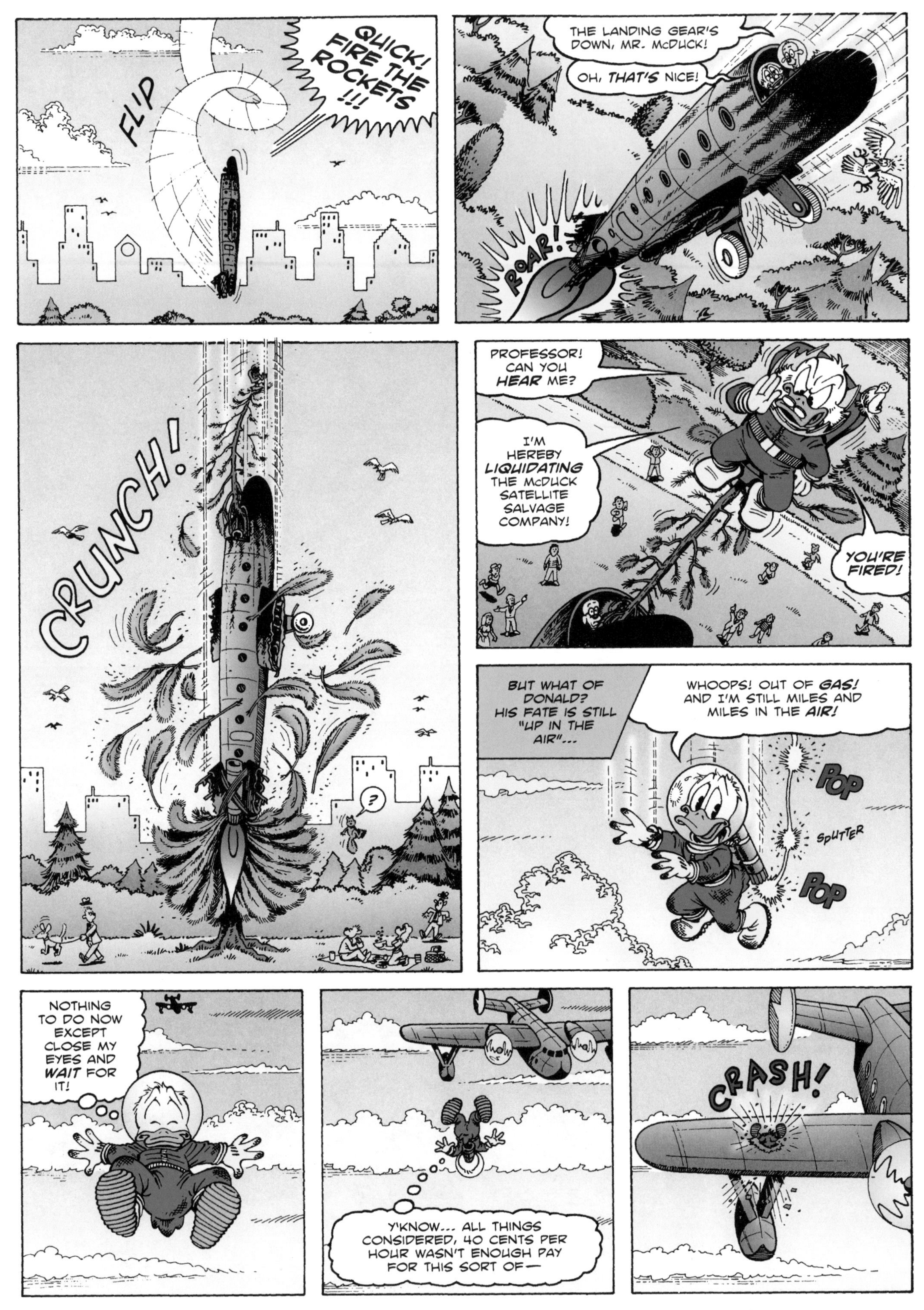
QUICK! FIRE THE ROCKETS !!!
FL'P
THE LANDING GEAR'S DOWN, MR. McDUCK!
OH, THAT'S NICE!
ROAR!
CRUNCH!
?
PROFESSOR! CAN YOU HEAR ME?
I'M HEREBY LIQUIDATING THE McDUCK SATELLITE SALVAGE COMPANY!
YOU'RE FIRED!
BUT WHAT OF DONALD? HIS FATE IS STILL "UP IN THE AIR"...
WHOOPS! OUT OF GAS! AND I'M STILL MILES AND MILES IN THE AIR!
POP
SPUTTER
POP
NOTHING TO DO NOW EXCEPT CLOSE MY EYES AND WAIT FOR IT!
Y'KNOW... ALL THINGS CONSIDERED, 40 CENTS PER HOUR WASN'T ENOUGH PAY FOR THIS SORT OF—
CRASH!

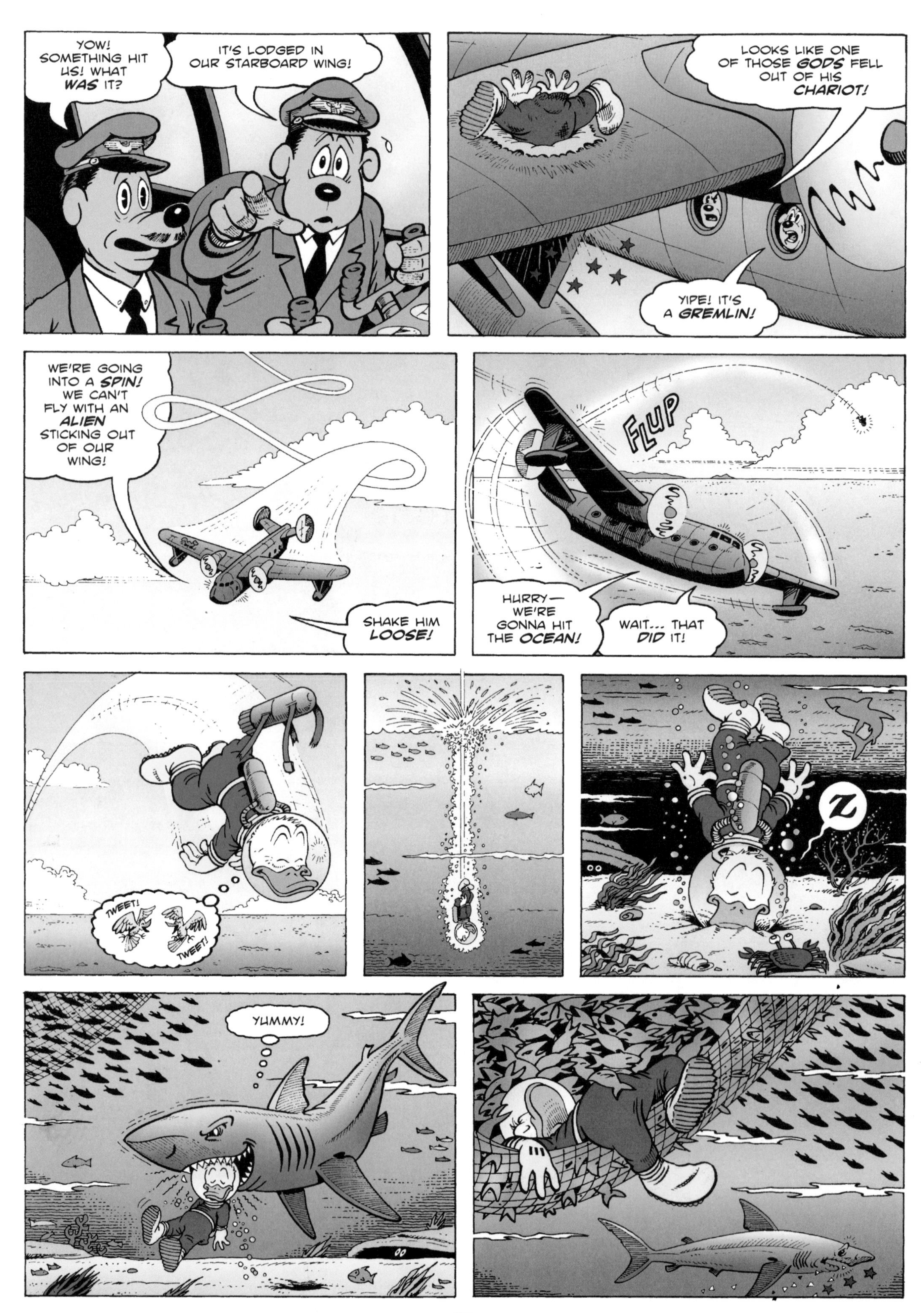

YOW! SOMETHING HIT US! WHAT WAS IT?
IT'S LODGED IN OUR STARBOARD WING!
LOOKS LIKE ONE OF THOSE GODS FELL OUT OF HIS CHARIOT!
YIPE! IT'S A GREMLIN!
WE'RE GOING INTO A SPIN! WE CAN'T FLY WITH AN ALIEN STICKING OUT OF OUR WING!
SHAKE HIM LOOSE!
FLUP
HURRY— WE'RE GONNA HIT THE OCEAN!
WAIT... THAT DID IT!
TWEET!
TWEET!
Z
YUMMY!

CANNERY
z
?
THUD!
z
BLINK
BLINK

AND SO...
I'VE SEARCHED THE PLANE TEN TIMES, MR. McDUCK! DONALD JUST ISN'T HERE!
NONSENSE! HE MUST BE!
KEEP OUT!
YARD SALE
1949 CARGO PLANE AS IS
UNLESS... WE WERE GOING SO FAST HE WAS THROWN INTO A SPACE/TIME WARP!
MR. McDUCK— YOUR NEPHEW DONALD IS CALLING COLLECT FROM SAN FRANCISCO!
WHAT? HOW DID HE GET THERE?
I KNEW IT! A SPACE/TIME WARP! LET ME TALK TO HIM!
HELLO? WOULD SOMEBODY EXPLAIN HOW I GOT TO SAN FRANCISCO?
YOU'VE GONE THROUGH A DIMENSIONAL WARP! WHEN IS IT WHERE YOU ARE? TODAY? TOMORROW?
UH... I THINK HE WANTS TO KNOW WHEN MY RELEASE DATE WILL BE!
THE SENTENCE FOR VAGRANCY IS TEN DAYS IN JAIL!
POLICE
THEY SAY IT'S TEN DAYS FROM NOW!
OH, NO! HE'S BEEN KNOCKED CLEAR INTO THE MIDDLE OF NEXT WEEK!!!
WHAT?! GIVE ME THAT PHONE! HE'S TRYING TO FLIMFLAM ME AGAIN!
LISTEN, NEPHEW! IF YOU THINK YOU'RE GOING TO CHISEL ME OUT OF AN EXTRA PAYCHECK BY GOING INTO THE FUTURE, YOU CAN FORGET IT!
DID YOU RAISE YOUR BAIL, PAL? PAL? HEY!

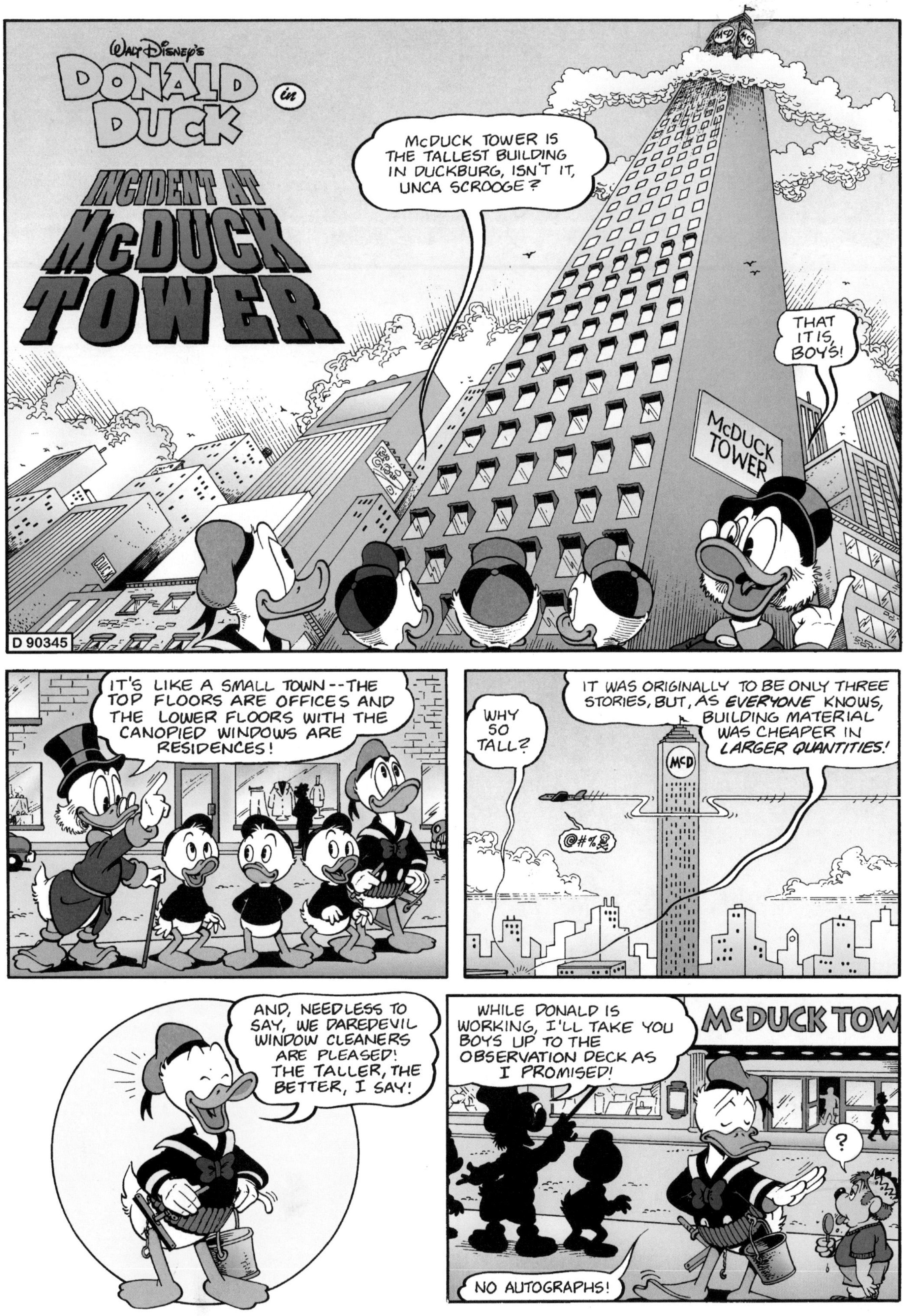
WALT DISNEY'S
DONALD DUCK
in
INCIDENT AT McDUCK TOWER
McDUCK TOWER IS THE TALLEST BUILDING IN DUCKBURG, ISN'T IT, UNCA SCROOGE?
THAT IT IS, BOYS!
McDUCK TOWER
D 90345
IT'S LIKE A SMALL TOWN--THE TOP FLOORS ARE OFFICES AND THE LOWER FLOORS WITH THE CANOPIED WINDOWS ARE RESIDENCES!
WHY SO TALL?
IT WAS ORIGINALLY TO BE ONLY THREE STORIES, BUT, AS EVERYONE KNOWS, BUILDING MATERIAL WAS CHEAPER IN LARGER QUANTITIES!
AND, NEEDLESS TO SAY, WE DAREDEVIL WINDOW CLEANERS ARE PLEASED! THE TALLER, THE BETTER, I SAY!
WHILE DONALD IS WORKING, I'LL TAKE YOU BOYS UP TO THE OBSERVATION DECK AS I PROMISED!
McDUCK TOW
?
NO AUTOGRAPHS!

BUT FIRST LET ME CALL MY OFFICE TO TELL THEM WHERE I -- OOPS!
WAK! STOP! DON'T LEAVE ME LIKE THIS!
FOR PETE'S SAKE, IT WAS JUST A NICKEL!
YES -- GO ON... IT WAS A NICKEL... SO WHAT'S YOUR POINT?
SKIP IT! I SPOKE WITHOUT THINKING!
McDU
SIGH! COME WITH ME! IF I KNOW OUR UNCLE SCROOGE, HE'LL BE BUSY FOR THE REST OF THE DAY!
HOW DID YOU BECOME A WINDOW WASHER, UNCA DONALD? AREN'T YOU SCARED OF HEIGHTS?
NO, NOT ANY LONGER!
I TAUGHT MYSELF TO BE FEARLESS! I BEGAN WITH THE WINDOWS ON THE FIRST FLOOR, AND SLOWLY WORKED MY WAY UP!
"UNTIL ONE DAY I FOUND MYSELF HAPPILY POLISHING THE BRASS KNOB ON THE TOP FLAGPOLE!"

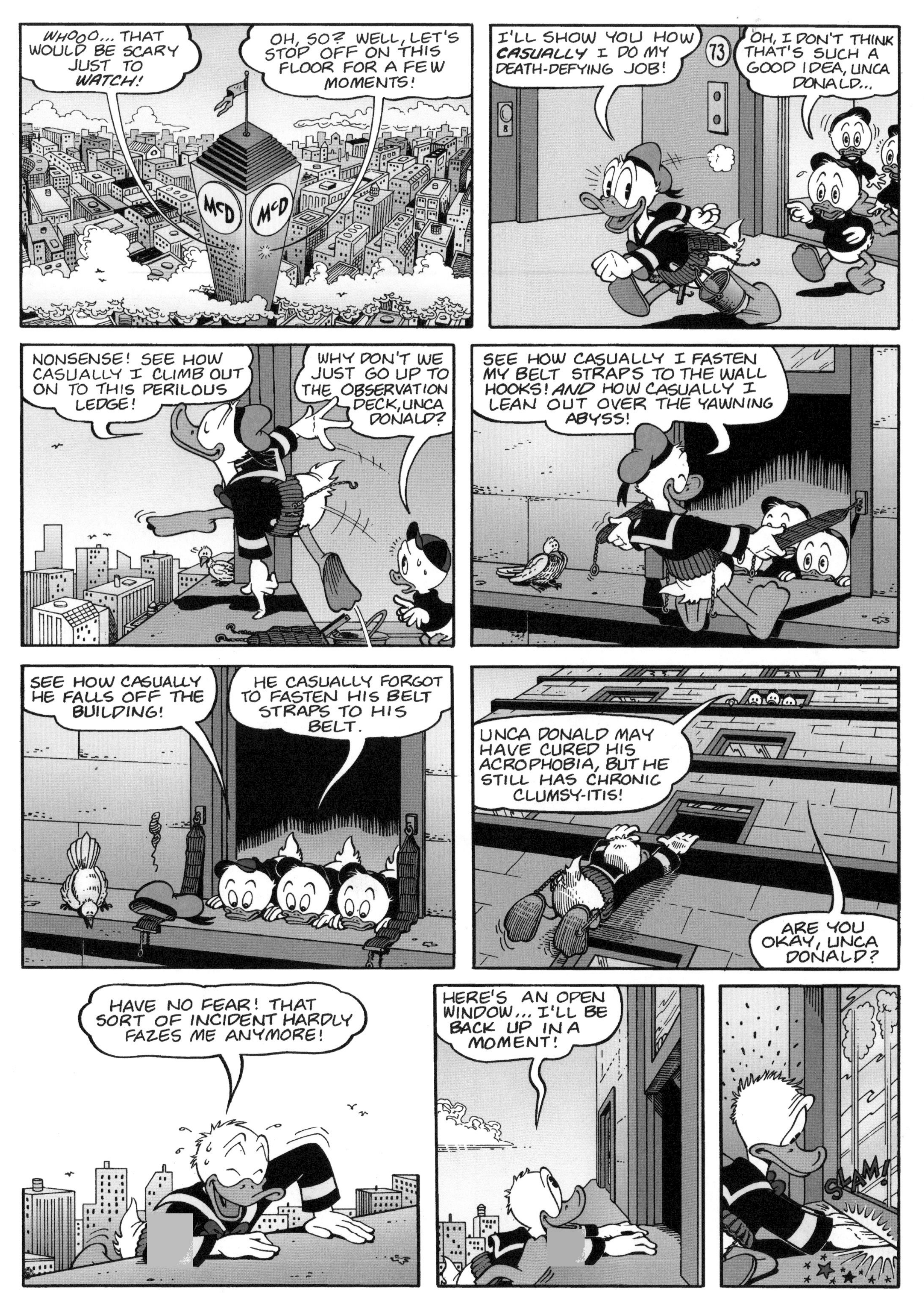
WHOOO... THAT WOULD BE SCARY JUST TO WATCH!
OH, SO? WELL, LET'S STOP OFF ON THIS FLOOR FOR A FEW MOMENTS!
McD
McD
I'LL SHOW YOU HOW CASUALLY I DO MY DEATH-DEFYING JOB!
73
OH, I DON'T THINK THAT'S SUCH A GOOD IDEA, UNCA DONALD...
NONSENSE! SEE HOW CASUALLY I CLIMB OUT ON TO THIS PERILOUS LEDGE!
WHY DON'T WE JUST GO UP TO THE OBSERVATION DECK, UNCA DONALD?
SEE HOW CASUALLY I FASTEN MY BELT STRAPS TO THE WALL HOOKS! AND HOW CASUALLY I LEAN OUT OVER THE YAWNING ABYSS!
SEE HOW CASUALLY HE FALLS OFF THE BUILDING!
HE CASUALLY FORGOT TO FASTEN HIS BELT STRAPS TO HIS BELT.
UNCA DONALD MAY HAVE CURED HIS ACROPHOBIA, BUT HE STILL HAS CHRONIC CLUMSY-ITIS!
ARE YOU OKAY, UNCA DONALD?
HAVE NO FEAR! THAT SORT OF INCIDENT HARDLY FAZES ME ANYMORE!
HERE'S AN OPEN WINDOW... I'LL BE BACK UP IN A MOMENT!
SLAM!

DID I JUST HEAR YOU SHUT THE WINDOW, GRETTA?
YES, IT WAS GETTING TOO DRAFTY!
?
!
IT'S THAT FRESH WINDOW WASHER AGAIN! HE'S ALWAYS FLIRTING WITH ME!
TEACH HIM A LESSON!
AH! THANK YOU! I DIDN'T THINK YOU'D EVER OPEN--
THWAP
I WAS BETTER OFF BEFORE SHE OPENED THE WINDOW-- AT LEAST MY FINGERTIPS WERE SAFE INSIDE!
ALL THESE OTHER OFFICES ARE VACANT AND THE WINDOWS ARE LOCKED! THIS IS GETTING... DISTURBING!
THERE'S UNCA DONALD! BELOW THIS WINDOW, TWO FLOORS DOWN!
FIRE HOSE
LOWER THIS HOSE TO HIM!

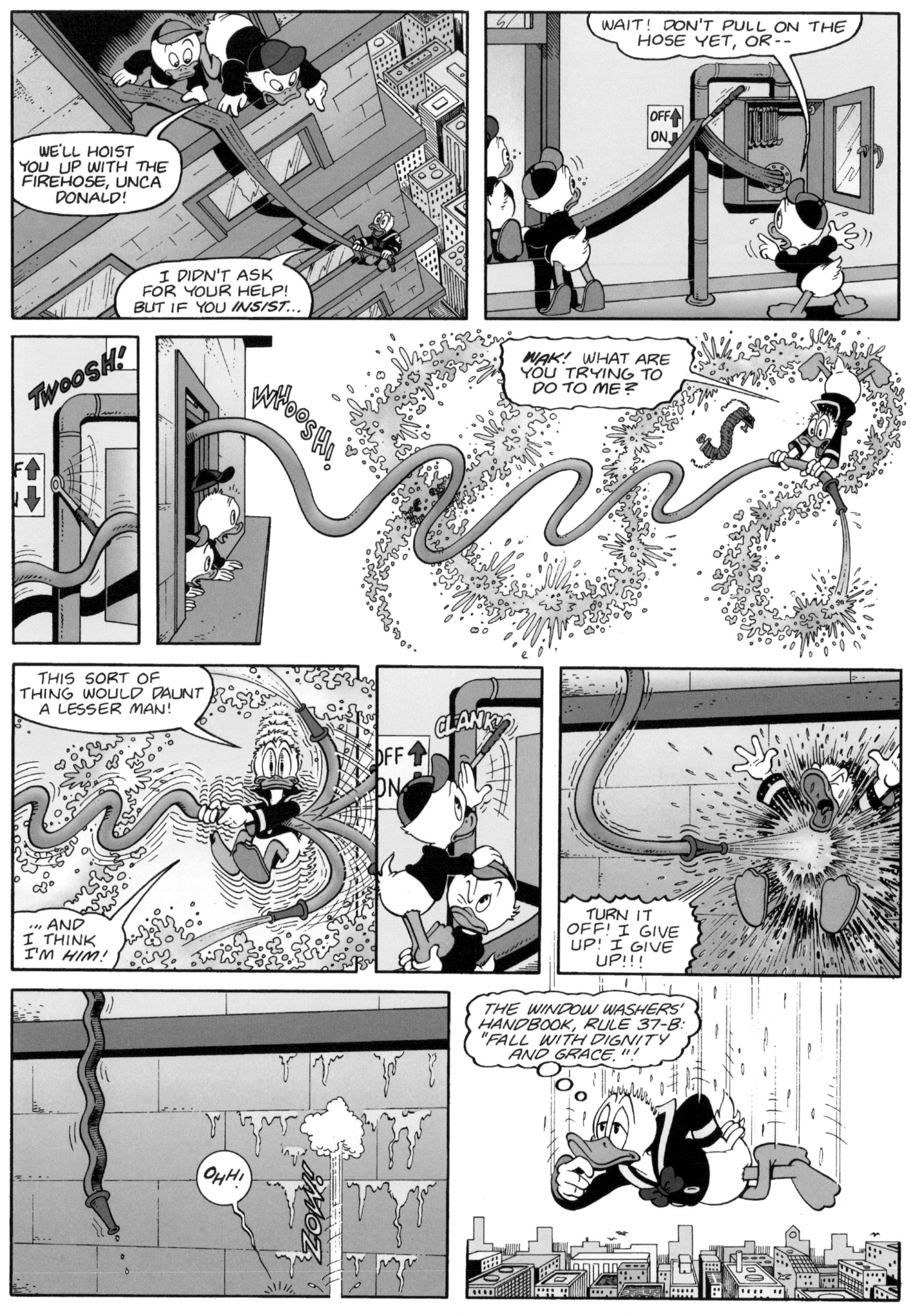
WE'LL HOIST YOU UP WITH THE FIREHOSE, UNCA DONALD!
I DIDN'T ASK FOR YOUR HELP! BUT IF YOU INSIST...
WAIT! DON'T PULL ON THE HOSE YET, OR--
OFF
ON
TWOOSH!
WHOOSH!
WAK! WHAT ARE YOU TRYING TO DO TO ME?
THIS SORT OF THING WOULD DAUNT A LESSER MAN!
...AND I THINK I'M HIM!
CLANK!
OFF
ON
TURN IT OFF! I GIVE UP! I GIVE UP!!!
OHH!
ZOW!
THE WINDOW WASHERS' HANDBOOK, RULE 37-B: "FALL WITH DIGNITY AND GRACE."!!

SPLAT!
THIS GUY WILL LET ME IN! I'M SAVED!
WHAT? A JUMPER? I CAN'T DEAL WITH HIS PROBLEM TODAY!
NURSE, COME AND SEE IF THIS MAN CAN JUMP AGAIN TOMORROW!
NOK NOK
NO MEDICAL INSURANCE? HOW DO YOU PLAN TO PAY FOR THIS CONSULTATION?
CASH! JUST LET ME IN!
SLAP
UP
POOR UNCA DONALD LANDED ON A LEDGE ON ONE OF THESE FLOORS, BUT WHICH ONE?
WRONG
DOWN
C'MON, MEN! THE DOCTOR WHO CALLED SAID THE JUMPER WAS ON THIS FLOOR!
JUMPER?! NOW WHAT?
McDUCK TOWER SECURITY CAN DEAL WITH OUR OWN JUMPERS! BACK OFF!
YEAH... AND IT PAYS A BONUS!
HEY! WE'RE THE POLICE! WE'LL HANDLE THIS EMERGENCY!

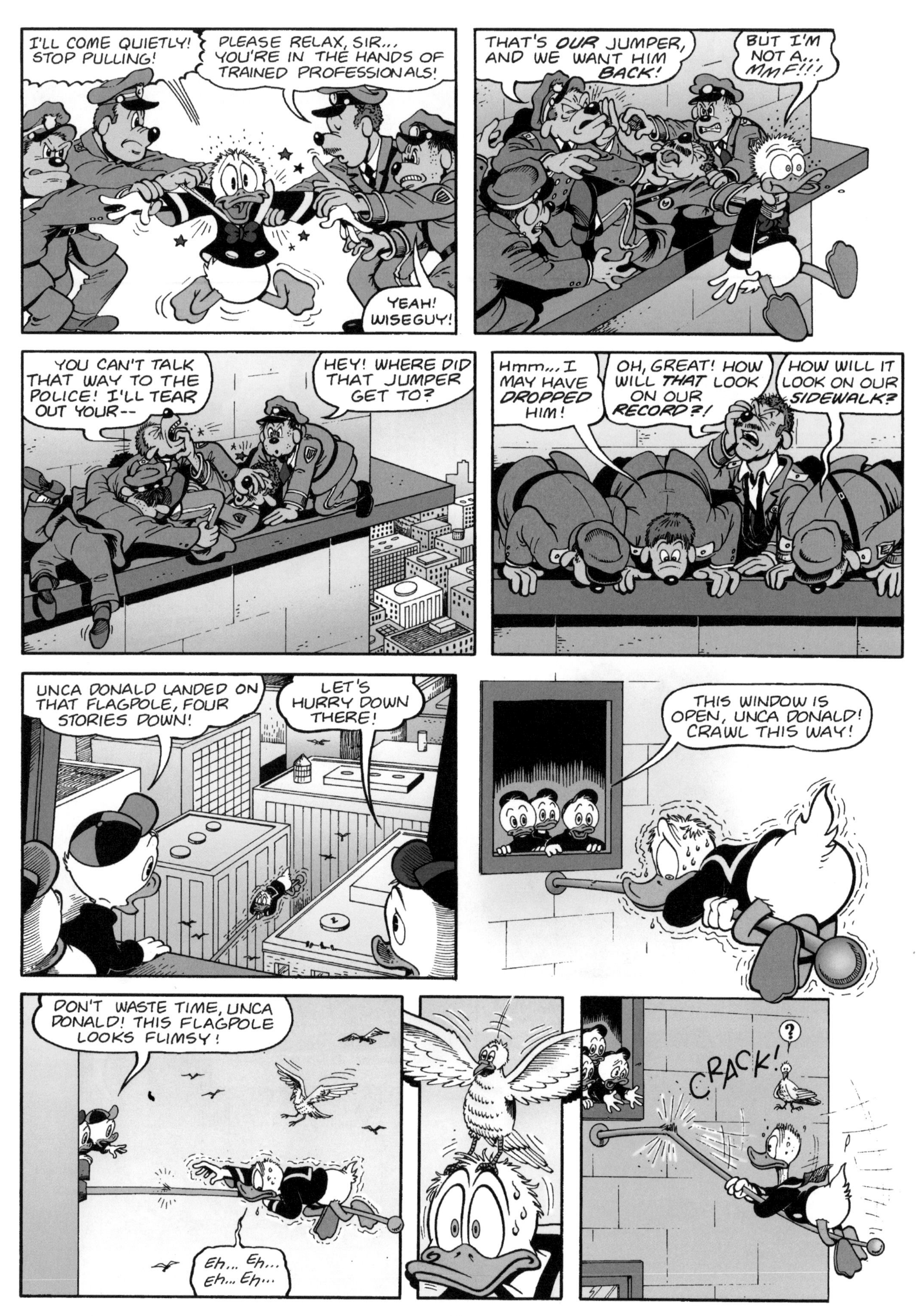

I'LL COME QUIETLY! STOP PULLING!
PLEASE RELAX, SIR... YOU'RE IN THE HANDS OF TRAINED PROFESSIONALS!
YEAH! WISEGUY!
THAT'S OUR JUMPER, AND WE WANT HIM BACK!
BUT I'M NOT A... MMF!!!
YOU CAN'T TALK THAT WAY TO THE POLICE! I'LL TEAR OUT YOUR--
HEY! WHERE DID THAT JUMPER GET TO?
Hmm... I MAY HAVE DROPPED HIM!
OH, GREAT! HOW WILL THAT LOOK ON OUR RECORD?!
HOW WILL IT LOOK ON OUR SIDEWALK?
UNCA DONALD LANDED ON THAT FLAGPOLE, FOUR STORIES DOWN!
LET'S HURRY DOWN THERE!
THIS WINDOW IS OPEN, UNCA DONALD! CRAWL THIS WAY!
DON'T WASTE TIME, UNCA DONALD! THIS FLAGPOLE LOOKS FLIMSY!
Eh... Eh... Eh... Eh...
CRACK!
?

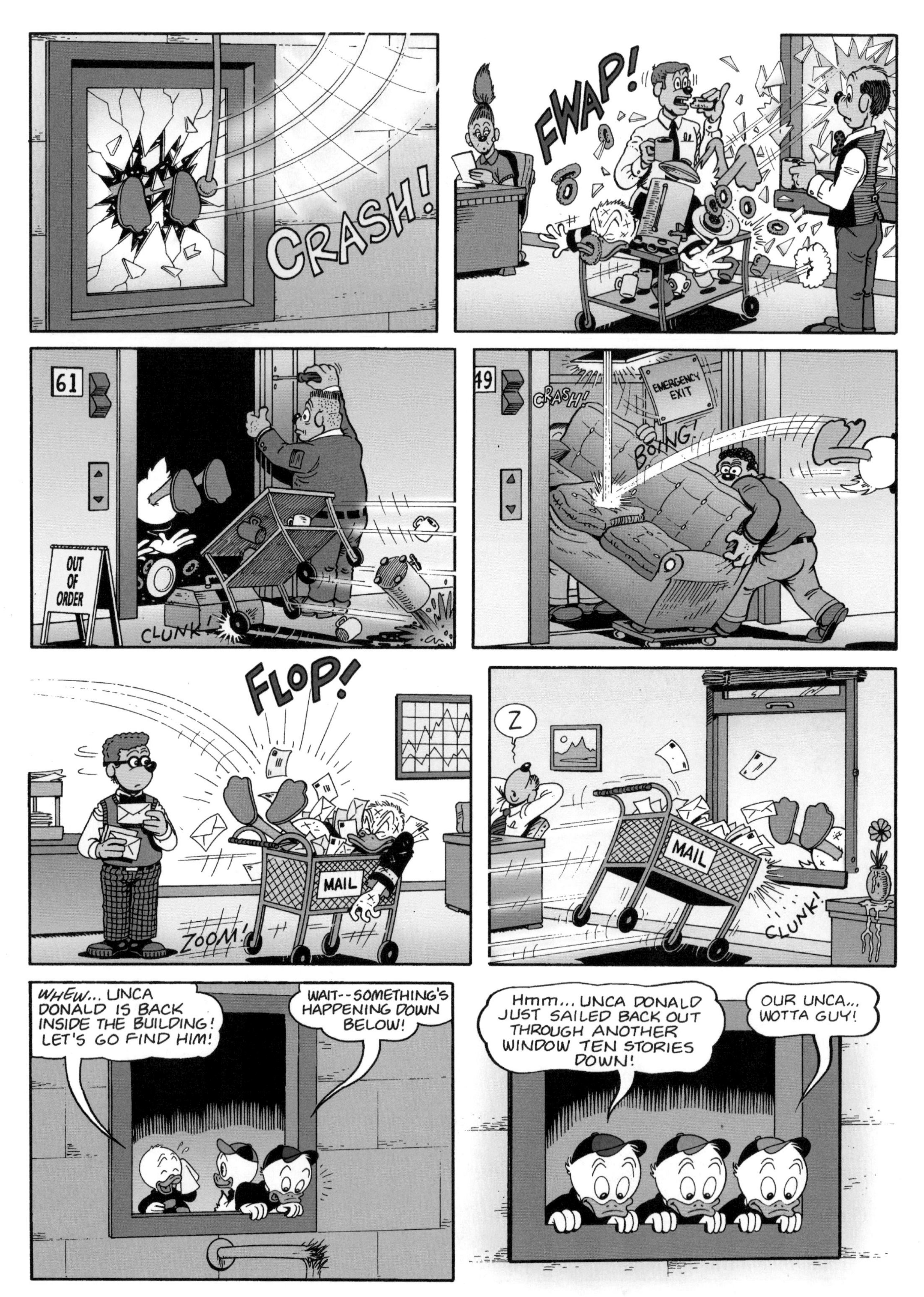
CRASH!
FWAP!
61
OUT OF ORDER
CLUNK!
49
CRASH!
EMERGENCY EXIT
BOING!
FLOP!
MAIL
ZOOM!
Z
MAIL
CLUNK!
WHEW... UNCA DONALD IS BACK INSIDE THE BUILDING! LET'S GO FIND HIM!
WAIT--SOMETHING'S HAPPENING DOWN BELOW!
Hmm... UNCA DONALD JUST SAILED BACK OUT THROUGH ANOTHER WINDOW TEN STORIES DOWN!
OUR UNCA... WOTTA GUY!

BOINK!
TWOING!
FOING!
ZOW!
BOYNG!
BWANG!
BEYOING!
WHIRRR!
WHIRRR!
TWOING!
BWANG!
RIP!
BOINK!
9.5
ZOOM!
FOING!
BYONG!
BEYANG!
TWOING!
RIP!
CRASH!
RIP!
CRASH!
FRESH FISH
SALE
COD
FRESH FISH
SNAG
CRASH
ON SECOND THOUGHT, SKIP THE PICKLED HERRING! IT LOOKS SPOILED!
PICKLED HERRING
ST. PETER... WHY IS HEAVEN FULL OF PARSLEY?
UNCA DONALD! ARE YOU OKAY?

I HOPE THIS LITTLE INCIDENT HASN'T PUT YOU OFF YOUR WINDOW WASHING CAREER!
NOT OUR FEARLESS UNCLE!
YAAHH!
WHAT? WHO? WHICH?
THIS CURB! IT'S SO HIGH! I'M GETTING VERTIGO! OH! OH!
HELP!
HELP ME DOWN... EASY... EASY... WHEW! THERE! FINALLY!
TOMORROW I'M APPLYING FOR A JOB AS A STREET CLEANER! I'M KEEPING MY WEBBED TOES ON SOMETHING I CAN'T FALL OFF!
RESH FISH
JOE'S DIN
FIND UNCA SCROOGE AND TELL HIM THAT UNCA DONALD IS KNOCKING OFF EARLY TODAY, AND...
WHIT!
WHAT THE--
SPLASH!
AREN'T YOU SUPPOSED TO BE WASHING WINDOWS?
End

WALT DISNEY'S
UNCLE $CROOGE
in
THE ISLAND AT THE EDGE OF TIME
TIME! TIME IS AN INTERESTING CONCEPT. IN PARTICULAR, IT IS A RELATIVE MATTER HAVING DIFFERENT MEANINGS FOR THE PEOPLE AND PLACES SCATTERED ALONG THE ETERNAL THREAD!
FOR EXAMPLE: AT THIS POINT IN TIME, NIGHT IS DESCENDING ON DUCKBURG, THUS ENDING ANOTHER DAY IN THE THRIFTY LIFE OF SCROOGE McDUCK. AND YET...
...AT THIS SAME MOMENT, DAYLIGHT STILL SHINES SOMEWHERE IN THE PACIFIC OCEAN, WHERE A NEW ADVENTURE FOR UNCLE SCROOGE WILL SOON BEGIN!
D 91071
AS WE MOVE FORWARD ALONG THE TIMELINE, WE CAN SEE THAT VOLCANIC ACTIVITY IS TAKING PLACE AND GIVING BIRTH TO A NEW ISLAND... NOT A PARTICULARLY UNUSUAL OCCURRENCE!
RUMBLE!
AND YET, THERE IS A DIFFERENCE!
THIS TIME THE MAGMA ERUPTING FROM THE EARTH'S CORE IS COMPOSED OF SOMETHING THAT MAKES THIS TINY ISLAND UNIQUE!
RUMBLE!
GOLD!
MEANWHILE, FOR SCROOGE McDUCK, IT IS TIME FOR REST. EVEN THE WORLD'S RICHEST DUCK CANNOT REMAIN PERPETUALLY VIGILANT!
AT TIMES SUCH AS THIS, SCROOGE RELIES ON HIS WORLD-WIDE INFORMATION SYSTEM.
AND RIGHT AT THIS INSTANT, THE SENSORS ABOARD A McDUCK MINING CORPORATION SATELLITE DETECT THE ISLAND ABORNING!
GOLD?
GOLD?!
GOLD!!!

SCROOGE IS PREPARED FOR EMERGENCIES LIKE THIS, FOR HE KNOWS TIME IS OF THE ESSENCE! AN ENTIRE ISLAND OF GOLD TRIGGERS INTENSE ACTIVITY IN SCROOGE'S SATELLITE AS IT STRUGGLES TO ESTABLISH A GROUND-LINK FOR ITS REPORT!
GOLD!
GOLD!
LOOK! GOLD!! THERE!!
HOWEVER, THE ELECTRONIC FERVOR SETS OFF AN EXPLOSION IN THE SATELLITE'S CIRCUITRY. PERHAPS SCROOGE SHOULDN'T HAVE USED SUCH LOW QUALITY DIODES...
BZZT!
BOOM!
...BUT AT THE TIME, THEY WERE ON SALE!
THE DISABLED SATELLITE PLUNGES EARTHWARD! ONLY TIME WILL TELL WHERE IT WILL FALL!
TIME EVENTUALLY TELLS DUCKBURG THAT IT IS THE DAWN OF A NEW DAY...
...WHICH MEANS IT'S TIME FOR SCROOGE TO JOURNEY THROUGH THE EARLY MORNING LIGHT!
Z.
FOR SCROOGE, TIME IS A MATTER OF DAILY ROUTINE-- AS HE CLIMBS TO HIS MIGHTY MONEY BIN AS HE HAS FOR 50 YEARS!
HANDS OFF!
SCRAM
GO AWAY!
WHILE SCROOGE SLEPT, THE FINANCIAL MACHINERY OF OTHER HEMISPHERES TOILED ON. HIS FIRST DAILY CHORE IS TO READ THE PREVIOUS NIGHT'S STOCK REPORTS, BUSINESS NEWS AND SATELLITE DATA.
WOW!
TIME IS RELATIVE! DAWN IN DUCKBURG IS DUSK OF THE SAME DAY IN AFRICA, AS NIGHT FALLS ON THE TRANSVAAL...
...BUT THIS DUSK IS ILLUMINATED BY A FIERY STREAK ACROSS THE HEAVENS!

IT'S GETTING LATE, SIR!
DRIVE ME HOME, THEN! THIS PROBLEM WITH IMPURITIES IN THE GOLD OF MY MAIN MINE WILL HAVE TO WAIT UNTIL TOMORROW!
BESIDES, THERE COULD BE WORSE PROBLEMS THAN FINDING STAR SAPPHIRES IN MY GOLD ORE!
GASP! WHAT IS THAT?
IT LOOKS LIKE A METEOR!
WHUMP!
IT STRUCK JUST OVER THAT SAND DUNE!
THAT'S MY LAND! LET'S GO INVESTIGATE! SOMETIMES METEORITES CAN HAVE DIAMONDS IN THEM!
IT APPEARS TO BE A SATELLITE THAT DROPPED FROM ORBIT! I CAN BARELY MAKE OUT THE LETTERING!
"McDUCK MINING COMPANY"?
McDUCK? McDUCK, YOU SAY?... HEH HEH! VERY INTERESTING!
TIME! TIME CAN ALSO BE A MEASUREMENT OF SPEED! AS IN PARSECS PER YEAR, MILES PER DAY, FEET PER HOUR...
ZOW
...OR CITY BLOCKS PER MINUTE!
TIME IS RELATIVE! THOUGH A DAY BEGINS EARLY FOR ONE SCROOGE McDUCK, THAT SAME DAY CAN — AND OFTEN DOES — BEGIN LATER — MUCH LATER — FOR ANOTHER DUCK...
D. DUCK
ZING!
...NAMED DONALD!
WAKE UP! WAKE UP! GET OUTTA BED!
?!

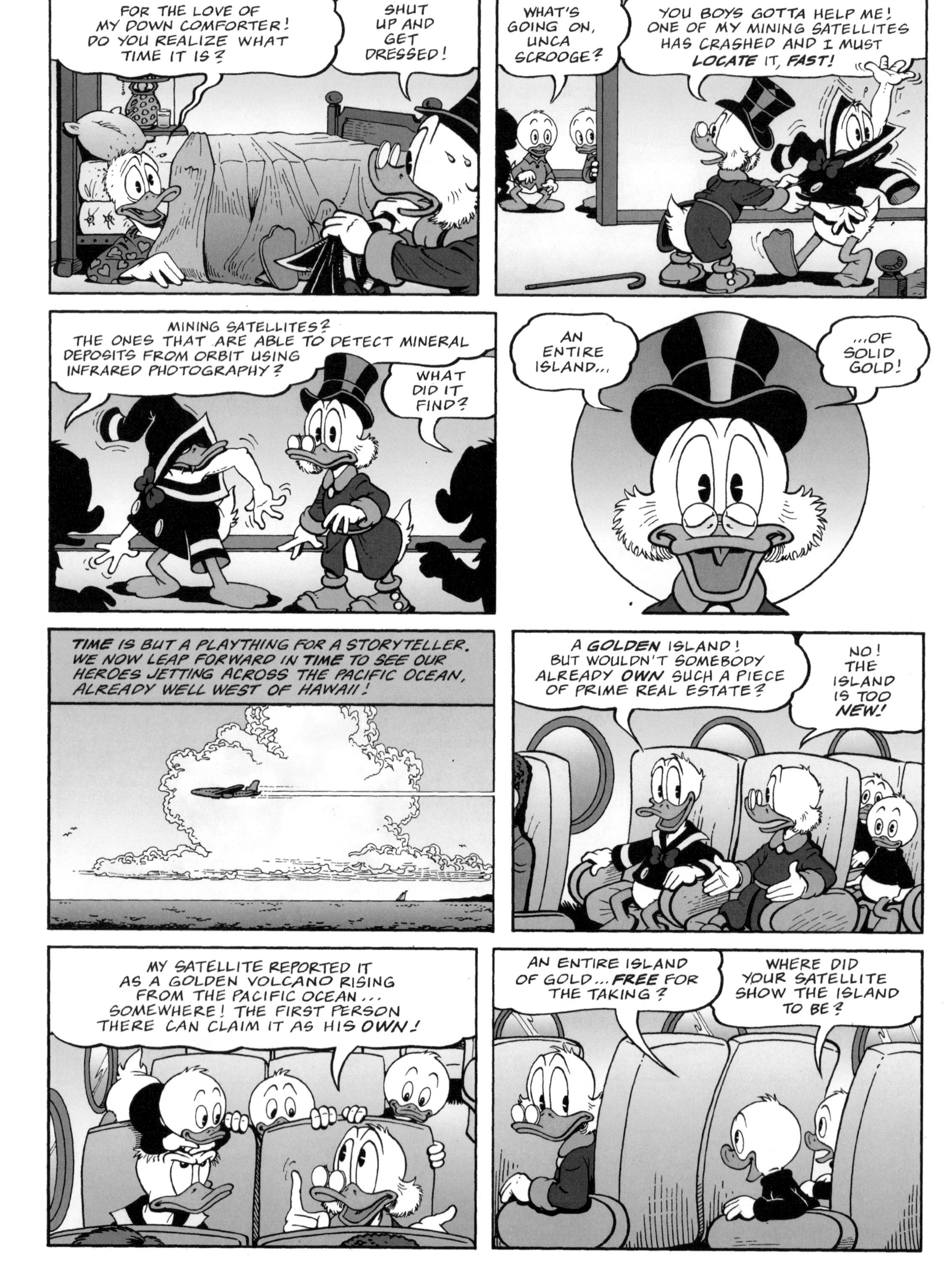
FOR THE LOVE OF MY DOWN COMFORTER! DO YOU REALIZE WHAT TIME IT IS?
SHUT UP AND GET DRESSED!
WHAT'S GOING ON, UNCA SCROOGE?
YOU BOYS GOTTA HELP ME! ONE OF MY MINING SATELLITES HAS CRASHED AND I MUST **LOCATE** IT, **FAST!**
MINING SATELLITES? THE ONES THAT ARE ABLE TO DETECT MINERAL DEPOSITS FROM ORBIT USING INFRARED PHOTOGRAPHY?
WHAT DID IT FIND?
AN ENTIRE ISLAND...
...OF SOLID GOLD!
TIME IS BUT A PLAYTHING FOR A STORYTELLER. WE NOW LEAP FORWARD IN **TIME** TO SEE OUR HEROES JETTING ACROSS THE PACIFIC OCEAN, ALREADY WELL WEST OF HAWAII!
A **GOLDEN** ISLAND! BUT WOULDN'T SOMEBODY ALREADY **OWN** SUCH A PIECE OF PRIME REAL ESTATE?
NO! THE ISLAND IS TOO **NEW!**
MY SATELLITE REPORTED IT AS A GOLDEN VOLCANO RISING FROM THE PACIFIC OCEAN... SOMEWHERE! THE FIRST PERSON THERE CAN CLAIM IT AS HIS **OWN!**
AN ENTIRE ISLAND OF GOLD... **FREE** FOR THE TAKING?
WHERE DID YOUR SATELLITE SHOW THE ISLAND TO BE?

THAT'S THE PROBLEM! IT MALFUNCTIONED BEFORE RELAYING THAT DATA, THOUGH IT SHOULD STILL HAVE IT STORED! I MUST FIND THAT SATELLITE!
MY EAST INDIES TRACKING STATION IN MANILA WILL KNOW WHERE IT FELL! THAT'S OUR FIRST STOP!
AND YOU'VE JUST LOST A FULL DAY IN YOUR SEARCH!
IT WAS MONDAY A MOMENT AGO, BUT NOW IT'S TUESDAY!
WHAT SORT OF GIBBERISH IS THAT?
WHAT THEY MEAN IS THAT WE JUST CROSSED THE 180TH MERIDIAN... THE INTERNATIONAL DATELINE!
IT'S THE LINE OF LONGITUDE WHERE EACH NEW DATE BEGINS!
HAH?
SUPPOSE IT'S MIDNIGHT IN DUCKBURG AND MONDAY IS BEGINNING! TO THE WEST, WHERE IT'S NOT YET MIDNIGHT, IT'S STILL SUNDAY! BUT EVERYWHERE EAST OF DUCKBURG IT'S WELL INTO MONDAY!
AT THAT MOMENT, IT WOULD BE THE MIDDLE OF THE DAY ON THE OPPOSITE SIDE OF THE EARTH! BUT HOW COULD THAT DAY BE BOTH SUNDAY AND MONDAY?
I GIVE UP! HOW?
THE INTERNATIONAL DATELINE IS HOW! WEST OF THAT POINT IS ALWAYS ONE DAY LATER THAN EAST OF IT!
!
Modern Tightwad
TIME! PEOPLE USE IT TO THEIR ADVANTAGES!
HEY! IF IT'S NOW TUESDAY INSTEAD OF MONDAY, YOU OWE ME ANOTHER FULL DAY'S PAY!
Modern Tightwad
WHAT IS THIS?
FOR IMAGINARY TIME I PAY IMAGINARY MONEY!
Modern Tightwad

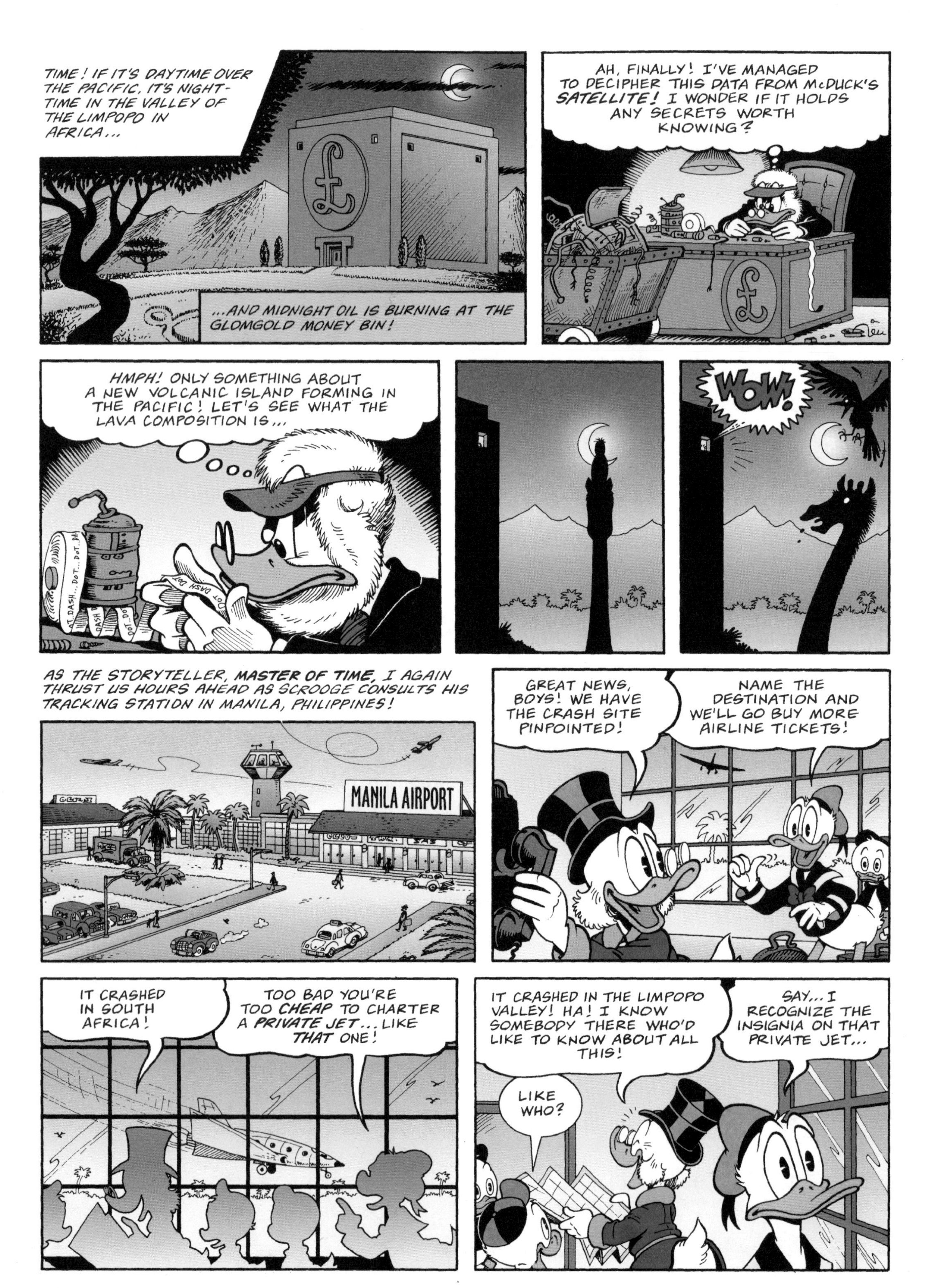

TIME! IF IT'S DAYTIME OVER THE PACIFIC, IT'S NIGHT-TIME IN THE VALLEY OF THE LIMPOPO IN AFRICA...
...AND MIDNIGHT OIL IS BURNING AT THE GLOMGOLD MONEY BIN!
AH, FINALLY! I'VE MANAGED TO DECIPHER THIS DATA FROM McDUCK'S SATELLITE! I WONDER IF IT HOLDS ANY SECRETS WORTH KNOWING?
HMPH! ONLY SOMETHING ABOUT A NEW VOLCANIC ISLAND FORMING IN THE PACIFIC! LET'S SEE WHAT THE LAVA COMPOSITION IS...
WOW!
AS THE STORYTELLER, MASTER OF TIME, I AGAIN THRUST US HOURS AHEAD AS SCROOGE CONSULTS HIS TRACKING STATION IN MANILA, PHILIPPINES!
MANILA AIRPORT
GREAT NEWS, BOYS! WE HAVE THE CRASH SITE PINPOINTED!
NAME THE DESTINATION AND WE'LL GO BUY MORE AIRLINE TICKETS!
IT CRASHED IN SOUTH AFRICA!
TOO BAD YOU'RE TOO CHEAP TO CHARTER A PRIVATE JET... LIKE THAT ONE!
IT CRASHED IN THE LIMPOPO VALLEY! HA! I KNOW SOMEBODY THERE WHO'D LIKE TO KNOW ABOUT ALL THIS!
LIKE WHO?
SAY... I RECOGNIZE THE INSIGNIA ON THAT PRIVATE JET...

FLINTHEART GLOMGOLD!
IS THERE AN ECHO AROUND HERE?
FLINTHEART GLOMGOLD? IN A JET HEADING TOWARDS THE PACIFIC? OH, MY WORD... I HAVE A BAD FEELING ABOUT THIS!
FG
HE'S REFUELING! DO YOU SUPPOSE HE KNOWS ANYTHING OF YOUR GOLDEN ISLAND?
FG FG
I HAVE TO FIND OUT!
HEY, BUDDY... LET ME TALK TO YOU FOR A MINUTE...
?
MANILA FUEL CO.
SHORTLY...
'SCUSE ME, SIR... I NEED TO CHECK YOUR GAUGES WHILE WE REFUEL YOUR PLANE!
WHAT? WELL, BE QUICK ABOUT IT!
SO WHEN WE REACH THIS ISLAND I'LL PARACHUTE DOWN TO IT! MY SEAPLANE WILL PICK ME UP LATER!
WHERE IS THIS ISLAND?
IT'S A NEW LAND MASS IN THE HAWAIIAN RIDGE ABOUT 125 MILES WEST OF KURE ISLAND!
I'M DONE, SIR! I'LL BE GOING!
AND GOOD RIDDANCE! WHY IS YOUR JET FUEL SO EXPENSIVE AROUND HERE?

DAGNABBIT! YOU'RE RIGHT! IT'S HIGHWAY ROBBERY! I ALWAYS REFUEL IN BORNEO! SIX HUNDRED MILES AWAY, BUT THE FUEL IS A NICKEL PER GALLON *CHEAPER!*
IT'S A PLEASURE TO MEET SOMEONE SO *FRUGAL!* I THOUGHT NOBODY BESIDES *ME* WOULD GO SIX HUNDRED MILES TO SAVE A NICKEL PER GALLON, THAT IS, NOBODY EXCEPT... EXCEPT...
...EXCEPT...
FLOOP!
GASP!
SCROOGE McDUCK! *GET OFF MY PLANE!*
MY PLEASURE, FLINTY! I'M ON MY WAY TO A CERTAIN *ISLAND!*
FG
ACK! OH, NO YOU'RE NOT, YOU OLD TURNIP-SQUEEZER! I'LL TEAR YOU INTO *TICKER TAPE!*
YOU AND WHAT GLEE CLUB?
WHAT'S THE PROBLEM HERE?
OFFICER! I... I... WAS INSPECTING THIS MAN'S AIR CARGO!
HUH?
HIS PLANE IS INFESTED WITH AUGER-NOSED PICKLE-HATER BEETLES! THEY'LL OVERRUN THE PHILIPPINES AND DESTROY YOUR ENTIRE CUCUMBER CROP!
HORRORS!
!
SIR, YOU AND YOUR PLANE WILL BE PUT INTO QUARANTINE FOR A MONTH!
AAK! *YOU CAN'T DO THIS!* THAT WHISKERED WEASEL IS *LYING!*

THAT WAS A DIRTY TRICK, UNCA SCROOGE! YOU SHOULDN'T HAVE TOLD THEM THAT!
YOU'RE RIGHT! I SHOULD'VE SAID AFRICAN KILLER BEES! GIGGLE!
BUT WHO CARES? I KNOW WHERE MY GOLDEN ISLAND IS NOW! WE NEED TO HIRE A PLANE AND FLY THERE DIRECTLY!
HERE'S A JET CHARTER SERVICE!
JET? ARE YOU NUTS? YOU KNOW WHAT JET FUEL COSTS IN THIS BURG?
CHARTER JETS
THERE'S NO LONGER ANY NEED TO HURRY WITH GLOMGOLD BEING HELD! WE'LL CHARTER THIS SEAPLANE!
Keoki's SEAPLANES
TIME! TIME MARCHES INEXORABLY ONWARD, AND EACH MOMENT BRINGS SCROOGE CLOSER TO THE ISLE OF GOLD!
WE'LL REACH THE AREA YOU DESCRIBED IN ABOUT SIX HOURS, MR. McDUCK!
THE ISLAND THERE... IS IT YOUR HOME?
NO — WE'RE FROM DUCKBURG ON THE WEST COAST OF AMERICA!
WHERE ARE YOU FROM, KEOKI? THE PHILIPPINES?
NO, LITTLE FRIEND! I COME FROM THE ISLAND OF WOKAWOKA IN THE SOUTH PACIFIC!
ALAS, IT IS A VERY POOR ISLAND! SEVERAL YEARS AGO, A HURRICANE WIPED OUT OUR CROPS AND LIVESTOCK AND WE DON'T HAVE THE MONEY TO REBUILD!
JEEPERS!

I SEND ALL MY CHARTER MONEY HOME TO FEED MY PEOPLE, BUT IT IS NOT ENOUGH! WOKAWOKA WILL NOT SURVIVE MUCH LONGER!
YOU KNOW, AFTER YOU CLAIM YOUR ISLAND, YOU SHOULD GIVE KEOKI A BONUS!
BONUS? WHAT'S THAT? GOT A BAD RING TO IT!
HEY! I HEAR A JET!
GLOMGOLD!
IT CAN'T BE!
RRROAR!
HIYA, SCROOGIE! WHEN YOU REACH MY ISLAND, DROP IN FOR TEA... AND I'LL TELL YOU SOME INTERESTING FACTS ABOUT MANILA!
F'RINSTANCE... MANILA IS ALREADY OVERRUN BY SWARMS OF AUGER-NOSED PICKLE-HATERS!
HOW ABOUT THAT, MISTER TOO-CHEAP-TO-RENT-A-JET?
?
THE TIME OF RECKONING DRAWS CLOSE! HOURS LATER, A PLUME OF VOLCANIC SMOKE IS SIGHTED!
THERE! THAT MUST BE THE GOLDEN ISLAND!
HURRY! LAND! MAYBE GLOMGOLD'S PLANE GOT LOST!
I'LL NEED TO CIRCLE AROUND THAT SMOKE!
DON'T WASTE TIME! IT'S ONLY SMOKE! FLY THROUGH IT!
YESSIR... YOU'RE THE BOSS!

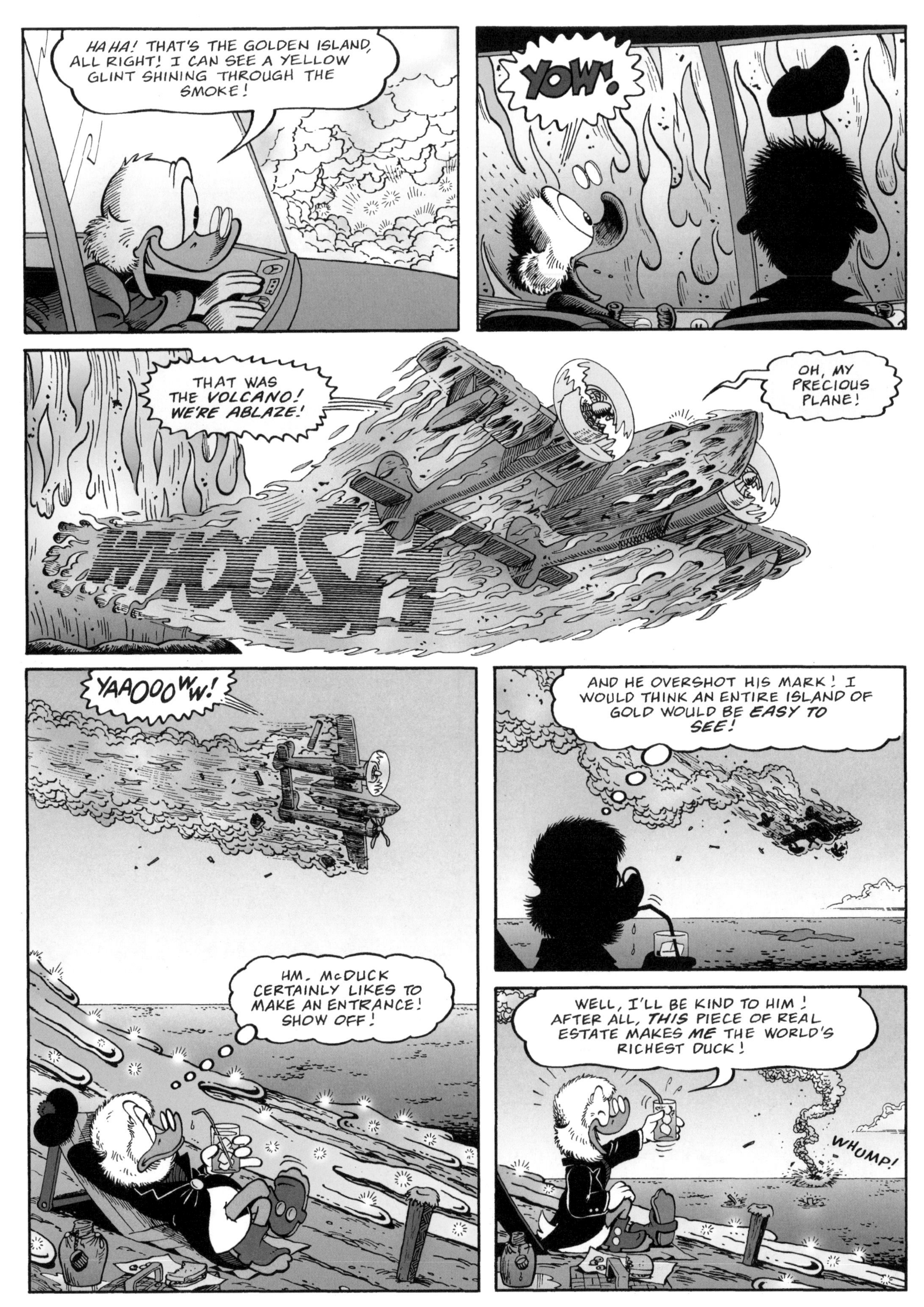
HA HA! THAT'S THE GOLDEN ISLAND, ALL RIGHT! I CAN SEE A YELLOW GLINT SHINING THROUGH THE SMOKE!
YOW!
THAT WAS THE VOLCANO! WE'RE ABLAZE!
OH, MY PRECIOUS PLANE!
WHOOSH
YAAOOOWW!
AND HE OVERSHOT HIS MARK! I WOULD THINK AN ENTIRE ISLAND OF GOLD WOULD BE EASY TO SEE!
HM. McDUCK CERTAINLY LIKES TO MAKE AN ENTRANCE! SHOW OFF!
WELL, I'LL BE KIND TO HIM! AFTER ALL, THIS PIECE OF REAL ESTATE MAKES ME THE WORLD'S RICHEST DUCK!
WHUMP!

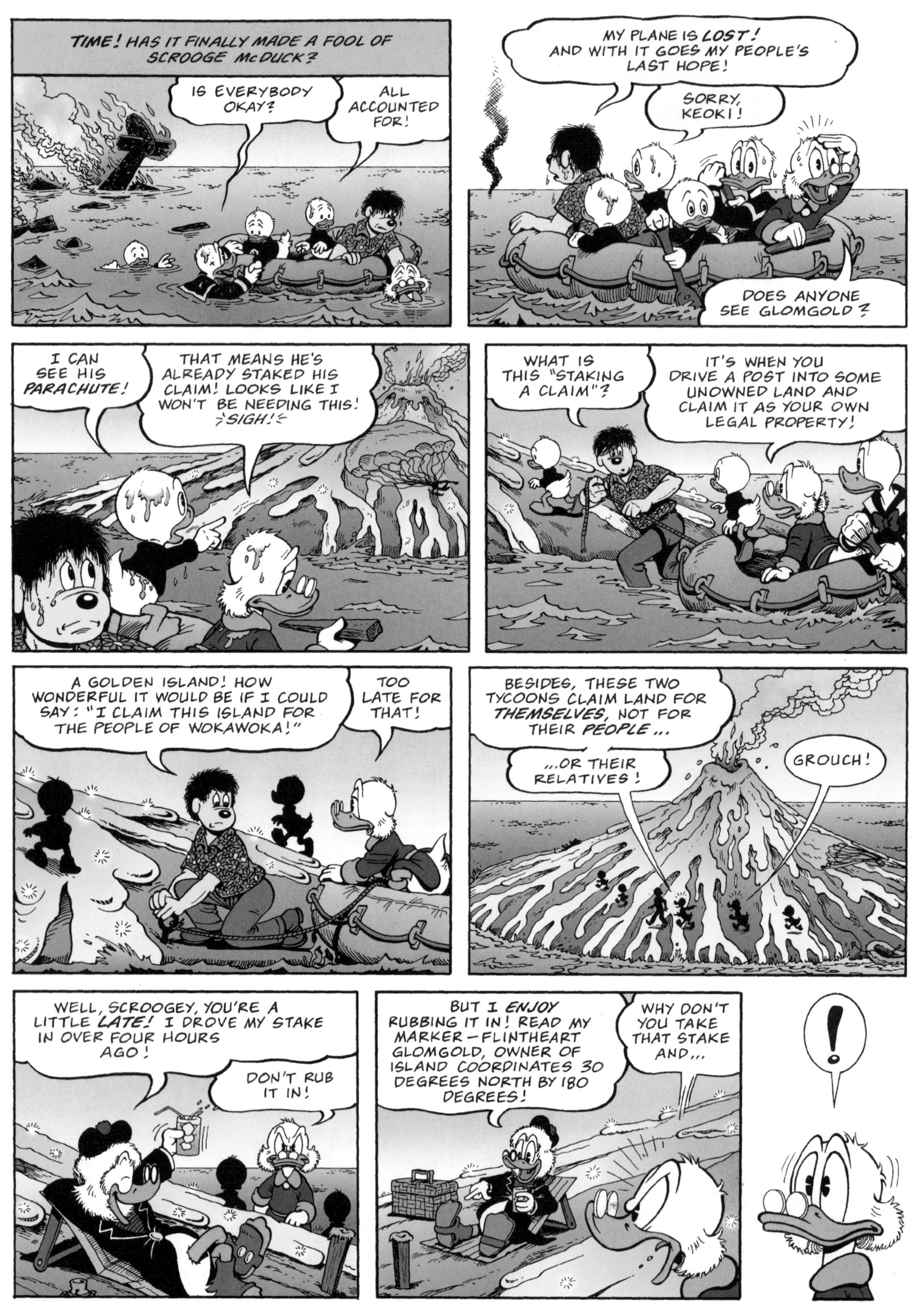
TIME! HAS IT FINALLY MADE A FOOL OF SCROOGE McDUCK?
IS EVERYBODY OKAY?
ALL ACCOUNTED FOR!
MY PLANE IS LOST! AND WITH IT GOES MY PEOPLE'S LAST HOPE!
SORRY, KEOKI!
DOES ANYONE SEE GLOMGOLD?
I CAN SEE HIS PARACHUTE!
THAT MEANS HE'S ALREADY STAKED HIS CLAIM! LOOKS LIKE I WON'T BE NEEDING THIS! SIGH!
WHAT IS THIS "STAKING A CLAIM"?
IT'S WHEN YOU DRIVE A POST INTO SOME UNOWNED LAND AND CLAIM IT AS YOUR OWN LEGAL PROPERTY!
A GOLDEN ISLAND! HOW WONDERFUL IT WOULD BE IF I COULD SAY: "I CLAIM THIS ISLAND FOR THE PEOPLE OF WOKAWOKA!"
TOO LATE FOR THAT!
BESIDES, THESE TWO TYCOONS CLAIM LAND FOR THEMSELVES, NOT FOR THEIR PEOPLE ...
...OR THEIR RELATIVES!
GROUCH!
WELL, SCROOGEY, YOU'RE A LITTLE LATE! I DROVE MY STAKE IN OVER FOUR HOURS AGO!
DON'T RUB IT IN!
BUT I ENJOY RUBBING IT IN! READ MY MARKER—FLINTHEART GLOMGOLD, OWNER OF ISLAND COORDINATES 30 DEGREES NORTH BY 180 DEGREES!
WHY DON'T YOU TAKE THAT STAKE AND...
!

'SCUSE ME... DID YOU SAY THE LONGITUDE WAS 180 DEGREES?
YEP! I CALCULATE THAT LINE RUNS SMACK DAB THROUGH THE CENTER OF MY ISLAND!
AND YOU STAKED YOUR CLAIM HERE ON THE *WEST* SIDE?
THAT I DID! EAT YOUR HEART OUT!
AND THIS IS THE *EAST* SIDE OF THE ISLAND, OVER THIS WAY?
YEAH — SO *WHAT?*
SO *THIS!*
I, SCROOGE McDUCK, CLAIM THIS ISLAND AS MY PROPERTY!
HEH HEH! LOOKS LIKE I'VE FINALLY DRIVEN YOUR DODDERING OLD UNCLE NUTS, LADS!
SCROOGE, YOU OLD HAS-BEEN! I ALREADY CLAIMED THIS ISLAND OVER FOUR HOURS AGO, REMEMBER?
TRUE ENOUGH!
BUT IF THE 180TH MERIDIAN BISECTS THIS ISLAND, SO DOES THE *INTERNATIONAL DATE LINE!*
OH, SO?
IT'S *WEDNESDAY,* THE 17TH OF THE MONTH, OVER ON YOUR *WEST* SIDE...
...BUT IT'S STILL *TUESDAY* THE 16TH HERE ON THE *EAST* SIDE!
I BEAT YOUR CLAIM BY AN *ENTIRE DAY!*
GLEEP!

AND I HAVE WITNESSES!
HE'S BEYOND CARING!
YES, UNCA SCROOGE! WITNESSES TO A PRIOR CLAIM TO BOTH OF YOURS!
WHAT ARE YOU YAMMERING ABOUT?!
REMEMBER, FIVE MINUTES AGO, WHEN KEOKI PUSHED THAT MOORING SPIKE INTO THE GROUND?
?
YES! HE SAID, "I CLAIM THIS ISLAND FOR THE PEOPLE OF WOKAWOKA"!
NO! NO! HE SAID NOTHING LIKE THAT! YOU HEARD AN OPTICAL ILLUSION!
SORRY, UNCA SCROOGE, BUT THIS ISLAND IS THE LEGAL PROPERTY OF THE PEOPLE OF KEOKI'S HOME ISLAND!
MOVE OVER, GLOMGOLD!
I CAN'T BELIEVE IT! MY PEOPLE ARE SAVED! WOKAWOKA WILL LIVE!
TIME! TIME PLAYS STRANGE JESTS ON THE AFFAIRS OF MEN! AS SCROOGE McDUCK HEADS HOME TO DUCKBURG, HE HAS MANY TIMELY CONCEPTS TO PONDER!
IT'S TIME THAT WILL WASH AWAY THE IGNOMINY OF SCROOGE'S DEFEAT! TIME HEALS ALL WOUNDS!
AND IT'S TIME THAT HAS PLAYED SCROOGE FOR THE FOOL IN HIS MERCILESS QUEST FOR WEALTH! TIME WOUNDS ALL HEELS!
AND IT'S TIME THAT IS THE ULTIMATE
IT'S TIME FOR YOU TO SHUT UP AND END THIS STORY!
End

Walt Disney's
UNCLE $CROOGE in WAR of the WENDIGO
PART ONE
WELL, BOYS, WELCOME TO THE GREAT WHITE NORTH!
THE GREAT WHITE NORTH LOOKS A LITTLE GREEN THIS MORNING!
D91192
WHITE, GREEN, OR POLKA DOT, IT WAS NICE OF YOU TO BRING US ON YOUR TOUR OF YOUR CANADIAN MILLS, UNCA SCROOGE!
WE CAN DO SOME NATURE STUDIES!
WE MIGHT EARN OUR MERIT BADGES IN LEARNING THE SQUAWKS OF THE COMMON LOON!
SEEMS LIKE YOU COULD DO THAT BACK HOME, LIVING WITH YOUR UNCLE DONALD!
JUST LOOK AT THE BEAUTY THAT SURROUNDS US ON ALL SIDES! CLEAN, UNSPOILED VISTAS!
PARADISE TO ALL FOUR COMPASS POINTS —
TAP! TAP!
McDUCK PULP MILL
WELL, THREE OUT OF FOUR ISN'T SO BAD! DON'T BE A WISE GUY!
I THOUGHT I WAS A COMMON LOON!

YOU AREN'T POLLUTING THE FOREST WITH THAT PULP MILL, ARE YOU, UNCA SCROOGE?
OF COURSE NOT!
I BUILT THE TALLEST SMOKESTACKS IN ONTARIO! THAT SMOG IS BLOWING FAR FROM THESE WOODLANDS!
BESIDES, SOON THERE WON'T BE MUCH FOREST LEFT HERE TO POLLUTE!
QUIET!
HOW ABOUT YOUR MILL'S WASTEWATER? WHAT'S IN IT?
LISTEN, SOMEBODY HAS TO HARVEST TREES TO EVEN PRINT YOUR WOOD-CHUCK GOODY-TWO-SHOES GUIDEBOOK!
THE GUIDEBOOK IS ON RECYCLED PAPER, OF COURSE! BUT YOU'RE RIGHT— WE DO NEED PAPER AND LUMBER!
GIVE POOR UNCLE SCROOGE A BREAK! MAKING LUMBER ISN'T EASY! WOOD DOESN'T GROW ON TREES, Y'KNOW!
WHEN I WANT YOUR HELP, I'LL ASK FOR IT!
IF YOU DON'T LIKE SEEING MY MILL, JUST CLOSE YOUR EYES AND ENJOY THE PEACE AND QUIET! SO RESTFUL, SO—
BLAM! BLAM!
WHAT THE DING-DONG DOOZLEFEATHERS WAS THAT?
SHOTGUN BLASTS! LET'S GO SEE!

WHAT WAS IT, JOE? TH-TH-THEM AGAIN?
YES! GULP! THEY WERE RIGHT BEHIND ME, EH?
THEM? THEM WHO?
WHO? THE WENDIGO, THAT'S WHO!
DO YOU KNOW WENDIGO?
!
SURE! I CAN TAKE A HINT! I DON'T HANG AROUND WHERE I'M NOT WANTED!
NOT "WHEN TO GO," YOU DOPE! WENDIGO! THE NORTH WOODS GREMLINS!
THE TRICKY DEVILS HAVE HAUNTED THIS LAND FOR CENTURIES!
THEY SNEAK UP BEHIND YOU, BUT WHEN YOU TURN AROUND, THEY'RE OUT OF SIGHT!
BRRR!
YOW! HALP!
THAT'S DEWEY! WHAT HAPPENED?
THE WENDIGO! THE WENDIGO GOT HIM!
I WARNED YOU ABOUT THAT WENDIGO TALK! YOU'RE FIRED! GET OUT!
WITH PLEASURE!
THAT'S MY PLANT MANAGER, RAVAGE DeFLORA!
WHAT ARE YOU DOING, DeFLORA?
I FINALLY CAUGHT ONE OF THESE RENEGADE BOY SCOUTS THAT ARE TERRORIZING THE MILL! THEY CALL THEMSELVES "JUNIOR WOODCHIPS"!
WE'RE JUNIOR WOOD-CHUCKS! AND WE'RE NOT TERRORISTS!
BUT THEY ARE MY NEPHEWS, DeFLORA! EXPLAIN YOURSELF!
OOPS! SORRY SIR!

FOR YEARS WE'VE GOTTEN MAIL FROM THESE MINIATURE NATURE BOYS ABOUT HOW WE'RE SUPPOSEDLY SPOILING THEIR PRECIOUS WOODS!
ARE YOU?
LOOK, KID, SAVING THE ENVIRONMENT IS FINE AND DANDY, BUT NOT IF IT COSTS ME MY JOB! HOW CAN YOU EVEN COMPARE THE TWO?
WE CAN'T IMAGINE!
ANIMAL LOVERS - BAH! GIVE BAMBI HALF A CHANCE AND HE'LL TAKE YOUR ARM OFF WITH ONE SNAP OF HIS GIANT FANGS!
WOODCHUCKS OR WENDIGO - WHAT ARE YOU DOING ABOUT THOSE GREMLINS?
MY GUARDS ARE WIMPS! THEY WON'T TRACK THOSE VANDALS INTO THE WOODS AND CATCH THEM!
HMM...
UH-OH!
DeFLORA, GET ME FIVE PACKS OF CAMPING GEAR!
RIGHT! WE'LL TRACK THEM DOWN AND PROVE THE JUNIOR WOODCHUCKS ARE NOT BEHIND THIS!
I'VE MATCHED WITS WITH MY SHARE OF LEGENDARY CRITTERS... YETI, HARPIES, MENEHUNE! THERE'S NOTHING IN THIS TIMBER-LAND I CAN'T HANDLE!
DEER HAVE FANGS? BIG FANGS?
OUR INTREPID BAND OF WENDIGO-BUSTERS TREKS INTO THE DENSE WOODLANDS EARLY THE NEXT MORNING! THEY CAN FEEL MYSTERIOUS EYES WATCHING THEM!
BUT THE WOODCHUCKS' WOODLORE SKILLS ARE UNABLE TO DETECT WHAT-EVER HAUNTS THIS LAND OF THE MAPLE LEAF!

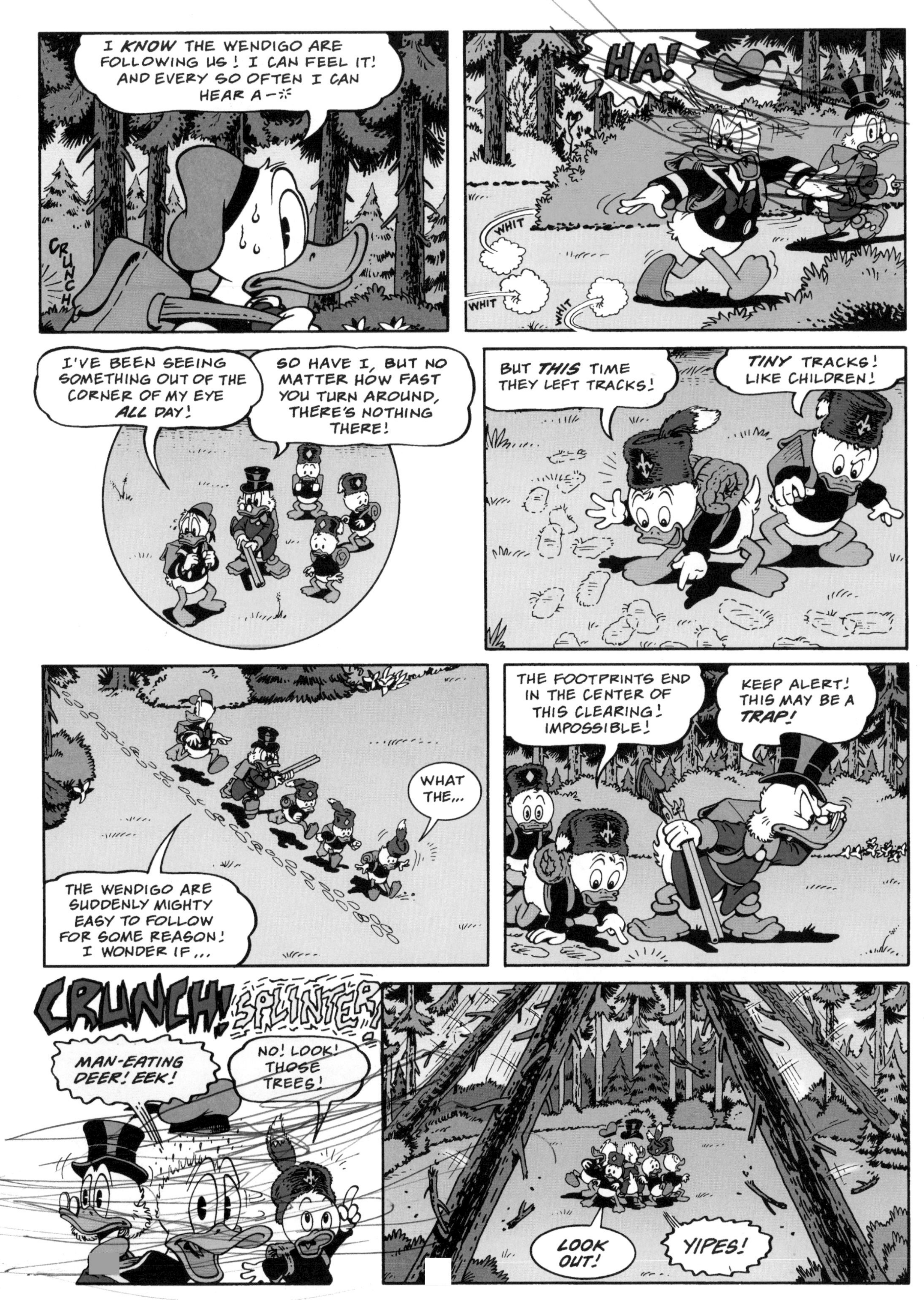
I KNOW THE WENDIGO ARE FOLLOWING US! I CAN FEEL IT! AND EVERY SO OFTEN I CAN HEAR A—
CRUNCH
HA!
WHIT
WHIT
WHIT
I'VE BEEN SEEING SOMETHING OUT OF THE CORNER OF MY EYE ALL DAY!
SO HAVE I, BUT NO MATTER HOW FAST YOU TURN AROUND, THERE'S NOTHING THERE!
BUT THIS TIME THEY LEFT TRACKS!
TINY TRACKS! LIKE CHILDREN!
WHAT THE...
THE WENDIGO ARE SUDDENLY MIGHTY EASY TO FOLLOW FOR SOME REASON! I WONDER IF...
THE FOOTPRINTS END IN THE CENTER OF THIS CLEARING! IMPOSSIBLE!
KEEP ALERT! THIS MAY BE A TRAP!
CRUNCH!
SPLINTER
MAN-EATING DEER! EEK!
NO! LOOK! THOSE TREES!
LOOK OUT!
YIPES!

CLAK!
CLAK!
CLAK!
WELL, I'LL BE A BOW-LEGGED MUSKRAT!
THE FALLING TREES HUNG TOGETHER!
WHAT A STUNT!
THIS LOOKS LIKE A WARNING TO GO HOME!
I'M CONVINCED! G'BYE!
COME BACK HERE, YOU COWARD!
THESE TREES WEREN'T CUT BY PEOPLE – THEY WERE CHEWED BY BEAVER!
TRAINED BEAVERS? DON'T BE SILLY! WHO COULD TRAIN BEAVERS TO CHEW TREES ON COMMAND?
SPLAT!
SPLAT!
SPLAT!
SPLAT!
?
THE SAME PEOPLE WHO CAN TRAIN BIRDS TO BOMB US WITH ROTTEN EGGS!
WE'D BETTER PITCH CAMP! IT'S LATE AND SOME OF US NEED TO WASH UP!
BUT COME MORNING, WE WON'T GO HOME! HEAR THAT, WENDIGO? SCROOGE McDUCK WON'T BE CHASED OFF HIS OWN LAND!
DID YOU HEAR WHAT NAME WAS SPOKEN? DOES HIS PALE FACE STIR YOUR MEM'RY? THIS MEANS TROUBLE FOR OUR PEOPLE! WE MUST TAKE HIM TO OUR LEADER!

NIGHT...
INSTEAD OF TELLING GHOST STORIES, LET'S READ WHAT OUR WOODCHUCKS GUIDEBOOK SAYS ABOUT WENDIGO!
I'LL TAKE FIRST WATCH!
THE NIGHT IS SO PEACEFUL AND SERENE! REMINDS ME OF MY DAYS ON WHITE AGONY CREEK BACK IN THE KLONDIKE!
LEGENDS SAY THE WENDIGO WERE ESPECIALLY ACTIVE AT NIGHT, WHEN THE EARLY FUR TRAPPERS SET UP THEIR CAMPS!
OH, SO? YOU MAY STOP READING NOW!
DURING THE GOLD RUSH I WOULD CAMP UNDER THE YUKON STARS AND WATCH MY CAMPFIRE LIGHT DANCE ALONG THE EDGE OF THE WOODS!
THE WENDIGO WERE SAID TO SURROUND THE HUNTERS' CAMPS, BUT STAY JUST BEYOND THE EDGE OF THEIR CAMP-FIRE LIGHT! SPOOKY, HUH?
THAT'S ALL! STOP! I DON'T WANT TO KNOW ANY MORE!!!
THOSE FLICKERING LIGHTS PLAY TRICKS ON OLD EYES! IT ALMOST LOOKS LIKE FIGURES STANDING IN THE GLOOM! I CAN SEE FEET...AND LEGS...AND...
GREAT SCOTT!
THEY WOULD TAUNT THE HUNTERS AND MAKE THEM EMPTY THEIR GUNS INTO THE DARKNESS!
I CAN'T HEAR YOU! I'M FAST ASLEEP! LISTEN! ZZZZ! I'M SNORING!
FREEZE, YOU VARMINTS! OR I'LL GIVE YOU A LOAD OF ROCK SALT IN YOUR BRITCHES!

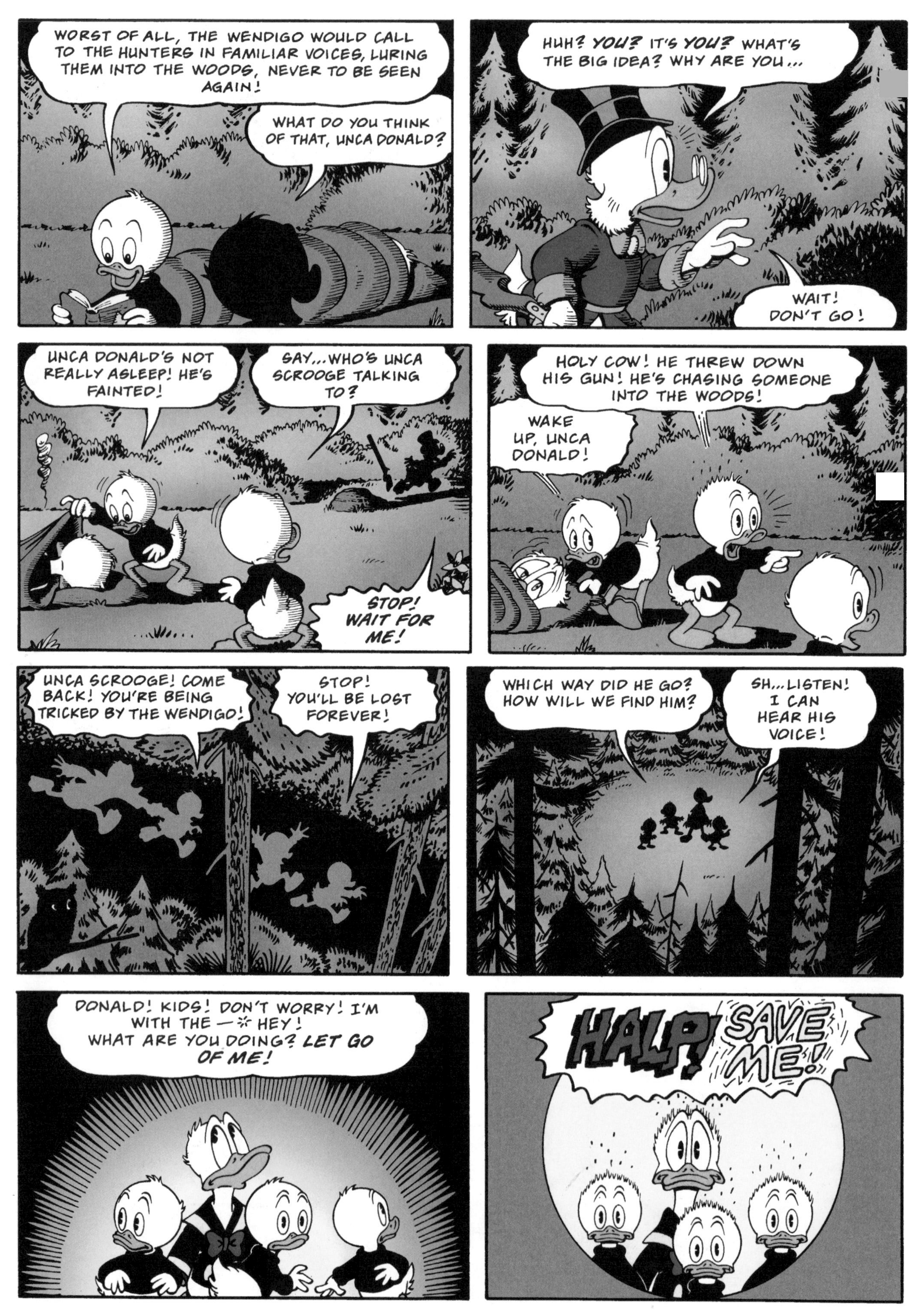
WORST OF ALL, THE WENDIGO WOULD CALL TO THE HUNTERS IN FAMILIAR VOICES, LURING THEM INTO THE WOODS, NEVER TO BE SEEN AGAIN!
WHAT DO YOU THINK OF THAT, UNCA DONALD?
HUH? YOU? IT'S YOU? WHAT'S THE BIG IDEA? WHY ARE YOU...
WAIT! DON'T GO!
UNCA DONALD'S NOT REALLY ASLEEP! HE'S FAINTED!
SAY... WHO'S UNCA SCROOGE TALKING TO?
STOP! WAIT FOR ME!
HOLY COW! HE THREW DOWN HIS GUN! HE'S CHASING SOMEONE INTO THE WOODS!
WAKE UP, UNCA DONALD!
UNCA SCROOGE! COME BACK! YOU'RE BEING TRICKED BY THE WENDIGO!
STOP! YOU'LL BE LOST FOREVER!
WHICH WAY DID HE GO? HOW WILL WE FIND HIM?
SH... LISTEN! I CAN HEAR HIS VOICE!
DONALD! KIDS! DON'T WORRY! I'M WITH THE — HEY! WHAT ARE YOU DOING? LET GO OF ME!
HALP!
SAVE ME!

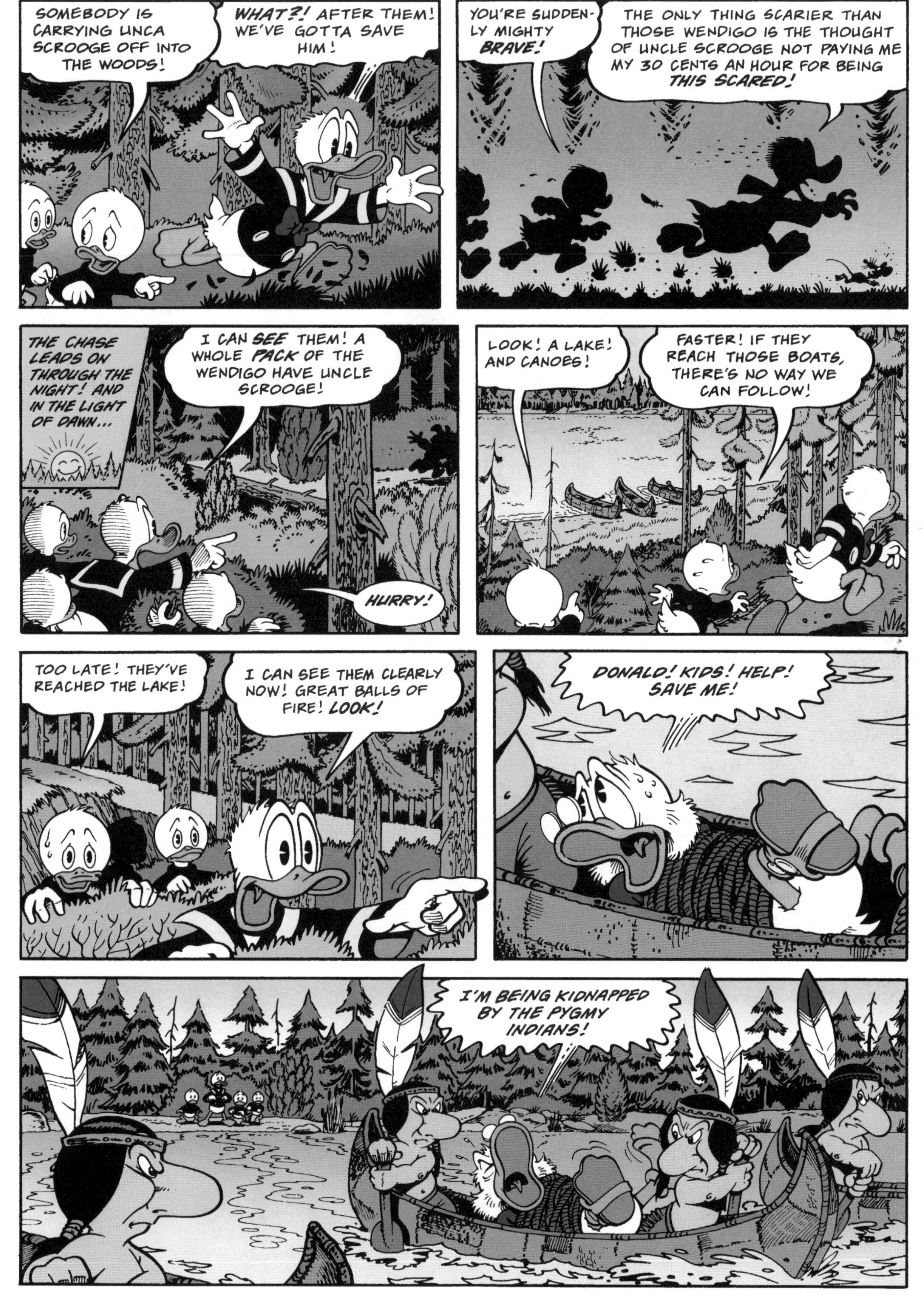

(End of Part One as originally serialized)

Walt Disney's
UNCLE $CROOGE in WAR of the WENDIGO
PART TWO
THE UNSEEN GREMLINS THAT ARE TERRORIZING UNCA SCROOGE'S PULP MILLS HERE IN CANADA AREN'T THE WENDIGO! IT WAS THE PEEWEEGAH! AND THEY TOOK UNCA SCROOGE CAPTIVE!
PEE-WEE-WHAT?
PEEWEEGAH! THEY'RE A TRIBE OF PYGMY INDIANS THAT LIVE ON UNCA SCROOGE'S NATURE PRE-SERVE UP NORTH!
WHY ARE THEY WAY DOWN HERE?
TO TERRORIZE MY PULP MILL! THAT'S WHY!
THEY'RE PEACEFUL NATURE LOVERS! THEY WOULDN'T DO THAT... WITHOUT A REASON!
PLANT MGR. RAVAGE DeFLORA
WHAT HAS THIS MILL BEEN DUMPING INTO THE AIR AND WATER, MR. DeFLORA?
FORGET THAT, SQUIRT! DON'T YOU WANT TO RESCUE YOUR UNCLE?
McDUCK PULP MILL
WELL, YES! THAT COMES FIRST!
GET MY HELICOPTER READY! WE'LL FLY IN AND SHOW THOSE RENEGADE SAVAGES WHO'S BOSS AROUND HERE!
#100,000,000!

SOON...
THERE'S THE HOOK-SHAPED LAKE THAT MARKS THE EDGE OF UNCLE SCROOGE'S PRESERVE!
LAND IN THAT CLEARING BELOW!
WE'LL HIKE TO THE PEEWEE-GAH VILLAGE! THIS HELICOPTER WOULD SCARE THEM OUT OF THEIR LITTLE MOCCASINS!
I'LL AWAIT YOUR RETURN!
...BUT NOT HERE! THEY'LL NEVER BE ABLE TO WALK BACK TO CIVILIZATION ON FOOT! HAH!
THEY'RE OUT OF SIGHT! NOW'S MY CHANCE!
WITH LUCK, THEY'LL ALL BE CAUGHT BY WILD INDIANS AND NEVER BE HEARD FROM AGAIN! THAT WOULD SUIT ME JUST FINE!
I'LL BUY UP McDUCK'S TIMBERLAND AND THIS USELESS "NATURE PRESERVE"! WHEN I'M DONE LOGGING I'LL BE A BILLIONAIRE AND THEY'LL CALL THIS THE NORTH PRAIRIE INSTEAD OF THE NORTH WOODS!
MEANWHILE, NEAR A SPOT IN THE LAND OF A THOUSAND LAKES KNOWN ONLY TO OUR HEROES...
THE VILLAGE SHOULD BE JUST AHEAD!
I HEAR ANGRY VOICES!
LOOK!
I DON'T KNOW WHAT'S GOTTEN INTO YOU SAWED-OFF INJUNS, BUT YOU CAN'T TREAT SCROOGE McDUCK LIKE THIS!
YOU HAVE LIED TO THE PEEWEEGAH! TOLD US FIBS AND MADE BIG FLIMFLAM! WE CALLED PALEFACE DUCK OUR BROTHER! YET WITH FORKED TONGUE HE DECEIVED US!

HOW WILL WE-
YOWCH!
POIT!
WE SHOULD HAVE WATCHED FOR ANIMAL SENTRIES!
THESE INDIANS CAN TALK TO EVERY ANIMAL IN THE FOREST!
SO, NOW PALEDUCK TRIBE IS ALL HERE! HERE TO FACE PEEWEEGAH JUSTICE! BRING THEM FORWARD TO THE COUNCIL! BRING THE PALEDUCKS WHO BETRAYED US!
WHAT ARE YOU LOONIES SAYING?
YOU SAID YOU WOULD KEEP OUR LAKES CLEAN! KEEP OUR AIR PURE AND OUR TREES GREEN! BUT YOU BUILD A MIGHTY WIGWAM THAT SPITS POISON OUT TO BURN US!
HE MEANS YOUR PAPER MILL, UNCA SCROOGE!
THESE RUNTS ARE A FEW ARROWS SHORT OF A QUIVER! I KEPT MY WORD TO THEM!
I MADE THIS A NATURE PRESERVE, OFF LIMITS TO HUNTERS AND DEVELOPERS! I'VE MADE SURE THE PEEWEEGAH LAND HAS STAYED AS PURE AS NEW SNOWFALL!
SO! MAC-DUCK ADMITS HIS EVIL! SNOW AND RAIN THAT NOW COMES FALLING BURNS OUR TREES AND TURNS THEM YELLOW! KILLS THESE NOBLE ANCIENT GIANTS!
RUBBISH! YOU CAN'T BLAME ME FOR THAT! MY PAPER MILL IS OVER TWO HUNDRED MILES FROM HERE!
?

I'M AFRAID THEY'RE RIGHT, UNCA SCROOGE!
THE SMOKE FROM YOUR MILL TRAVELS HERE AND TURNS INTO "ACID RAIN"! THOSE SCORCHED TREES ARE THE PROOF!
THE LAKE HAS A SOOTY SCUM ON IT!
THE FISH ARE PROBABLY DROWNING!
ER... DID YOU SAY "DROWNING"?
YES! CHEMICALS HAVE TAKEN THE OXYGEN OUT OF THE WATER!
YOUR MILL USES SOLVENTS TO SOFTEN WOOD INTO PULP! AND YOUR MEN USE POISONS TO KILL THE UNDERBRUSH!
!
!
ALL THAT GETS INTO THE RIVER NEAR YOUR MILL, AND IT FLOWS THROUGH ALL THESE LAKES ON ITS WAY TO HUDSON BAY!
THESE THREE DUCKS WHOSE SIZE IS NORMAL SPEAK WITH TONGUES THAT SHOW MUCH WISDOM! ME SUSPECT THAT IN THIS DUCKSKIN SOMEHOW HIDE-UM A PEEWEEGAH!
ALL RIGHT SHORTY! ALL RIGHT! I'LL KEEP MY PROMISE! RELEASE US AND I'LL CLOSE MY PULP MILL!
WE ARE NOT TRICKED TWICE SO SIMPLY! WHAT IF PALEFACE DUCK IS FIBBING? BUILDS MORE SMOKY POISON WIGWAMS? OF OUR TRUST THEY MUST PROVE WORTHY!
OH, BROTHER! NOT AGAIN! WHERE'S THE EXIT?
OUR NOBLEST WARRIOR IS ALWAYS READY FOR DEEDS OF HONOR! JUST NAME IT!

OKAY, GIVE ME SOME WEAPONS! I SUPPOSE I MUST BATTLE ANOTHER KING STURGEON SPOILING YOUR FISHING? OR IS IT A BIG BOSS BASS?
I FEAR NOW THERE ARE NO STURGEON! NO BASS OR TROUT OF ANY SIZE! AND THE NIGHTFALL BRINGS NO SINGING OF THE WHIPPOORWILLS OR BULLFROGS!
NONE COULD STAND THE STINGING WATERS, SO THEY LEFT US, TO OUR SORROW!
I'M SORRY, DARN YA! HOW CAN WE PROVE IT SO YOU'LL LET ME HELP YOU?
WHEN WE TRACKED THE SMELLY WATER TO YOUR LODGE OF SMOKE AND POISON WE DID SEE A FEARSOME MONSTER WHOSE GREAT JAWS COULD EAT A MOUNTAIN!
WAH! WAH! WAH!
LET THE PALEDUCK KILL THAT MONSTER TO AGAIN BE TRUSTED BROTHER!
?
NEPHEW?
ARE YOU WRITING ALL THIS DOWN, NEPHEW?
WHILE THE OTHERS REMAIN CAPTIVES, TWO WARRIORS LEAD DONALD ON HIS QUEST OF HONOR! FINALLY, THE NEXT MORNING...
WHERE IS THIS MONSTER? I FEEL SILLY TRAMPING AROUND LIKE BIG CHIEF BEAK-ON-THE-PUSS!
SHH!
THERE!
OH, MY GALLSTONES! IT'S A GIANT STRIP MINE STEAM SHOVEL!
McDUCK MINING

BEHOLD BEAST THAT EATS THE MOUNTAINS! GO, OH MIGHTY PALEDUCK WARRIOR, IN PEEWEEGAH TRIBAL WARDUDS! GO AND SLAY BIGFOOT'S BIG BROTHER!
HOW EMBARRASSING!
I'LL JUST TELL THEM UNCLE SCROOGE SAID TO KNOCK OFF EARLY, THEN GO BACK AND MAKE LIKE A HERO! THIS'LL BE A CINCH!
LOOK! IT'S ONE OF THOSE PYGMY INDIANS RAVAGE DeFLORA TOLD US TO WATCH OUT FOR, EH?
KINDA BIG FOR A PYGMY, AIN'T HE?
PYGMY INJUNS MUST COME IN ALL SIZES, EH?
LET'S GET HIM, EH? DeFLORA POSTED A REWARD FOR THOSE SAVAGES!
'SCUSE ME, FELLAS, I WAS WONDERING IF I COULD TALK TO YOU FOR A SEC...
WHUPS!
WHUMP!
OUR ONE HOPE, OUR MIGHTY SAVIOR HAS BEEN FELLED BY JUST ONE WALLOP! WHEN IT COMES TO PALEDUCK WARRIORS, THEY NOT MAKE-UM LIKE THEY USED TO!
SPUT-SPUTTER! FINE THING TO DO TO THE BOSS' NEPHEW... THROW A MEDIUM-SIZE HILL AT HIM!
RUMBLE
NOW WHAT? AN EARTHQUAKE?
WAK!

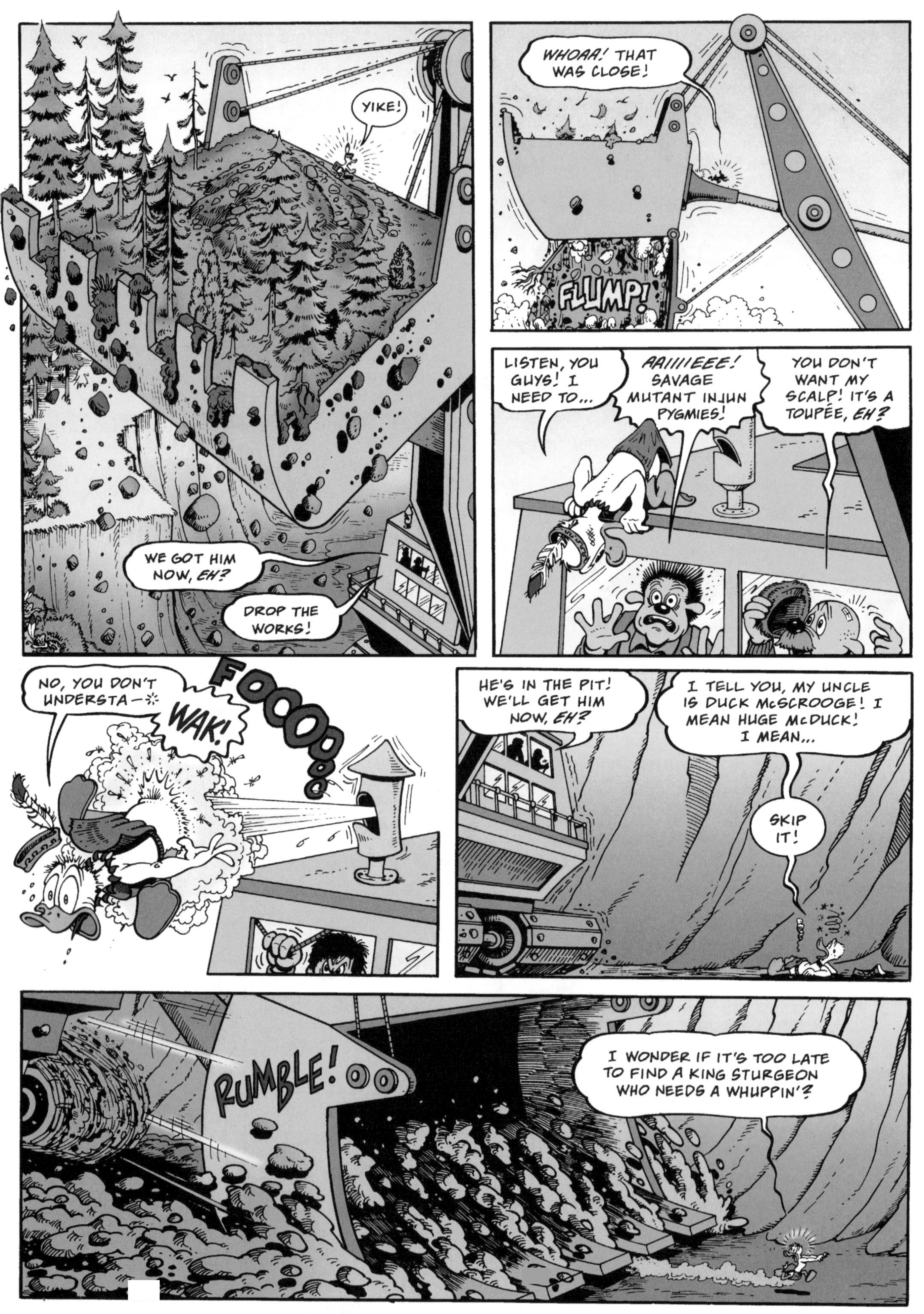
YIKE!
WE GOT HIM NOW, EH?
DROP THE WORKS!
WHOAA! THAT WAS CLOSE!
FLUMP!
LISTEN, YOU GUYS! I NEED TO...
AAIIIIEEE! SAVAGE MUTANT INJUN PYGMIES!
YOU DON'T WANT MY SCALP! IT'S A TOUPÉE, EH?
NO, YOU DON'T UNDERSTA—
FOOOOOOOO
WAK!
HE'S IN THE PIT! WE'LL GET HIM NOW, EH?
I TELL YOU, MY UNCLE IS DUCK McSCROOGE! I MEAN HUGE McDUCK! I MEAN...
SKIP IT!
RUMBLE!
I WONDER IF IT'S TOO LATE TO FIND A KING STURGEON WHO NEEDS A WHUPPIN'?

LOOK OUT, EH? YOU'VE UNDERMINED THE MINE!
RUN FOR YOUR LIFE!
CRASH!
!!!
WAH! WAH! WAH!
YOU HAVE SENT THE MOUNTAIN EATER TO JOIN ALL HIS FIERCE ANCESTORS! YOU ARE BROTHER TO PEEWEEGAH!
CAN THE POETRY, HIAWATHA, AND GIVE ME BACK MY CLOTHES!
NOW YOU MUST GO HOLD A POWWOW WITH THE CHIEF OF SMELLY WIGWAM! TIME IS PRECIOUS — WE MUST HURRY! GO AS SWIFT AS SOARING EAGLES!
SURE, BUT HOW?
IF I WERE A JUNIOR WOODCHUCK, I'D PROBABLY BE ENJOYING THIS!
SOON...
SO, MR. McDUCK IS STILL A PRISONER OF THOSE PYGMY NATURE-NUTS?
YES, BUT HE SENT ME WITH THIS LETTER TELLING YOU TO CLOSE DOWN THE MILL IMMEDIATELY!

(End of Part Two as originally serialized)

Walt Disney's
UNCLE $CROOGE
in WAR of the WENDIGO
PART THREE
RUMBLE!
GREAT STUMBLING CATASTROPHES! THE INDIANS ARE LEADING THE FOREST ANIMALS IN AN ATTACK ON MY MILL!
PALEDUCK TYCOON, YOU WILL WITNESS! WITNESS HOW THE FORCE OF NATURE TAKES ITS VENGEANCE ON YOUR WIGWAM! YOU WILL SEE WITH YOUR OWN EYEBULBS!
YOU'RE ATTACKING UNCA SCROOGE'S MILL? WE THOUGHT YOU WERE A PEACEFUL PEOPLE!
PEACEFUL ARE PEEWEEGAH PEOPLE! NOT RAISE HAND AGAINST THEIR BROTHERS!
BUT WE TELL THE WOODLAND CREATURES WHY THEIR HOMES THE RAINS ARE BURNING! TELL THEM WHY THEIR LAKES ARE DYING!
DON'T YOU KNOW HOW CREATURES TRUST YOU? TRUST YOU TO PROTECT THE FORESTS? NOW WE TELL THEM OF YOUR MENACE! NOW YOU WILL HEAR AWESOME THUNDER, SEE THE FORCE OF NATURE'S VENGEANCE!

HE TALKS PRETTY, BUT IT DOESN'T SOUND GOOD!
YOU SAID IT! IMAGINE IF EVERY ANIMAL ON EARTH KNEW WHAT A DANGER MANKIND IS! THEY'D WIPE US OUT IN A DAY!
IT'S NOT LONG BEFORE THE WOODS AROUND THE McDUCK MILL ARE FILLED WITH SHADOWY FORMS CREEPING NEARER AND NEARER...
McDUCK PULP MILL
MEANWHILE, INSIDE...
I'M WARNING YOU, DeFLORA! SHUT DOWN THIS MILL BEFORE YOU MAKE THESE HALF-PINT INDIANS REALLY MAD!
DON'T MAKE ME LAUGH!
THERE'S NO TELLING WHAT THEY'LL DO! THEY CAN TALK TO ANIMALS!
I'M SO SURE! WELL, I CAN TALK TO ANIMALS TOO! WANNA SEE?
HEWWO, WIDDLE SQUIRRELY-WHIRL! COME IN AND VISIT UNCA RAVAGE! HE'LL MAKE YOU INTO A NICE FUR HAT, YOU NASTY LITTLE...
CHUCK! CHUCK!
YOW!
KER-FLUMP!
I WARNED YOU! THIS IS ONLY THE BEGINNING!
LOOK OUT! THERE'S A PACK OF BERSERK RODENTS HEADED FOR THE CONTROL ROOM!
CONTROL ROOM
THEY CAN HAVE IT! IT'S FILLED WITH MAD BEES AND HORNETS!
BUZZZ!
...ONLY THE BEGINNING!

AGH!
WHAT'S THAT STENCH? GO UP ON THE ROOF AND CHECK THE AIR CONDITIONERS!
YEAH, BOSS!
WHUPS!
KEEP THE MILL OPERATING! I WON'T BE INTIMIDATED!
WE CAN'T, SIR! THE ENTIRE WOOD SUPPLY IS RUINED!
ARE YOU CRAZY? THAT'S TOP QUALITY TIMBER!
NOT ANY MORE, EH?
PEK PEK PEK PEK PEK PEK PEK PEK PEK PEK PEK
OW! MY EYES! WHERE'S ALL THIS SMOKE COMING FROM?
THE SMOKESTACKS ARE COMPLETELY CLOGGED, SIR!
CLOGGED? HAS THIS PLACE GONE BATTY?
YESSIR! THAT'S IT EXACTLY, SIR!
HEY! NOW WHAT?
THE WASTEWATER PIPES ARE CLOGGED UP TOO, SIR!
YOU'D BETTER GIVE UP, DeFLORA!
YOU'RE NO MATCH FOR NATURE ON A RAMPAGE!
OH, YEAH? JUST WATCH ME, DUCK!

I'LL SHOW THEM WHO'S KING OF THE FOREST!
STOKE THE FURNACES WITH PURE DIOXIN, OUR DEADLIEST PLANT KILLER!
GAG
KOFF
ERP
YUK
ICK
GAG
BLAA
KOFF
CHOKE
THAT'LL CLEAR OUT THOSE BATS! THAT SMOG WILL PEEL BOWLING BALLS!
AND PUMP ACID INTO THE DRAIN PIPES! FULL STRENGTH! THAT'LL CLEAR OUT THOSE SLIMY FROGS!
YOU'VE GONE NUTS, DeFLORA!
YOU'LL KILL EVERY TREE IN THE PROVINCE!
SO WHAT? IF YOU'VE SEEN ONE TREE, YOU'VE SEEN THEM ALL!
HSSSSSSSSS!
McDUCK OWNS PLENTY OF OTHER TIMBERLAND, AND WITH HIM MISSING, I'M IN CONTROL OF IT ALL!
BOSS! THE BOILERS AND DRAIN PUMPS STOPPED!
WHAT HAPPENED TO THE ELECTRICITY?
LOOK! THERE'S A TRILLION BIRDS ON THE POWERLINES!
THEY'RE MOVING ALONG THE SYSTEM, SECTION BY SECTION!
THIS IS SERIOUS! I'M CALLING THE ARMY!
CRASH!
DRAT! WHAT'S WRONG WITH THE PHONES?
HA! YOU SHOULD SEE WHAT'S UP ON THE PHONE LINE!
I DIDN'T EVEN KNOW MOOSE COULD CLIMB POLES!

THAT'S IT! I QUIT!
ME TOO! I'M NOT GONNA TRY TO FIGHT THE ENTIRE ANIMAL KINGDOM!
LET'S HEAD FOR THE CITY!
NEARBY...
LOOK, UNCA SCROOGE! THE ANIMALS HAVE ROUTED YOUR WORKMEN!
BUT MY MILL IS STILL STANDING! MAYBE THEY'LL SPARE IT!
SAY, WHAT HAPPENED TO THE RIVER THAT USED TO BE HERE?
THERE'S YOUR ANSWER!
A THOUSAND BEAVER HAVE BUILT A GIANT DAM TO DIVERT THE RIVER AND STOP YOUR MILL FROM DUMPING POISON INTO IT!
GREAT SCOTT! IF THAT DAM BREAKS, IT'LL WIPE OUT MY MULTI-MILLION-DOLLAR MILL! AND I LET MY INSURANCE LAPSE! ACK!
MEANWHILE, BACK AT THE BESIEGED MILL...
GIVE UP, DeFLORA, YOU'RE LICKED!
NEVER, DUCK! I STILL HAVE ONE ACE UP MY SLEEVE!
THOSE ANIMALS MAY NOT FEAR ME OR MY MACHINES, BUT THERE'S ONE THING ANIMALS FEAR ABOVE ALL! FIRE!
RUN, YOU VERMIN! RUN! BWAH-HAH-HAH-HAH-HAH!
WHOOSH!
HE'S LOST HIS HEAD! I'M GETTING OUT OF HERE WHILE THE GETTING'S GOOD!

LOOK! DEFLORA HAS STARTED A FOREST FIRE!
THIS ISN'T FAIR! I COULD HAVE STOPPED THAT MANIAC IF YOU INDIAN MIDGETS HAD LET ME!
MADNESS STALKS THE POISON WIGWAM! AT THE FOREST FLAMES ARE LEAPING! SOON THE WOODS WILL ALL BE BURNING! NOTHING WORSE THAN THIS COULD HAPPEN!
I WISH NOT TO BE LIKE PALEFACE! THEY ARE LOVERS OF DESTRUCTION! WE HAVE VOWED TO THE GREAT SPIRIT NOT TO HARM OUR BROTHERS' LODGES!
BUT TO SAVE OUR LAND FROM BURNING, I MUST DESTROY POISON WIGWAM! KNOCK OUT KEY LOG, DAM WILL TUMBLE, WASH AWAY THE EVIL BURNING!

WITH THIS ACT BREAKS VOW MOST SACRED! THIS IS END OF THE PEEWEEGAH!
WAH! WAH! WAH!
GLOM!
?
CHIEF, I WILL NOT LET YOU DO THAT! YOU WERE RIGHT TO NOT TRUST PEOPLE LIKE ME! WE NEVER VOWED NOT TO DESTROY YOUR "LODGES"!
THE FORESTS JUST LOOKED LIKE WOOD TO US... FOR MAKING PAPER WE USE ONCE AND THROW AWAY!
I WILL NOT LET YOU DESTROY MY MILL!
I'LL DO IT MYSELF...

ATTA BOY, UNCA SCROOGE!
GRUNT!
HURRY! THE WOODS AROUND THE MILL ARE ABLAZE! IT'S SPREADING FAST!
THERE SHE GOES! RUN FOR IT!
RUMBLE!
IF THAT DOESN'T STOP THE FOREST FIRE, NOTHING WILL! YOU'VE DONE ALL YOU CAN!
NOT QUITE! THERE'S ONE LAST DETAIL!
ROAR!
RAVAGE DeFLORA!! I DON'T KNOW IF YOU CAN HEAR ME, BUT...
ROAR!
ROAR!
YOU'RE FIRED!
McDUCK PULP MILL
?

WAR OF THE
ENDS... AND AS
WAR, THERE
WELL, THE MILL IS A TOTAL LOSS!
AND DeFLORA MANAGED TO DUMP HIS ENTIRE CHEMICAL ARSENAL! THIS PLACE WILL BE STONE DEAD FOR 20 YEARS!
McDUCK
THAT MEANS BY THE TIME YOU GET OUT OF JAIL, THIS MAY BE A FOREST AGAIN!
MR. McDUCK, SIR, THERE'S SOME MIS-UNDERSTANDING!
AND YOU MADE IT WHEN YOU DECIDED TO MAROON US IN THE WILDERNESS AND TAKE CONTROL OF MY TIMBERLAND!
TAKE HIM AWAY!
POST 37
R.C.M.P
REGIONAL
I COULD HAVE PREVENTED THIS MESS IF THE ANIMALS HAD LET ME! MOTHER NATURE HAD NO RIGHT TO TAKE IT ALL AWAY FROM ME! IT'S NOT FAIR!
OH, PALEFACE DUCK OF BIG WAMPUM, HOW YOU THINK YOU GOT YOUR RICHES? DID MAN PUT GOLD IN THE YUKON FOR YOU TO DIG OUT WITH SHOVEL?
NO, BUT...
DID MAN FILL YOUR MINES WITH DIAMONDS? DID MAN FILL YOUR WELLS WITH OIL? DID MAN PLANT THE ANCIENT FORESTS THAT TURNED TO COAL FOR YOUR DIGGING?
N-NO, B-BUT...
SCROOGE MAC-DUCK, YOU OWE YOUR RICHES TO THE MOTHER NATURE SPIRIT! THIS DAY SPIRIT HAS DECIDED TAKE-UM BACK THIS TINY PORTION!

SOME BIG MOUTHS HAVE BEEN TELLING PYGMY INDIANS AN AWFUL LOT ABOUT MY PRIVATE BUSINESS!
YOU SMOKE PEACE PIPE WITH GREAT SPIRIT, SHE MIGHT SMILE AGAIN ON PALEDUCK!
YOU MEAN, IF I STOP WRECKING THE ENVIRONMENT, IT WOULD BE A GOOD INVESTMENT IN MY OWN BUSINESS FUTURE, EH, CHIEF?
HEY! WHERE'D THE PEEWEEGAH GO?
DISAPPEARED WITHOUT A SOUND! LIKE THE WENDIGO LEGENDS!
GONE WITH THE WENDIGO!
CHIEF! THE GREAT SPIRIT HAS BEEN GOOD TO ME! I'LL MAKE THAT INVESTMENT!
I'LL INSTALL POLLUTION CONTROLS IN ALL MY FACTORIES! AND I'LL PLANT TWO TREES FOR EVERY ONE I CUT! YOU'LL SEE!
I HOPE THE PEEWEEGAH LAST UNTIL THEIR LAND IS CLEAN AGAIN!
IF WE DON'T TAKE CARE OF THE ENVIRONMENT, IT'LL BE THE END OF ALL OF US! NOT JUST THE PEEWEEGAH!
IT'LL COST UNCA SCROOGE A LOT TO CLEAN UP ALL HIS FACTORIES!
IT'LL PAY OFF IN MANY WAYS! HE'LL SEE!
?!
OH, SO? DO YOU THINK UNCA SCROOGE WILL EVER LEARN TO APPRECIATE THE NON-FINANCIAL PROFITS?
MAYBE HE'S LEARNING ALREADY!
End

SUPER SNOOPER STRIKES AGAIN!
Donald Duck Adventures [series II] 34, March 1993.
Layout by Bob Foster; color by Cris Palomino and Egmont.

D.U.C.K. SPOTTER'S GUIDE:
Starting now, Rosa's famous dedication (see page 161) is hidden on covers, too. Here, check the row of windows on the house to the lower right.

Walt Disney's
Donald Duck
in
SUPER SNOOPER STRIKES AGAIN!
BOY! AREN'T THESE "SUPER SNOOPER" COMICS JUST GREAT?!
LOOKIT— HE'S SMASHING THE BAD GUY WITH AN ASTEROID!
WISTFUL UNION
!
?
AND THE CHAIN REACTION WIPES OUT A SOLAR SYSTEM! NEATO!
D 91076
NOW HE'S SWATTING THE VILLAIN WITH A WHOLE GALAXY! NIFTY!
NIX! HERE COMES UNCA DONALD!
SO! WASTING YOUR TIME READING THOSE STUPID SUPER-HERO COMICS AGAIN, EH?
SNATCH!
THIS MR. "SUPER SNOOPER" SOLVES ALL HIS PROBLEMS WITH VIOLENCE AND DESTRUCTION! WHY DON'T YOU READ COMICS THAT RELY ON PLOT AND CHARACTER...
...LIKE "MARVIN MONKEY"?
COMICS ABOUT A TALKING MONKEY??
AW! THAT'S KID STUFF!
SOMEDAY YOU'LL REALIZE IT'S "SUPER SNOOPER COMICS" THAT'S KID STUFF!

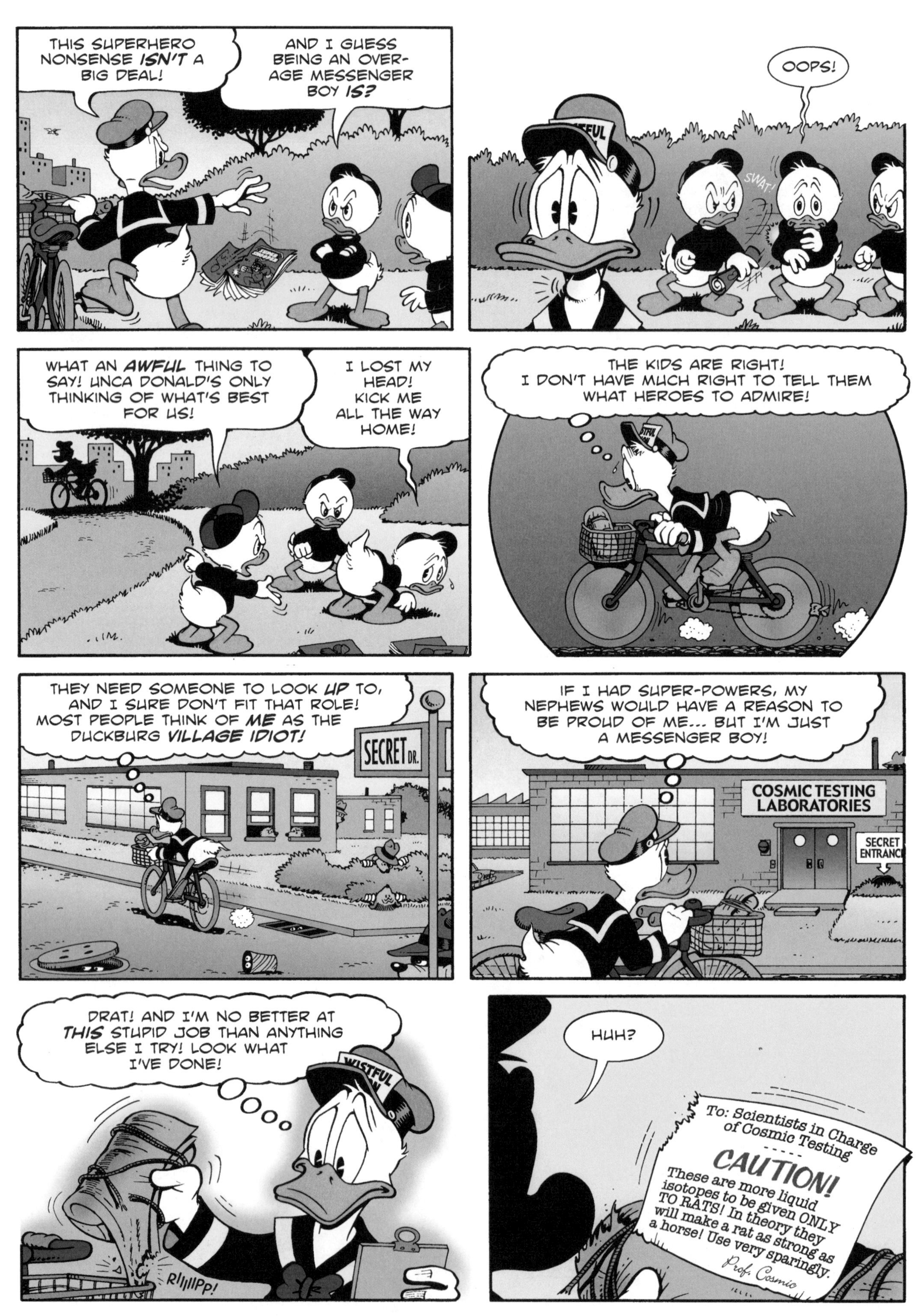
THIS SUPERHERO NONSENSE ISN'T A BIG DEAL!
AND I GUESS BEING AN OVER-AGE MESSENGER BOY IS?
OOPS!
SWAT!
WHAT AN AWFUL THING TO SAY! UNCA DONALD'S ONLY THINKING OF WHAT'S BEST FOR US!
I LOST MY HEAD! KICK ME ALL THE WAY HOME!
THE KIDS ARE RIGHT! I DON'T HAVE MUCH RIGHT TO TELL THEM WHAT HEROES TO ADMIRE!
THEY NEED SOMEONE TO LOOK UP TO, AND I SURE DON'T FIT THAT ROLE! MOST PEOPLE THINK OF ME AS THE DUCKBURG VILLAGE IDIOT!
SECRET DR.
IF I HAD SUPER-POWERS, MY NEPHEWS WOULD HAVE A REASON TO BE PROUD OF ME... BUT I'M JUST A MESSENGER BOY!
COSMIC TESTING LABORATORIES
SECRET ENTRANC
DRAT! AND I'M NO BETTER AT THIS STUPID JOB THAN ANYTHING ELSE I TRY! LOOK WHAT I'VE DONE!
WISTFUL
RIIIIPP!
HUH?
To: Scientists in Charge of Cosmic Testing
CAUTION!
These are more liquid isotopes to be given ONLY TO RATS! In theory they will make a rat as strong as a horse! Use very sparingly.
Prof. Cosmic

SOUNDS LIKE THIS IS THE STUFF "SUPER-SNOOPERS" ARE MADE FROM! I WONDER IF IT'S SAFE FOR PEOPLE!
I'LL RISK IT! ANYTHING TO BE A HERO TO HUEY, DEWEY AND LOUIE!
GLUG! GLUG!
FEH! ALL I FEEL IS SICK! THIS STUFF TASTES LIKE STALE SKUNK OIL!
SECRET DELIVERIES
KNOCK! KNOCK!
NO SPIES ALLOWED
AH! ANOTHER SHIPMENT FROM PROF. COSMIC! GIVE THIS BOY A TIP!
OKAY: MY FRIEND, NEVER WEAR RADIOACTIVE UNDERWEAR!
WHA—?! THAT DIZZY PROF. COSMIC SENT ANOTHER HALF-EMPTY CANISTER OF ISOTOPES!
THESE SCIENTIST TYPES ARE JUST PLAIN GOOFY!
GOSH! I'M RUNNING LATE! I NEED TO HURRY HOME TO FIX THE KIDS' SUPPER AND START DOING THEIR LAUNDRY!
?
ZOW!
DONALD DUCK
ZOW!
SCREECH!

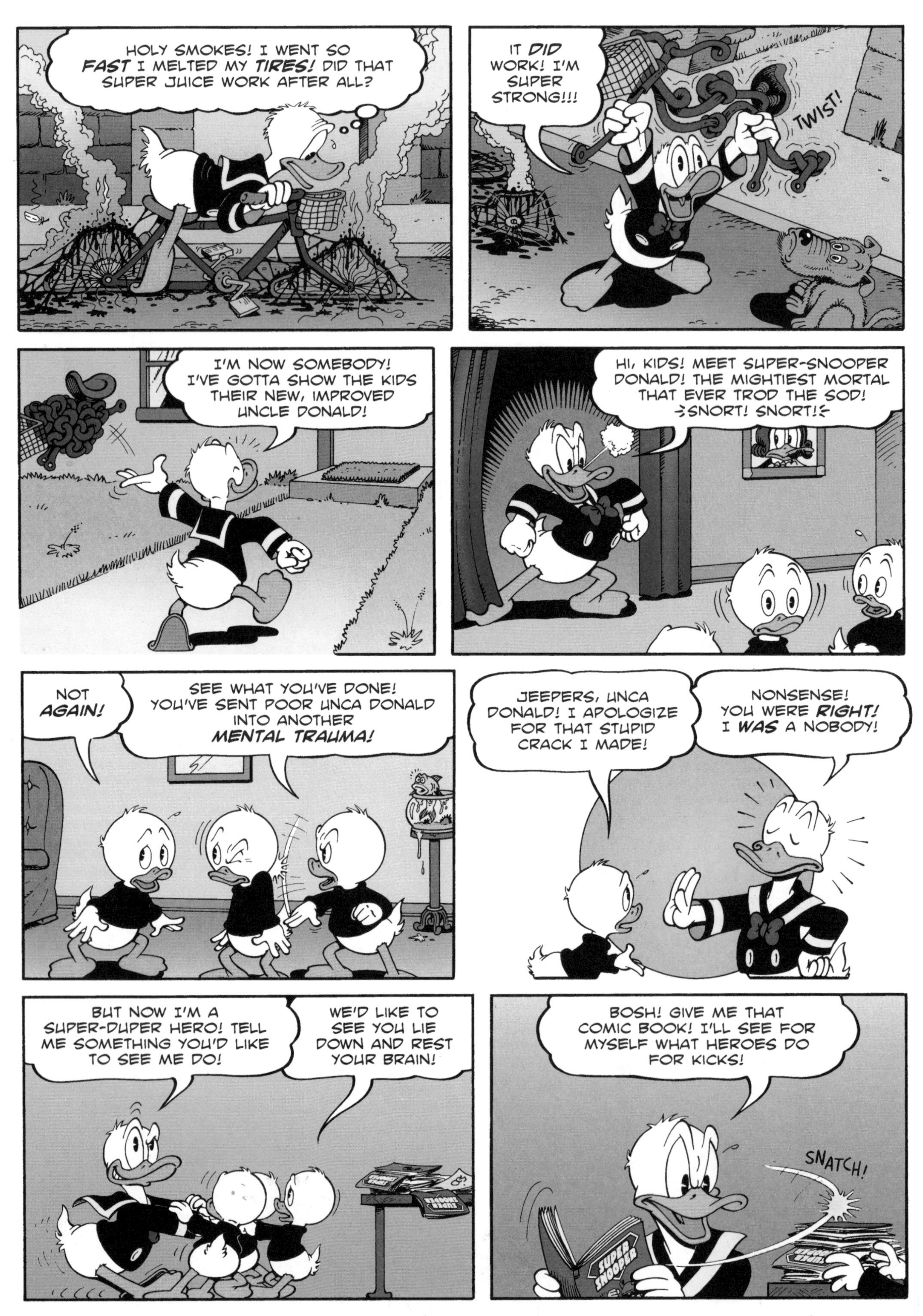
HOLY SMOKES! I WENT SO FAST I MELTED MY TIRES! DID THAT SUPER JUICE WORK AFTER ALL?
IT DID WORK! I'M SUPER STRONG!!!
TWIST!
I'M NOW SOMEBODY! I'VE GOTTA SHOW THE KIDS THEIR NEW, IMPROVED UNCLE DONALD!
HI, KIDS! MEET SUPER-SNOOPER DONALD! THE MIGHTIEST MORTAL THAT EVER TROD THE SOD! SNORT! SNORT!
NOT AGAIN!
SEE WHAT YOU'VE DONE! YOU'VE SENT POOR UNCA DONALD INTO ANOTHER MENTAL TRAUMA!
JEEPERS, UNCA DONALD! I APOLOGIZE FOR THAT STUPID CRACK I MADE!
NONSENSE! YOU WERE RIGHT! I WAS A NOBODY!
BUT NOW I'M A SUPER-DUPER HERO! TELL ME SOMETHING YOU'D LIKE TO SEE ME DO!
WE'D LIKE TO SEE YOU LIE DOWN AND REST YOUR BRAIN!
BOSH! GIVE ME THAT COMIC BOOK! I'LL SEE FOR MYSELF WHAT HEROES DO FOR KICKS!
SNATCH!
SUPER SNOOPER

HA! THIS HERE SNOOPER RUNS CLEAR AROUND THE EARTH IN AN INSTANT SO HE CAN SMASH THE BAD GUY FROM BEHIND!
SUPER SNOOPER
YOU KIDS STAY RIGHT THERE! I'LL BE BACK IN A HALF INSTANT!
BUT, YOU...
I SWITCHED TO SUPER-SPEED SO FAST THE KIDS DON'T EVEN KNOW I'M GONE YET!
ZOOM!
THIS IS WILD! EVERYTHING LOOKS FROZEN SINCE I'M MOVING WITH SUPER VELOCITY!
ZOOM!
YET, I FEEL LIKE I'M RUNNING AT NORMAL SPEED! MY BRAIN IS THINKING SUPER-FAST SO I DON'T RUN INTO THINGS!
ZOW!
WAIT A NANOSECOND! IF THAT'S TRUE, THEN THIS TRIP WILL SEEM TO ME TO TAKE AS LONG AS IT WOULD IF I WERE NOT SUPER!
EVEN IF IT SEEMS LIKE AN INSTANT TO THE KIDS, IT WILL SEEM LIKE MONTHS TO ME! OR EVEN YEARS!
SCREECH!
I'LL HAVE TO DO SOMETHING DIFFERENT TO IMPRESS THE KIDS!
ZOW!

...CAN'T DO THAT, UNCA DONALD!
I COULD, BUT IT WOULD BE TOO BORING! I'LL DO SOMETHING ELSE!
ZOW!
OH, RIGHT! HE DOESN'T FEEL LIKE RUNNING AROUND THE EARTH IN AN INSTANT!
YEAH! THAT'S TOO BORING! SURE!
I'LL SHOW YOU! NAME SOMETHING ELSE "SUPER SNOOPER" WOULD DO, AND I'LL MATCH IT!
HE'D LIE DOWN AND REST HIS TIRED BRAIN AND...
HERE'S WHAT I NEED! THE BIG SHOW-OFF IS USING MOUNT EVEREST TO POUND THE BAD GUY INTO OATMEAL!
I'LL BRING YOU A MOUNTAIN! ALERT THE MEDIA! WAKE THE NEIGHBORS!
NO! STOP!
WOOSH!
?! WHERE'D HE GO?
HE MUST HAVE DUCKED UNDER THE PORCH! LET'S HUMOR HIM UNTIL THIS TRAUMA PASSES! SHH!
ZOOM!
I KNOW THIS ROCKY ISLAND OFF THE COAST THAT NOBODY WILL MISS!
WOOSH!
"SUPER SNOOPER" CAN MOVE A WHOLE MOUNTAIN RANGE WITH HIS EARLOBE! ONE ISLAND IS A BREEZE!
SPLASH!

HOOHAH! THIS IS A CINCH!
EAT YOUR HEART OUT, "SUPER SNOOPER"!
LEMME JUST FLY THIS SALTWATER MOUNTAIN HOME AND— SAY, WHAT GIVES??
THIS GANG-DANGED THING IS BREAKING APART! THIS NEVER HAPPENED IN THE COMIC BOOKS!
I CAN'T CARRY THIS OVER DUCKBURG! I'D RAIN BOULDERS ON THE CITY LIKE A GRANITE HAILSTORM!
SPLASH!
UH... LISTEN, KIDS... LIFTING A MOUNTAIN IS OUT! I'LL DO SOMETHING ELSE! JUST NAME IT!
CURING BONKUS OF THE CONKUS
NO, WE WOULDN'T WANT YOU LIFTING A DIRTY OL' MOUNTAIN!
WHAT WE'D REALLY LIKE TO SEE IS HOW GOOD YOU ARE AT BEING TUCKED INTO BEDDY-BYE!
I'LL SHOW YOU IF IT'S THE LAST THING I DO! GIVE ME THAT @*#% COMIC BOOK!
HEY KIDS! MAKE BIG MONEY!
SUPER SNOOPER

HERE! LOOK! "SUPER SNOOPER" IS LIFTING A SINKING OCEAN LINER OUT OF THE SEA!
SUPER SNOOPER
UP, UP AND AWAAAAY!
WATCH OUT FOR NAILS UNDER THE PORCH, UNCA DONALD! YOUR CLOTHES ARE GETTING TORN!
ZOOM!
SHH!
SUPER SNOOPER
A SHIP WILL HAVE A SUPER STRUCTURE TO HOLD IT TOGETHER WHEN I LIFT IT!
ZOW!
HERE'S THE ANDRIA DUCKIA THAT SANK IN DUCKBURG BAY YEARS AGO! I'LL FLY IT HOME!
WAIT TILL MY NEPHEWS SEE THEIR SUPER-UNCLE NOW!
THIS WOULD KNOCK THEIR SOCKS OFF... IF THEY WORE ANY!
Z
I WONDER IF I SHOULD LIFT THIS UNDER ONE POINT ON ITS HULL? IT MIGHT BE KINDA RUSTY AFTER SO MANY...
!
CRACK!
SLAM!
SPLASH!

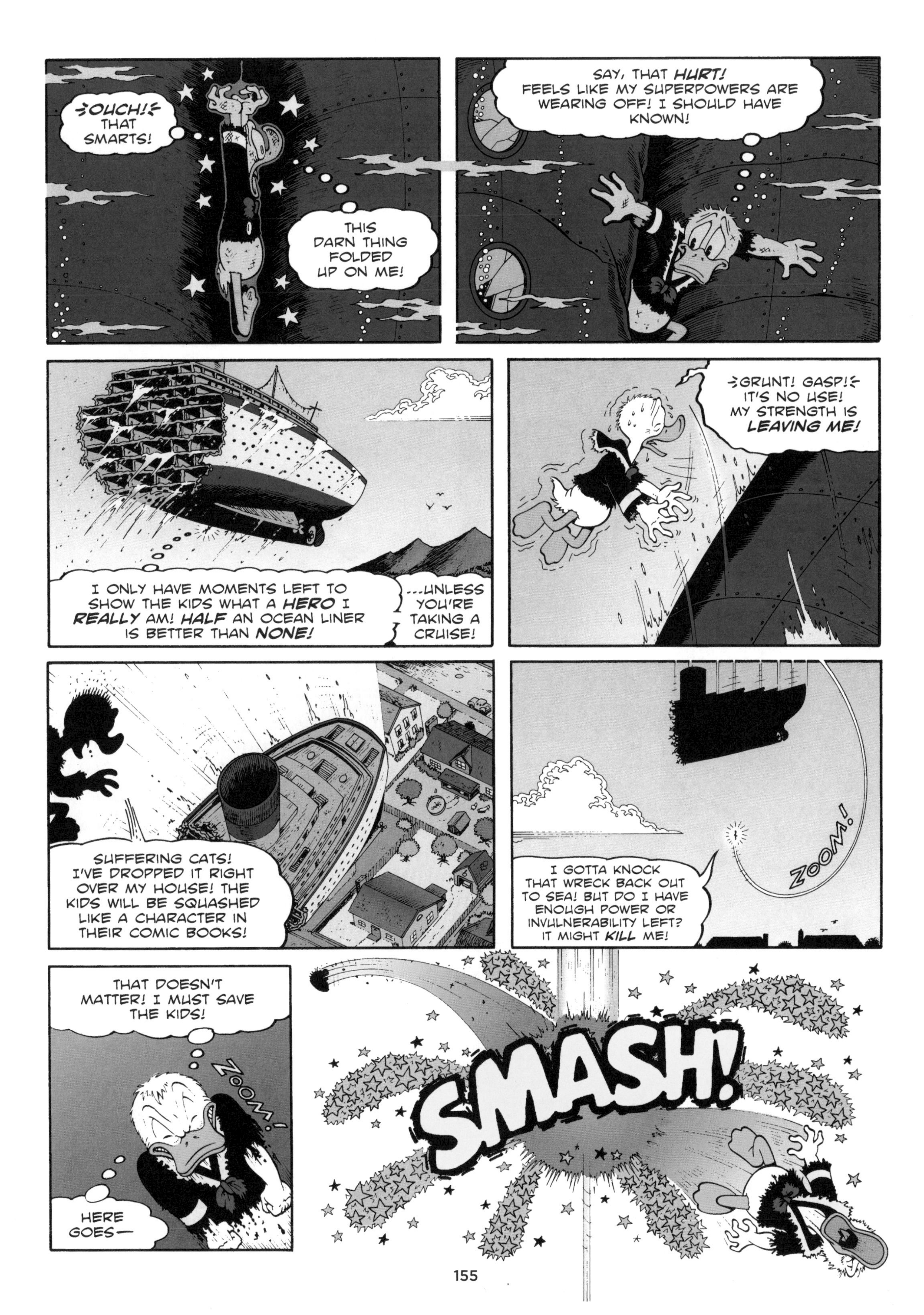

OUCH! THAT SMARTS!
THIS DARN THING FOLDED UP ON ME!
SAY, THAT HURT! FEELS LIKE MY SUPERPOWERS ARE WEARING OFF! I SHOULD HAVE KNOWN!
I ONLY HAVE MOMENTS LEFT TO SHOW THE KIDS WHAT A HERO I REALLY AM! HALF AN OCEAN LINER IS BETTER THAN NONE!
...UNLESS YOU'RE TAKING A CRUISE!
GRUNT! GASP! IT'S NO USE! MY STRENGTH IS LEAVING ME!
SUFFERING CATS! I'VE DROPPED IT RIGHT OVER MY HOUSE! THE KIDS WILL BE SQUASHED LIKE A CHARACTER IN THEIR COMIC BOOKS!
I GOTTA KNOCK THAT WRECK BACK OUT TO SEA! BUT DO I HAVE ENOUGH POWER OR INVULNERABILITY LEFT? IT MIGHT KILL ME!
ZOOM!
THAT DOESN'T MATTER! I MUST SAVE THE KIDS!
ZOOM!
HERE GOES—
SMASH!

POW!
BWAM!
CRASH!
WHAT WAS THAT?!
THAT'S UNCA DONALD! HE MUSTA JUMPED OFF THE ROOF THINKING HE COULD FLY!
HELP HIM! HELP HIM!
I'LL NEVER FORGIVE MYSELF IF HE'S HURT!
POOR, POOR UNCA DONALD!
UNCA DONALD! SPEAK TO US!
WE DON'T CARE THAT YOU'RE NOT LIKE "SUPER SNOOPER"!
WE LIKE YOU JUST THE WAY YOU ARE!
HE SAYS HE CAN'T REMEMBER A THING SINCE LAST TUESDAY!
WEIRD! JUST LIKE THE OTHER TIME!
AND SO—
Y'KNOW... THESE "MARVIN MONKEY" COMICS AREN'T SO BAD!
NOT BAD? THEY'RE GREAT!
YEAH! THESE STORIES ARE CLEVER AND EXCITING AND FUNNY!
MARVIN SOLVES HIS PROBLEMS WITHOUT HITTING PEOPLE WITH ASTEROIDS!
MARVIN MONKEY
MARVIN MONKEY
MARVIN MONKEY

OUT! OUT!
PLEASE, UNCLE SCROOGE! I JUST NEED TO BORROW A FEW BUCKS TO BUY A NEW BIKE SO I CAN GET BACK TO WORK!
McDUCK BANK No. 37
McDUCK BANK No. 37
MY OLD BIKE GOT TIED INTO A KNOT... SOMEHOW!
POOR UNCA DONALD! DO YOU SUPPOSE HE THINKS WE'RE ASHAMED OF HIM OR SOMETHING?
WE SHOULD TELL HIM MORE OFTEN THAT WE THINK HE'S PRETTY SPECIAL!
HONK!
HE MAY NOT BE AS RICH OR AS CLEVER AS UNCA SCROOGE...
HE MAY NOT BE AS SMART OR SKILLED AS GYRO GEARLOOSE...
AND HE MAY NOT BE AS GOOD-LOOKING OR SUCCESSFUL AS COUSIN GLADSTONE!
NO, BUT HE'S STILL GOT THEM ALL BEAT!
TRIP!
IT WAS UNCA DONALD WHO TOOK IT UPON HIMSELF TO RAISE HIS THREE ORPHANED NEPHEWS!
SINGLE-HANDED, AND ON HIS INCOME!
AND WE'VE SOMETIMES BEEN UNGRATEFUL AND HORRIBLE TO HIM!
I'D SAY UNCA DONALD IS A PRETTY SUPER KINDA GUY!
AGREED!
YEAH! SUPER SNOOPER MAY BE THE MIGHTIEST MORTAL TO EVER TROD THE SOD...
BUT HE'S NO DONALD DUCK!
DD
Hero!
End

Donald and Scrooge one-shot album, 1992. New color by Scott Rockwell. Look for "mementos" from "The Master Landscapist," "On Stolen Time," "Treasure Under Glass," "Return to Xanadu," and "Incident at McDuck Tower," as well as last volume's "The Money Pit."

D.U.C.K. SPOTTER'S GUIDE:
The dedication is in the wood grain on the front of the chest.

Behind the Scenes

BY Don Rosa

The top half of Page 9 for "The Master Landscapist" as first published—but not as first drawn. See page 17 for Rosa's original, more complex version.

THE MASTER LANDSCAPIST *p. 9*

This was the very *first* story I ever did for Egmont! And for this first of what I hoped would be a long career, I decided to use the tried-and-true Donald Duck plot that we Carl Barks fans often refer to as the "brittle-mastery-of-Donald-Duck syndrome." In this style of plot, often used by Mr. Barks, we suddenly learn that Donald has acquired a world-class skill of mastery in some special ability, be it glass-blowing or house-wrecking or... landscaping. And, as usual, his pride and arrogance eventually prove his downfall—so in the next issue, we see that Donald is again an average guy in search of an average job.

"The Master Landscapist" is only a ten-page gag story; but let me tell you, the short stories were the toughest for me to do! I always had a two-page list filled with ideas for future long adventure sagas for Donald or Scrooge; but I had to *force* myself to create ten-page story ideas as needed, one by one. It seems easy for me to create stories based on the actual facts of history, since "historical fiction" is the genre that interests me. It was Barks' longer adventures—as well as old adventure movies on TV—that were my favorites as a kid, and still are. So that's what my mind tended to run to. I envied the writers who could do short gag stories one after another and still always fill them with enough action and humor to be fun. Frankly, whenever I found myself doing one of these gag shorts, I felt like I was in my own "brittle-mastery-of-*Don-Rosa* syndrome" (!!!), and the entire project might be in danger of crashing into ruin around me just as it does with Donald.

The one completely unique aspect of "The Master Landscapist" involves the bottom half of the ninth page. Anyone familiar with my work knows that I enjoy filling scenes with incredible amounts of (what I call) "needless and irritating detail." My first version of this half-page panel was *rejected* by my new Egmont editor, and I was required to completely redraw the scene on my own time.

I've always figured that my editor was trying to teach me an early lesson to not fill my art with so much eye-numbing detail by making me redo it at my own expense. But later, when the editors saw that their "trick" had failed—and I continued to fill each and every panel with 150% more ink lines than were needed—I guess they just gave up on me and let me draw the only way I knew. But I imagine that European stock analysts have been wondering why sales of aspirin and eyedrops took a sharp increase starting in 1990. *I* know it's because readers were esperiencing the side effects of my "needless and irritating detail."

Fantagraphics' *Don Rosa Library* gives you a bonus! I saved a copy of the rejected bottom half of page 9, and it is presented in this volume in both versions!

D.U.C.K. SPOTTER'S GUIDE: "D.U.C.K." ("Dedicated to Unca Carl from Keno," Keno being my actual first name) is the special dedication to Carl Barks that I hide somewhere on the first page of most of my stories. I'm sure you've been eagerly awaiting my telling you where to look for it in "The Master Landscapist."

Well... stop looking! This story being the very first I did for Egmont, the dedication is missing from the first panel. I even seem to recall putting it in one of the pine trees there—perhaps landscapist Donald did not appreciate the aesthetic quality of my placement and clipped it out. (Or I just erased it.)

ON STOLEN TIME *p. 19*

This may be one of my oldest plot ideas. Ever since I was a kid, I'd daydreamed of what it would be like to try to move around in a world where time was standing still, and all physical objects were "frozen" as solid as granite. I'd think of how difficult and dangerous it would be to even walk across the front lawn, with the blades of grass as stiff and sharp as a field of daggers. I later saw episodes of TV science-fiction shows—such as *The Twilight Zone* and *The Outer Limits*— which featured this sort of idea, with characters moving about in frozen time.

For my second Egmont story, I used the opportunity afforded by Barks' wacky inventor Gyro Gearloose to finally use this plot idea I'd had for so long. Gyro could invent something that could freeze time and enable the user to move through that frozen world of which I had long dreamed. And that something would be a "stopwatch," as just the right thing for "stopping time."

But in retrospect, I wish that I'd had Gyro invent some doohickey that would simply freeze *motion*—and do so only within, say, a few miles' radius. I mean, stopping *time itself*?! *All* over the universe?! That's too silly an idea! It's more like something you'd see in a superhero comic, fer Pete's sake! Besides, consider the way I did it in my tale. With everything supposedly frozen solid in time-suspension—even if the user of the stopwatch is not affected, how does he move around? Aren't all of the air molecules frozen around him?!

After I did "On Stolen Time," I found out that the time-stands-still idea was also the basis for a short story titled "The Girl, the Gold Watch and Everything," by the famous mystery writer John D. MacDonald. MacDonald avoided my frozen-air-molecule problem in his story. Rather than *freezing* time, MacDonald's magic pocketwatch would only make time move incredibly *slowly* for the usei which was why it was not a "stopwatch" like my notion. The magic pocketwatch user would have difficulty moving through the air around him when he slowed time down—it would feel like moving through water, and would even burn him with air friction if he tried to move too quickly. Much more clever than my idea! Well, it's that darn Gyro Gearloose's fault—*he* invented my darn stopwatch!

One gag in here that I now don't like involves that very idea I'd long ago had about how dangerous "frozen" grass blades would be. When I first started doing these Duck stories, I would make cheap gags mentioning their "beaks" or "feathers." But as time went on, I became uncomfortable with those jokes; because I knew that I had always envisioned Barks' Ducks as caricatures of human beings, not as giant talking ducks. So I no longer like making specific references to their physical appearance. That now seems as weird to me as if Obelix would tell Asterix that his nose was inhumanly large. Or like Captain Haddock asking Tintin why his eyes are only tiny black dots on his head.

So I now regret the "On Stolen Time" gag about how the nephews can't run over the frozen grass because they don't wear shoes due to their webbed feet. Ugh—that's just plain creepy!

(NO) D.U.C.K. SPOTTER'S GUIDE: Still no hidden dedication, so don't make yourself crazy trying to find it! But again, I *think* I put the dedication there in pencil and later inked over it—I clearly recall writing it on one of those loose bills lying at the base of the stacks of money in panel one.

TREASURE UNDER GLASS *p. 33*

This was one of several stories that I wrote in 1988 while waiting for the Walt Disney Company to approve a previous one that Gladstone Publishing had submitted for approval. That one was "His Majesty, McDuck"—and that one became my final story for Gladstone before I was forced to quit working for them (see Volume 2 of this *Library* for all the details).

So what of "Treasure Under Glass"? I did not want to complete the story for Disney Comics, Inc., the in-house Disney publisher that took over from Gladstone when Disney rescinded Gladstone's license to publish Donald and Scrooge comics. So I set the script aside and figured it was scrapped—not knowing that I would one year later be invited to work for Egmont in Europe. Thus, in 1990 I dusted off the unsold script and happily completed the art chores for Egmont!

This story is another example of how I love to find actual facts of history on which to base my stories—to my way of thinking, this makes a far more interesting tale than something simply created out of the writer's pure imagination. I wanted to do a tale about hunting for sunken treasure around the Florida Keys, that string of islands located off the southern tip of Disney World—er, I mean, Florida. But how could I put a new twist on the old sunken-treasure adventure?

My research soon told me that hunting for sunken treasure was not just a modern-day activity. There had been sunken treasure hunters since about five minutes after the first sunken treasure sank! And in the olden days, when treasure ships were lost on reefs in the shallow waters of the Caribbean Sea and the "Spanish Main," these treasure seekers had little trouble locating their lost galleons. They could see them through the clear waters, resting peacefully on the shallow seabed—often with their masts actually jutting above the waves to mark their locations! Finding them couldn't have been easier!

But recovering their treasures was still a difficult task. The problem was the *opposite* of the problem faced by modern-day treasure galleon seekers. Nowadays the treasure seekers can salvage the treasure, but they don't know where the shipwrecks are. Four centuries ago, the treasure hunters knew where the sunken treasure ships were, but they had no diving equipment to enable them to get down to the tons of gold and jewels that were literally in plain sight under a few fathoms of water! That must have been rather frustrating!

After Spain lost one particularly huge treasure armada off Key West in the Hurricane of 1622 (I'm sure you heard about it—it was in all the papers), King Philip IV sent a salvage fleet to the Florida Keys to find the lost treasure; but there was little they could do in those days other than to simply *locate* the sites of the sunken galleons.

Therefore, I thought, how about if I sent Scrooge *not* in search of a sunken treasure, but in search of the charts of the Spanish treasure-salvage fleet? So be it!

As usual for me, every single historical fact in this story is true, including the ancient diving bell and the salvage fleet's lost flagship, the *Candelaria*. The only "artistic/literary" license I took may have been the depiction of the *Candelaria* as a typical comic-book sunken galleon. In actuality, the *Candelaria*—wherever it may really lie wrecked—is now nothing more than a pile of old cannons, an anchor and some slowly rusting iron nails. All other parts of her, including her treasure charts, would have dissolved into nothingness several centuries ago. But to obey that law of nature would take all the fun out of sunken treasure galleon stories in comic books!

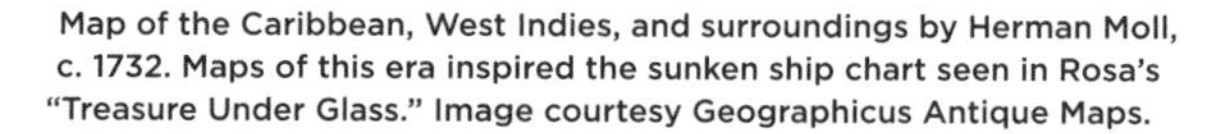
Map of the Caribbean, West Indies, and surroundings by Herman Moll, c. 1732. Maps of this era inspired the sunken ship chart seen in Rosa's "Treasure Under Glass." Image courtesy Geographicus Antique Maps.

Incidentally, I designed "Treasure Under Glass" so I could eventually do sequels to it, sending Scrooge in search of some of the treasure sites that he discovers on the *Candelaria's* chart. However, I only got around to doing one sequel: "The Last Lord of Eldorado," to come in Volume 7 of this series.

By the way, my original script for "Treasure Under Glass" ended with what is now the second-to-last page—the last scene being the half-page panel where we find the pirates marooned inside the overturned glass dome. I remember that much for certain; but I don't recall why my editor or I decided to extend the story one more page. Perhaps the editor needed me to show the pirates being taken into police custody? Whatever the case, I never liked the closing gag I came up with for the new last panel, with Scrooge using his cane to whack Donald on the hand. In retrospect, the only kind of "corporal punishment" that's funny is a swift kick in the butt.

(NO) D.U.C.K. SPOTTER'S GUIDE: This time, the place where I distinctly recall hiding the dedication was in the waves in the lower left of panel one. But they apparently sprang a leak and sank. Chronologically speaking, however, this is the last story I ever did where I left out the dedication! You'll have plenty of dedications to find in most of the following stories, so sharpen your eyeballs!

RETURN TO XANADU *p. 53*

When Egmont hired me in 1990, one of the things the editors said they definitely wanted me to do—something for which their readers had been clamoring for years—were *sequels* to favorite old Barks stories! Now, I'll be the first to agree that doing an add-on to some venerated Carl Barks classic does *not* necessarily do it honor! Those stories don't *need* sequels! They are complete and time-proven! And yet... what could be more *thrilling* for me than to find myself telling a "book two" of a beloved tale that I grew up reading over and over again? Even now the idea gives me goose-bumps!!! I am too weak to resist that offer... Sorry! Well... I'm really not sorry—I love these sequels!

As a matter of fact, since "Return to Xanadu" contains a surprise as to *which* Barks story it follows up on, you might want to read "Xanadu" first before continuing with this introduction. As we say: **spoiler warning follows!**

For the first Barks sequel I did for Egmont, I decided to send the Ducks *back* to Tralla La, the happy valley they had first visited in Barks' untitled 1954 adventure (*Uncle Scrooge* 6). Why did I pick that tale as my first choice? Because Barks' original was obviously a spoof of "Shangri-La," created by James Hilton in his famous 1933 book *Lost Horizon*, which was adapted into an even more famous 1937 Frank Capra movie. That movie is one of the absolute greatest films of all time, and Barks created his parody of Shangri-La for one of his absolute greatest stories. So, as a Barks fan and movie buff, this was easily my first choice!

The classic film *Lost Horizon* (1937)—parodied in Carl Barks' "Tralla La" and Don Rosa's "Return to Xanadu"—features a mystical land of milk and honey in which youth springs eternal, grave illness can be healed, and life is generally a little slice of heaven... until our heroes' arrival, that is. Poster image courtesy Heritage Auctions.

But I realized that Scrooge, Donald, and the boys already knew where Tralla La was—and they wouldn't *want* to return there, as they had departed "persona non grata" in Barks' original adventure. Therefore, the only way I could get them there was by accident, not knowing where they were headed... and the only way that could happen is if they traveled there *underground* in a cave or such. Well, Barks' story had clearly established that there were many caves in the valley of Tralla La, as well as the outlet tunnel for the whirlpool in the valley's lagoon. Aha! I had my method of accidental entrance—an underground river!

Next, *why* would the Ducks be messing around in caves in Tibet? Scrooge would be again in search of some fabled treasure, of course, and the only famous lost treasure in that part of our globe is the lost treasury of the Cathay Empire—the loot of Genghis Khan. But wait—Carl Barks already *did* a story titled "The Lost Crown of Genghis Khan" (*Uncle Scrooge* 14, 1956). Since that crown would obviously be part of the Cathay treasure trove, I reread that adventure. The plot involved Scrooge regaining the

RETURN TO XANADU
Norwegian *Donald Duck & Co.* 1991-13, March 1991; first American printing on *Uncle Scrooge* 262, January 1992. Color by Egmont.

D.U.C.K. SPOTTER'S GUIDE:
There's no dedication on this cover.

Scrooge and Lah Deedah enjoy a cuppa in Carl Barks' original Tralla La tale (*Uncle Scrooge* 6, 1954).

crown from a Yeti who had stolen it from Scrooge's agents; but when asked where his agents found the crown *originally*, Scrooge only replied "that is a story for another time." *Perfect!* So, now I needed to go and do research on Genghis Khan and his Cathay empire...

The last custodian of the treasure of Cathay would have been Genghis' grandson Kublai Khan—so I got out a copy of Samuel Taylor Coleridge's famous poem about Kublai's legendary retreat, "Xanadu." And read it. And that's when the hairs on my neck got all tingly! The poem tells of Xanadu being a land of milk and honey, a small hidden valley paradise surrounded by a ring of tall mountains, and containing a river that disappeared into caves in a "tumult"! The poem was describing Barks' valley of Tralla La in detail!!! There was the entire first half of my story, all waiting for me in a famous poem written nearly 200 years earlier! Wow!!!

Yes, I was now working primarily for a non-English-speaking audience, but do you think I could ignore such a remarkable coincidence? Besides, perhaps some of the older readers might be familiar with the poem. Coleridge's "Kubla Khan" is one of the most famous English poems, despite the fact that he never finished it. Maybe my Scrooge sequel sort of finishes it?

Actually, I do hope there aren't any readers who think doing sequels is easy—they are actually far *more* difficult than creating a whole new story from scratch that doesn't require the endless cross-referencing to the original in art and plot details. For instance, in doing "Return to Xanadu," not only was I confronted with the problems of plot logic I described above, but I also knew that what I should not do is introduce any totally new ideas into the well-known comic book reality of Barks' Tralla La. Once I managed to get the Ducks into the valley, any conflicts or problems that arose thereafter had to be some logical outgrowth of elements in the original story, not based on any new idiotic ideas that I might toss into the mix.

So I had to figure a process by which our heroes could enter Tralla La through the underground river passage, but somehow be unable to leave by that same route... I recall that problem stumped me for two full days! And then, having finally gotten them back into Tralla La, the next problem was to devise a new situation, a new crisis for the happy valley, that would develop Barks' original ideas into both a new danger and a new solution. Note how my plot involved the cessation of the whirlpool, a danger mentioned in Barks' original; and my solution involved the very bottle caps that solved the problem in Barks' tale. I was (and am!) pretty happy at how I handled my first Barks sequel for Egmont... I only hope you agree a bit.

During development, this story felt so important to me that I had an urge to give it even more significance. So I considered using it as a springboard for another story set in Tralla La, which would have involved a plot that Duck fans were asking me to undertake 24 years ago, and for which I still get a few requests. Take a look at the sequence (overleaf) and see if you can guess what that as-yet-unrevealed "Secret of Tralla La" is! For various reasons, I never ended up producing the idea as a story.

D.U.C.K. SPOTTER'S GUIDE: *Yes*! In "Return to Xanadu" is the "Return of the Dedication"!!! And that's especially appropriate for this Barks sequel! Look in the bristles at the end of the whisk broom in the lower left of panel one.

INSANE DETAILS TO LOOK FOR: Tralla La's looks and inhabitants; the absence of metal from the valley, apart from a vast bottle cap cache; and Scrooge's long-ago yak trading: all originate in the untitled story usually remembered as simply "Tralla La" (*Uncle Scrooge* 6, 1954).

The Crown of Genghis Khan and its history come, appropriately, from "The Lost Crown of Genghis Khan!" (*US* 14, 1956). Scrooge's memento shelves at the story's start also display the Goose Egg Nugget ("Back to the Klondike," Uncle Scrooge *Four Color* 356, 1953); the Treasure of Sir Quackly McDuck ("The Old Castle's Secret," Donald Duck *Four Color* 189, 1948); the Philosopher's Stone and the Treasure of King Minos ("The Fabulous Philosopher's Stone," *US* 10, 1955); the Candy-Striped Ruby ("The Status Seeker," *US* 41, 1963); Jason's Golden Fleece ("The Golden Fleecing", *US* 12, 1955); an old Spanish helmet ("The Prize of Pizarro," *US* 26, 1959); gold bars from the *Flying Dutchman* ship ("The Flying Dutchman," *US* 25, 1959); sand from King Solomon's mines ("The Mines of King Solomon," *US* 19, 1957); and a 1916 quarter ("The Secret of Atlantis," *US* 5, 1954). (*Continued on Page 169*)

An unused script page for Page 1 of Rosa's "Return to Xanadu" shows a working title—"Prisoners of Paradise"—that ended up being used as a phrase elsewhere in the story.
All script images courtesy Don Rosa.

Rosa's storyboard-script panels from an aborted "Return to Xanadu" sequence, showing a clue that might have warranted a sequel (see page 165). Guess what the clue is!

When "Return to Xanadu" made its U.S. debut in *Uncle Scrooge* 261-262 (1991-92), the story was split into two parts—with this *partially* new Rosa page opening Part 2. Letters by Teresa Davidson.

Marco Polo meets Kublai Khan in a medieval illuminated manuscript. Image courtesy Egmont Serieforlaget AS

NO KHAN DO: We can't leave "Return to Xanadu" without one last look at the source. Here to give us some background is Professor Øystein Sørensen of the University of Oslo, contributing author from our Norwegian parent edition, Egmont Serieforlaget AS' *Don Rosa Collection*:

The Mongols conquered China in the 13th century. The conquest took time; the invaders started in the north and pushed slowly into wider terrain. In the 1270s, China's Song Dynasty ended; the Mongolian rulers established the Yuan Dynasty as its successor. From 1259, the Mongols' great Khan—their supreme leader—was Kublai Khan, grandson of Genghis. In the 1260s, Kublai took up residence in the city we know today as Beijing.

Kublai Khan's reign as Chinese emperor was marked by constant conquests; most successful, but a few notably not. The Mongol rulers tried twice to conquer Japan, in 1274 and 1281, and the efforts were famously disastrous. Even nature encumbered Kublai: in the second invasion attempt, an onrushing Chinese fleet was wrecked not by Japanese resistance, but by a storm at sea. It is no coincidence that the Japanese word kamikaze means "holy wind."

Kublai Khan gained worldwide fame for his power and riches, thanks largely to reports by European visitor Marco Polo. Of especial interest was the splendor associated with Kublai Khan's summer home, the Inner Mongolian region of Shangdu—better known as Xanadu.

In popular legend, Kublai's residence there evolved into a locale at once luxurious and inaccessibly remote. It is this Xanadu that was captured by English Romantic poet Samuel Coleridge (1772-1834):

Or, a vision in a dream.
A Fragment.

In Xanadu did Kubla Khan
A stately pleasure-dome decree:
Where Alph, the sacred river, ran
Through caverns measureless to man
Down to a sunless sea.
So twice five miles of fertile ground
With walls and towers were girdled round:
And there were gardens bright with sinuous rills,
Where blossomed many an incense-bearing tree;
And here were forests ancient as the hills,
Enfolding sunny spots of greenery.

But oh! that deep romantic chasm which slanted
Down the green hill athwart a cedarn cover!
A savage place! as holy and enchanted
As e'er beneath a waning moon was haunted
By woman wailing for her demon-lover!
And from this chasm, with ceaseless turmoil seething,
As if this earth in fast thick pants were breathing,
A mighty fountain momently was forced:
Amid whose swift half-intermitted burst
Huge fragments vaulted like rebounding hail,
Or chaffy grain beneath the thresher's flail:
And 'mid these dancing rocks at once and ever
It flung up momently the sacred river.
Five miles meandering with a mazy motion
Through wood and dale the sacred river ran,
Then reached the caverns measureless to man,
And sank in tumult to a lifeless ocean:
And 'mid this tumult Kubla heard from far
Ancestral voices prophesying war!

The shadow of the dome of pleasure
Floated midway on the waves;
Where was heard the mingled measure
From the fountain and the caves.
It was a miracle of rare device,
A sunny pleasure-dome with caves of ice!

A damsel with a dulcimer
In a vision once I saw:
It was an Abyssinian maid,
And on her dulcimer she played,
Singing of Mount Abora.
Could I revive within me,
Her symphony and song,
To such a deep delight 'twould win me,
That with music loud and long,
I would build that dome in air,
That sunny dome! Those caves of ice!
And all who heard should see them there,
And all should cry, Beware! Beware!
His flashing eyes, his floating hair!
Weave a circle round him thrice,
And close your eyes with holy dread,
For he on honey-dew hath fed,
And drunk the milk of Paradise.

— Samuel Taylor Coleridge

THE DUCK WHO FELL TO EARTH
Donald Duck Adventures [series II] 37, June 1993. Layout by Bob Foster; color by Jo Meugniot and Digikore Studios.

D.U.C.K. SPOTTER'S GUIDE:
Check out the flames near Donald's right boot.

It's up to "Prof. Duck" (our Donald) and Professor Mollicule to rescue a hair-dissolving explosive from a scheming spy in Carl Barks' "Donald Duck's Atom Bomb" (*Walt Disney Giveaway* Y-1, 1947).

THE DUCK WHO FELL TO EARTH *p. 83*

Like "On Stolen Time," this story uses a plot idea that I'd had for many years. I don't refer to the idea of salvaging old satellites, but of the fall from orbit of a man wearing a space suit. I'd been trying to find a use for the idea in one of the comics adventure stories that I'd done in the mid 1970s for fanzines (those amateur magazines we comics fans would create just for fun!).

As I developed this story, I originally planned for the inventor of my low-speed sub-orbiter to be Gyro Gearloose. But it was decided that the refurbished airplane was far too low-tech for Gyro, and also that the scientist in this tale was just too *stupid* to be Barks' brilliant inventor. Gyro is scatter-brained and impractical, but he's not *stupid*! So I changed the Gyro role to that of the nutty "Professor Mollicule" that Mr. Barks had used in an obscure little comic-pamphlet titled "Donald Duck's Atom Bomb" which was given away with breakfast cereal in 1947. I always get a kick out of using some old Barks character whenever I can, especially when I know that only the most knowledgeable comics buffs will recognize the character, as in this case.

I'm actually not very fond of this story—it's a bit too science-fictiony a Duck story for my taste (as was the earlier time-stop tale!), but my main personal objection to my own story is: *when is it happening?* As many of you know, I write and draw my Duck stories as taking place sometime in the 1950s. That's when I was reading those old Dell comics where Unca Carl's stories originally appeared, and that's my favorite period of the Duck Man's work. Besides that, if I am to stick to Barks' version of Scrooge McDuck as having been a Mississippi riverboat worker in 1880 or a Montana cowboy in 1882 or a Yukon sourdough in 1897, I can't see how I could set my stories in the present day. The poor guy would be about 150 years old! Furthermore, when all my stories are set 60 years ago, it makes me feel as if I was putting my own stories into a time machine and sending them back to myself as a child to read on the living room sofa in the house where I grew up! But the editors naturally wanted the stories to be taking place in the current year so as to not confuse the younger readers. Therefore, I had to regard the 1950s time frame of my stories as a "private joke" for myself (and for the sharp-eyed readers who spot the clues I sometimes hide in the art).

But... what's my point here? Oh, yes—it's that *this* story violated my own rules! It concerns satellites falling from orbit, and includes a TV weatherman showing viewers an image taken by a weather-satellite camera. These are things not known until the 1970s. Well, maybe that makes this an "imaginary story"? (*Continued on Page 174*)

Two "Duck Who Fell to Earth" storyboard-script pages from an early stage in the creative process when Gyro Gearloose was given the role of the professor.

Don Rosa and his editor decided the airplane was not hi-tech enough to be one of Gyro's inventions, and that the role in the story called for a much wackier professor.
All script images courtesy Don Rosa.

From *The Pertwillaby Papers* episode 128, "Sub-Zero." Lance Pertwillaby's Empire State Building antics foreshadow Donald's later mishaps on McDuck Tower (see page 102). *The Pertwillaby Papers* © and courtesy Don Rosa.

The first European publication dummy for "Incident at McDuck Tower" (1991, left) shows non-Rosa dialogue at Page 4, Panel 1. The story's American debut in *Uncle Scrooge* 268 (1992, right) repeats this wording, altered only to change Gitte into Gretta. For more recent U.S. printings of the story, Rosa's original intent was restored (see page 98).

You decide for yourself. As for me, I've had Fantagraphics editor David Gerstein "recolor" a big-screen view of the TV weatherman to make it black and white—because a monochrome TV screen, even if it's awfully big for the 1950s, seems a little *more* 1950s when it's monochrome.

(NO) D.U.C.K. SPOTTER'S GUIDE: Don't look! For the last time in this volume, it ain't there! But I distinctly recall *intending* to hide the dedication in that junkyard flower that a mouse is staring at in panel one.

INCIDENT AT McDUCK TOWER *p. 95*

This 1991 story is yet another remake of a sequence that I had already done with my own comics characters. The 1975 fanzine version involved my hero, Lancelot Pertwillaby, being thrown off the Empire State Building rather than McDuck Tower, but what happened to him was exactly what happens to Donald in pages 8 and 9 of this version.

This is another of the slapstick "gag" stories... and there's really not much more to say about it. I do know that it was a *pain* to draw! My so-called "art" is generally not so hot—I can do facial expressions and overly-complex action scenes pretty well, and I don't have too much trouble with background outdoor landscapes. But what I am particularly bad at drawing is buildings and cars and any other manmade items. I just don't know how to go about it correctly. Since my only training is in civil engineering, you'd think that I would be able to draw such things well—but all I know is how to render truss designs or structural load diagrams in very technical methods. That's more of a hindrance than a help to a cartoonist! Drawing aerial views of all these Duckburg skyscrapers was an awful job to give myself! Readers don't necessarily even look at the background in a comic panel... it's "just there," but they'd notice if the background was simply blank. For me, drawing those @#$%& backgrounds in each panel was about 85% of the labor in drawing a story!

Ever since I drew this tale, you'll notice that I started finding ways to get these Ducks *out* of Duckburg! If I sent Scrooge on a treasure hunt to an ancient castle, I didn't need to worry about square corners or straight lines; if I sent him on an archaeological dig in Egypt, the background would only be palm trees and sand dunes. A story set at sea would have backgrounds of only water and fluffy clouds. If only I could have thought of some treasure to search for at the North Pole! That story would have been filled with panels whose backgrounds were only a single horizontal line. O, bliss.

As I try to think of what else I can say about this simplistic story, I might mention how confusing and often aggravating it was to write comics that were published in dozens of languages that I couldn't read. To this day, I never know when the stories are being correctly translated—or, as in this case, if the "official script" is accurate to my original storyboard-script. In the case of "Incident at McDuck Tower," I didn't find out what mysterious and inexplicable changes were made in my script until I read the first English language edition a couple of years later.

We have corrected several speech balloons in this new version to match my original script. But if you were a reader of this story when it first appeared, you were probably rather puzzled when you got to panel 1 on page 4. The first balloon in my original script was "Did I just hear you shut the window, Gitte?" But the dialogue that appeared in the official script—and, therefore, in all early printings around the world—was "Don't ever speak to me like that again, Gitte!" The first American publication anglicized Gitte—an Egmont staffer in Denmark at the time—to Gretta, as we have also done here; but otherwise, the oddity was left intact. Wondering about "life's little mysteries" like this one is probably what turned my red hair white!

D.U.C.K. SPOTTER'S GUIDE: Um... not very clever—the dedication is simply written on a sign on a building in the lower left of panel one. Maybe it's an ad for "D.U.C.K. Toothpaste"?

THE ISLAND AT THE EDGE OF TIME *p. 105*

This story has some unusual aspects. My main memory of it is of the trouble I had trying to explain the plot. I had a misguided notion that it would be interesting to base a story on the strange anomaly that exists at the "International Dateline" in the center of the Pacific Ocean, where there are

THE ISLAND AT THE EDGE OF TIME
Uncle Scrooge 276, March 1993. Layout by Bob Foster; color by Jo Meugniot and Digikore Studios with David Gerstein.

D.U.C.K. SPOTTER'S GUIDE:
It's on four of the rope hooks, starting with the one under Huey.

always two different dates existing side by side. Huh? Well, if that sounds confusing, try reading this story, but I don't guarantee you'll be any less confused when you're done. I can tell you that the story was originally intended to only be the usual ten pages, but it soon stretched to 14 pages as I wrestled with explaining the whole International Dateline phenomenon to young readers who might not have ever even heard of it. After all, it sounds like science-fiction or time travel! In fact, I'm still not too clear on it myself; so if anyone reads this story and understands it, I hope they'll drop me a note and explain it to me.

Another confusing aspect of this story, at least for its original audience, involved my use of Carl Barks' great rival for Scrooge McDuck: Scrooge's "evil twin," Flintheart Glomgold. I later found out that in the Disney Duck stories that had been created for decades in Europe after the American publishers ceased, the writers had always placed Flintheart as living in Duckburg. But in my stories I always have Flinty living where Barks situated him in his original classics that I grew up reading—in the Valley of the Limpopo River in the country of South Africa. I suspect that when this story first appeared in 1991, many European readers were quite puzzled by why their Duckburgian Glomgold suddenly had a giraffe wandering through his yard.

A final amusing oddity involves another script change made by my earliest Egmont editors—even though it is one that I "un-changed" for the first U. S. edition, so American readers have never known about it until now! I seem to recall that as I developed the script, I purposely enlarged the role of the narrator in the storytelling, making him as overblown and pompous as possible. Then, on the last page, I carried this to its natural conclusion—with Scrooge turning to the narrator, "breaking the fourth wall" of reality, and telling him "It's time for you to shut up and end this story!" However, the wording that was typed up into the "official script" had Scrooge screaming (at me?) "It's time to end this story! It's *too long*!" Hmm—*length* hadn't been part of Scrooge's complaint before. Was that the editor trying to give me a subtle hint? Well, if so, I tend to agree with that sentiment! (Not one of my favorite stories!)

D.U.C.K. SPOTTER'S GUIDE: The dedication is hidden in the same fashion that I had intended to hide it in "Treasure Under Glass," but didn't. Look in the waves in the lower left of panel one.

INSANE DETAILS TO LOOK FOR: The design of Glomgold's Money Bin, and the scenery around it, derive from its debut in Barks' "The Second-Richest Duck" (*Uncle Scrooge* 15, 1956). Auger-nosed pickle-hater beetles were seen in "Forbidden Valley" (*Donald Duck* 54, 1957).

The Glomgold Money Bin stands out from the Limpopo landscape in Carl Barks' "The Second-Richest Duck" (*Uncle Scrooge* 15, 1956). The same scenery was lovingly replicated for various Rosa Glomgold adventures.

Carl Barks' "Land of the Pygmy Indians" (*Uncle Scrooge* 18, 1957) introduced the Peeweegahs and their Longfellow-like poetic dialogue.

WAR OF THE WENDIGO *p. 119*

There were actually *two* different types of requests made of me by the editors of the Egmont publishing branches—besides sequels to Barks stories, they also would sometimes request that I create a story based on, or to raise awareness of, a local current event. For example, Norway asked me for a story that would tie into their 1994 "Year of the Book": this became "Guardians of the Lost Library," to appear in Vol. 5 of this series. Soon thereafter came their 1994 Winter Olympics—thus "From Duckburg to Lillehammer," also coming up in our Vol. 5.

"War of the Wendigo" was both a requested subject and another requested Barks sequel rolled into one. Northern Europe—Scandinavia in particular—has a problem with acid rain, so in 1991 Egmont asked me to do a story dealing with this very serious subject. And when they did, the *first* idea that came to my ecological brain was that such a story *must* star Barks' guardians of the woodlands, the *Peeweegah Indians*! Of course, we in North America have the same acid rain problem: mostly in Canada, where the Peeweegahs lived in Barks' "Land of the Pygmy Indians" (*Uncle Scrooge* 18, 1957). As with the story of Tralla La and "Return to Xanadu," I could create a revisitation to another of Barks' isolated societies happily untouched by modern civilization, one of Barks' favorite subjects.

I don't think it was a conscious decision on my part, but as with "Return to Xanadu," the Barks connection was not revealed until about a third of the way through the adventure, at the end of Chapter 1. Chapter 1? Yes, this was the *first* Duck story I ever did that was designed to be presented in three separate chapters, serialized in three weekly issues of the Egmont weekly comics.

I didn't like the idea of continued stories, forcing my plot and action to be contained in separate eight-page segments affecting the plot's pacing. As Fantagraphics' readers will likely be aware, we've never had weekly Duck comics here in America; but our various monthly or bimonthly titles could contain any length of story without cutting them up into awkward pieces. Still, I was happy (beyond words!) to be still doing Duck comics at all after the tribulations of 1989-90, so I went along with Egmont's multi-part plans. I only begged for an extra chapter to hold my overblown ideas: they had expected me to do 16-page two-parters, but I ended up going one step longer.

Soon after "War of the Wendigo" I had the bright idea of doing extra art for three-chapter stories, the extra art being half-pages of additional (but nonessential) humor or action that would fill those top halves of the first pages of Chapters 2 and 3. This way, when my three-part stories

DAH-dah-DAH-dah-DAH-dah-DAH-dah ...

Henry Wadsworth Longfellow (1807-1882)—inspiration to Carl Barks and Don Rosa—with the inimitable rhythmic meter that he originally developed for his "Song of Hiawatha." Image courtesy Egmont Serieforlaget AS.

were reprinted as *one*-parters in other countries, they would flow smoothly without the interruption of inexplicable half-page panels at inappropriate times. Needless to say, these Fantagraphics *Don Rosa Library* volumes will show you all the stories in their one-part versions—and then *also* offer you the multi-part half-page chapter-opening art separately. However, for "War of the Wendigo"—since I never created a true one-part version—we'll just hafta suffer through the three-part incarnation, with its annoying half-page recap panels that do nothing other than repeat what was in the small last panel on the previous page. Sorry!

I put a great deal of extra work into the dialogue of "War of the Wendigo" in order to be faithful to the original Barks classic! In Barks' tale, the Peeweegahs all spoke in free-verse poetry in a rune-o-meter rhythm imitating that of Henry Longfellow's "Song of Hiawatha" poem. (Another story related to an English poem!) What this involves is that each Peeweegah word balloon must contain four lines of dialogue, with each line made up of eight beats of rhythm; the first beat of each line having emphasis, and then the remaining seven beats alternating in emphasis and de-emphasis. In other words, each line should have the rhythm of "DAH-dah-DAH-dah-DAH-dah-DAH-dah," and there should be four such lines in each balloon.

Barks' Peeweegah dialogue was *splendid*; when read aloud, it sounded like music. My version of Barks' Peeweegahs don't speak as nicely as did his... I assure you, writing good poetry is not simple work, and my English Peeweegahian dialogue sometimes hit a "clinker"!

Still, I knew that I was writing this story for Europe, and all of my extra effort would be wasted until an American Disney publisher reprinted my story for American readers. "War of the Wendigo" was duly announced to appear in *Uncle Scrooge* 278 (1993), at which time Disney Comics, Inc.—Disney's in-house publisher—was handling the series.

But then outside events intervened. In 1993, Disney was also at work on *Pocahontas* (1994), an animated feature that tackled the theme of racism, portraying hostility between British colonists and Native Americans. An editor felt that while the studio figured out how to treat this touchy subject, Disney Comics should avoid printing any stories involving ethnic groups—particularly American Indians. Of course, my story featured not just the Peeweegahs, but their conflict with bigoted mill workers who treated them like primitives.

It didn't matter, at first, that the story was anti-racist or that the Peeweegahs were the good guys: my "War of the Wendigo" was put on the shelf in our own country. An unrelated story replaced it in *Uncle Scrooge* 278. In 1995, when Gladstone Publishing asked to print the tale, the same editor said that would only be permitted if the Peeweegahs were colored *blue* and referred to not as Native Americans, but as "forest spirits." I didn't want to change Barks' noble Pygmy Indians, so it looked like I'd never see this story used in a language I could read.

But this story *about* a story has a happy ending. By the time Gladstone decided to drop their Disney license in 1999, an unchanged "War of the Wendigo" was finally greenlit for reprint, so Gladstone managed to feature it in the final comic book they published. Later, in 2007, the subsequent American Disney comics licensee Gemstone reprinted the story again, pairing it with Barks' original Peeweegah adventure—and giving me an opportunity to create a new cover illustrating *both* stories!

D.U.C.K. SPOTTER'S GUIDE: This is the only serialized story wherein I hid the dedication in the first page of *each* chapter, so you have three different "D.U.C.K."s to find, one in each of the three first panels! Chapter 1: look at the flower in the lower left. Chapter 2: check the waves at the canoe's nose in the lower right. Chapter 3: examine a Peeweegah's headband in the lower left.

INSANE DETAILS TO LOOK FOR: Every detail about the Peeweegahs, including their language and lifestyle, come directly from Barks' "Land of the Pygmy Indians" (*Uncle Scrooge* 18, 1957). When Scrooge refers to his past confrontations with yeti, Harpies, and menehune, the callbacks are to Barks' "The Lost Crown of Genghis Khan!" (*US* 14, 1956), "The Golden Fleecing" (*US* 12, 1955), and "Hawaiian Hideaway" (*US* 4, 1953), respectively.

SUPER SNOOPER STRIKES AGAIN! *p. 147*

Our final story is a sequel to another old Barks classic that holds a special place in my heart. The original "Super Snooper" story appeared in what was the oldest comic that I grew up with, *Walt Disney's Comics and Stories* 107 from 1949. It was a coverless copy, two years older than I was; just one of the thousands of my older sister's comics that I grew up with literally from birth!

That original "Super Snooper" story was Barks' gentle slap at the superhero comics that actually were then disappearing from the American comic book racks after their first heyday during World War II. Who would then dream that those unwanted superhero comics would not only later *return* to American comics, but would eventually take over the American market as being the only suitable content for comic books?! And finally result in the glut of violent "grim vigilantes" that now populate the relatively few comics sold in America. Yes, relatively few compared with Europe or Asia. American comics are still profitable to the publishers since they bypass the newsstand distributor and are sold directly to comic shops on a non-return basis. 50 years ago American comic books sold millions of copies per issue, but now a modern successful comic in American sells only about 20,000 copies over all of North America! And consider further: for an American comic to sell as well *per capita* as *Donald Duck* comics sell and are read in many European countries, it would need to sell around *70 million copies* per month! So *Batman* and *The Uncanny X-Men* are no big deal compared to *Donald Duck*!

And *that* was exactly the angle I wanted to play up in my "Super Snooper" sequel. I wanted to show that we Barks Duck fans think that the superheroes and their violence, mayhem, and pointless action are no match for the qualities of plot, characterization and humor found in most any Duck comic. I wanted to show that Superman is no match for Donald Duck!

But this story is yet another example of the frustrations that arise when my original script is changed. I wrote this story clearly as a *sequel*—with Donald, the nephews and the scientists all making constant references to Barks' original tale as an event that had previously happened to all of them. Even the title I used for the story indicates it's a sequel! But apparently the translators in several European countries were not Barks fans, and they chose to *remove* all of these references in my dialogue. As a result, there were a number of angry Barks fans and comic reviewers accusing me of *swiping* Barks' "Super Snooper" plot and trying to pass it off as my own! And I don't blame them for having thought that—they naturally assumed that my stories were being presented as I wrote them. But after mentioning these ancient script-change problems in several of this volume's stories, I will also say that this monkey business is long in the past, and I now happily have close communication with most translators.

The pedigreed Smugsnorkle Squattie—in Carl Barks' Donald Duck story for *Walt Disney's Comics and Stories* 70 (1946)—is either an immensely smart dog, or an immensely stupid one. We're not sure which.

D.U.C.K. SPOTTER'S GUIDE: Look at the windows of the building in the upper right of panel one.

INSANE DETAILS TO LOOK FOR: All references to the Super Snooper character and title refer to "Super Snooper" in *Walt Disney's Comics and Stories* 107 (1949). Certain poses of Donald drinking the super-serum and acting like a superhero reflect "Super Snooper," too. But those details aren't very insane, are they?

So how about that sleepy-looking dog at panel two of Page 4? It's a "Smugsnorkle Squattie," a supposedly super-smart breed of pooch that Donald tried to train in *Walt Disney's Comics and Stories* 70 (1946). The Squattie looks more bored than insane, but I've heard tell that Squatties only seem calm on the *outside*. Inside they're raging. •

KLONDIKE
GAZETTE
GLASGOW
PARIS
LOUIS
DAWSON
CAPE
TOWN
PERTH

The
Rosa
Archives

This cartoon has been a problem for me since 1991—due to unauthorized use! Fans see it on websites that never requested permission to use the image. Few seem to know how it came about.

The drawing was originally my contribution to a fanzine feature which invited many cartoonists to illustrate the line "Hey, Daisy! Whatever happened to Scrooge?" It was a joke feature—it was meant to be funny to see all the different odd ideas that various cartoonists would offer to illustrate the quote. Some were funny, some were rather vulgar; but, since I have such a serious view of these characters, I offered a scene of what might be said in the far future over Scrooge's grave. With my stories set in the 1950s, there's no way that Scrooge could do everything that Barks' stories said he did and still be alive today.

Anyway, some people took my contribution and started reprinting it without permission and out of context, making it look like I was trying to show a depressing scene for no reason!

I am delighted to finally, in this book set, have the above image used with my explanation. By this time it has also made the journey from its birth as a fanzine drawing to an "official" DIsney comics image, having been purchased and published in Gemstone's *Walt Disney Treasures—Uncle Scrooge: A Little Something Special* (2008).

—Don Rosa

PART 3: "The Invader of Fort Gutenberg"

When we last left off, our hero had just produced *Uncle Scrooge* comics for several different Disney licensees in quick succession. There was Gladstone Publishing in the United States. There was Oberon (today called Sanoma) in the Netherlands. Then there was Disney Comics Inc. in the United States again, Disney's brief in-house replacement for Gladstone.

But none of these could continue. At the time, domestic United States policy would not let me keep my original artwork, which I needed to sell to supplement my income. Oberon was permitted to let me keep it—but the Oberon editors didn't like my artwork, so I couldn't go on working for them, either.

At last I decided to throw myself on the mercies of the world-spanning Gutenberghus Publishing Service (today Egmont): the world's largest Disney comics licensee, based in Denmark. I sent them an old-fashioned telegram. A day or two later I received a telephone call from someone who said her name was Nancy Dejgaard and that she was calling from Copenhagen. I was talking on the phone with someone on the other side of the Atlantic Ocean?

Right away I suspected this was a practical joke by a friend who knew I wanted to contact Gutenberghus. This Nancy Dejgaard said that she was the head of the production center of all the Gutenberghus Disney comics, and that my telegram had been passed on to her. And that yes, she would very much like for me to work for Gutenberghus! (Now I *knew* this had to be my practical-joker pal.)

I asked what sort of stories she wanted me to do (praying it would not be short gag stories, which was all the Dutch wanted)—she said I could do any kind of stories I preferred (!). I asked if I would have my artwork returned—she was a bit puzzled and said that no artist had ever wanted their artwork back before, but sure, they'd send my art back (!!!). Then she asked me how much I needed to be paid—and I told her the rates that Gladstone used to pay me. She thanked me and said she'd have to think about the pay rate and call me back.

I was confused—if this was a practical joke, it was a very cruel one. My friends should know how much the idea of creating Scrooge stories meant to me. But I also realized something else—I had quoted Gladstone's page rates, which were far below the industry average. If this Gutenberghus was such a big publisher, surely they could afford to at least pay me the average page rate for comic work. So that afternoon I sent another telegram to Gutenberghus asking if I could please increase my requested page rate to that industry average amount which I named.

Nancy Dejgaard was Editor-in-Chief of the comics department at Gutenberghus in Copenhagen—responsible for development of the Egmont-created Disney comics—from 1988 through 1993, when she retired. Photo © and courtesy Egmont Serieforlaget AS

Soon came another phone call from Nancy Dejgaard. She mentioned the page rate I had first requested... *and*

A handful of the earliest Gutenberghus comics to reprint Don Rosa stories, 1989-1991. Typical for the time, the covers feature 1970s Disney character models drawn in an approximation of late-1980s Spanish and Franco-Belgian cartooning styles. Only two of the covers—Norwegian *Donald Duck & Co.* 01/90, drawn by Daniel Branca, and German *Micky Maus* 17/90, drawn by Marçal Bresco—hint at the Carl Barks-inspired Duck work that appeared inside the magazines. The *Micky Maus* 17/90 cover actually illustrates Rosa's "Return to Plain Awful."

the one mentioned in my *second* telegram. My blood went cold—this proved to me that this was not a practical joke by a cruel friend! They could not know the contents of my telegrams. So I *was* actually speaking to the head of the giant Gutenberghus Disney comics production center in Copenhagen! Nancy went on to say that neither page rate I'd mentioned was proper, and she said that, for starters, Gutenberghus would pay me an amount which I recall was about twice as much as my top request.

What I did not know was that my old Gladstone stories were already being used in Gutenberghus comics! Those stories were Disney property and could be used by any Disney publisher on Earth without notifying me or paying royalties, so I never dreamt that my work was already appearing in comics from the world's biggest Disney comic publisher! She also said that their readers liked my complex adventures and weird art! Then I realized that the only reason Nancy had asked me how much I needed to be paid was that she was afraid I would want too much!!! She was afraid I needed to be overpaid to persuade me to produce stories based the Carl Barks characters I loved with all my heart! Isn't that ironic?!?! What a world!

Nancy soon proved to be a wonderful person to work for! She soon learned that I was not really a professional cartoonist, nor did I pretend to be. I was just a fan who was living a dream. And she let me do just what she'd said—I could produce any sorts of Scrooge or Donald stories I wished (within certain page count restraints, of course).

That was the beginning of the rest of my life. I knew my stories would never be particularly popular with the Gutenberghus readers—they were used to seeing work by the best Disney comics people in the world. I knew I didn't have the ability to compete with all those experienced, skilled and trained artists. But no matter—I was now one of the Duck comics writers and artists for the world's biggest Disney comics publisher, doing the kinds of stories I liked, and getting paid a good page rate. There was nothing I wanted more out of life!

I wondered what it was like in Europe!? I was starting to get the idea that maybe Disney comics were still a bit popular there, as they had been in America when I was young. Ah, but if the idea of talking on the telephone to someone in Europe was fantastic, I always knew that my actually ever visiting Europe was something that couldn't possibly ever happen.

Or could it?

I need to say a few words about this company before I go on. Its founder, Egmont Petersen, had begun his publishing empire with only a small printing press on the kitchen table. As his corporation grew, selfless as he always was, he named it Gutenberghus (House of Gutenberg) in honor of the inventor of the printing press. In 1992, the still-expanding corporation decided to rename itself after its illustrious founder. This being an international corporation, the company name needed to sound grand in any language. The way someone explained it to me at the time, it was decided that "Petersen" sounds a bit odd in certain tongues (I try not to let my imagination run away), but the name "Egmont" sounded classy in all languages. Well, I don't know about that... in English "Egmont" doesn't "roll off the tongue" very sleekly, but whatever you call it, this is a big, successful worldwide media company, and I will call it Egmont from this point on.

So, there I was writing and drawing my crude-looking Donald Duck stories for this huge European company. This was wonderful—little Gladstone Publishing could not afford to keep me busy, but Egmont said they could use as much work as I could produce. There was only one limit to my level of income—my own speed. And that could hardly be called "speed"... it was mighty slow! I had never been trained to be a professional artist, one of the key elements of which is to learn how to work quickly and efficiently with the minimum of lines. I learned to draw as a way to amuse myself telling stories, not earn a living. And the slower I drew, the longer I was entertained. But I'd always known that creating Disney comics was no way to get rich! I would have stayed with the Keno Rosa Co., my now-closed family construction firm, if money had been all I was interested in. Creating Donald and Scrooge comics was my lifelong dream. So, if I could never maximize my possible income due to my extremely slow work speed, I didn't worry about it.

Now, if had known then that someday people would be asking me to write mini-autobiographies, I would have kept a diary. But it's been said that people who keep diaries write about things they hope to someday do; other people don't keep diaries, because they are too busy doing what they hope to do. I guess that would be me in those years, so I can only offer you jumbled memories of some very magnificent experiences in these early days.

And the first magnificent experience would have been in January 1991, when Egmont invited me to attend a Disney conference in Paris, and then also make a tour visiting the offices of their main publishing branches in Denmark, Sweden and Norway. An all-expense paid trip for myself and my wife to Europe! I never even thought I'd see Canada in my lifetime—and now we're on our way to Europe! A four-country tour, no less!

International fame preceded Don Rosa's first trip abroad. Quite a few photos from his initial visit to Europe involve fans and signature queues, here in Gothenburg, Sweden at the Book and Library Fair, 1991.
Photo © and courtesy Øyvind Braaten

Having broken the trans-Atlantic barrier, Don Rosa was soon to reappear in Norway. In 1992, he was given the Norwegian Comics Association honors award for 1991. Photo: Rolf Oehman/Aftenposten/Scanpix Norway/Sipa USA

In Paris I met my editor Nancy Dejgaard, who was as charming in person as she had been on the phone. I recall doing some sightseeing... the Arc de Triomphe, the Eiffel Tower, landmarks I never thought I'd see, but then I sat in this "Disney Conference" for days and days. It was Disney showing us their upcoming movies and so forth, none of which was of much interest to me. While I was watching scenes from *The Rescuers Down Under* (1990), my wife Ann was visiting more landmarks such as the Louvre with her camcorder. I would get to see the Mona Lisa on videotape when I got home.

After Paris we went to Copenhagen to visit Egmont's headquarters. After that to the main branch publishing offices in Oslo and Stockholm. I lump these three visits together because, now 20 years later, I can't separate all the new sights and new people in my poor brain due to the absolute mindboggling nature of what I was seeing...

Disney comic books were *popular* in Europe! While working for Gladstone Publishing, I had discovered that there were Disney comics still being published around Europe and the rest of the world, even though they had disappeared from wide American distribution in the 1970s. But I never in a million years would have imagined they were so *popular* in Europe! I was told that one out of every four people in a country like Norway read the weekly *Donald Duck* comic.

What? Weekly? Disney comics were *weekly* in Europe??? Oh, yes—weekly all *over* Europe. Have been for fifty years. Nonstop. Even longer in some countries. And here were entire multi-floor offices devoted to publishing those weeklies and monthlies and specials and albums and calendars and a plethora of top-selling Disney comics publications. I don't think anyone can visualize my face as I walked through corridors of offices all filled with Disney comics and toys and posters of the characters I grew up with and loved, but whose comic strip adventures I thought had disappeared from the face of the entire earth as they had disappeared in America. But no! The golden age of Disney comics still lived on... and even far more abundantly than they had ever been in America where the comics began!

And I walked down streets in Stockholm or Oslo seeing newsstands and magazine shops, sometimes three or four in sight at a time. And when I walked into such a shop, the first thing I saw was a wall of Duck comics! And I was told that in a country like Norway, the *Donald Duck* weekly was not merely the best-selling comic book, it was the best-selling *anything*! No other publication outsold the Disney comics.

And these Disney comics were virtually all stories of Barks' Ducks. Can you possibly imagine what a revelation this was for me?!?! The greatest joy of my life had been the Barks Disney comics of my youth. So much so that, even though I thought Disney comics were a thing of the past, when a miniscule Disney comic publisher sprang up in the USA, I liquidated my family's near-century-old company just for the opportunity to create stories that—to my knowledge—the world no longer wanted. But now... I am being shown that the beloved comics of my youth are still incredibly popular everywhere outside of America! I think I felt like Dorothy did when her dull Kansas farmhouse, all she ever knew, plopped down in the Land of Oz!

Comics maestro Svein Erik Søland at Egmont's Norwegian office, 2007. A longtime friend and advocate of Rosa, Søland would work on Rosa-related projects into the 2010s. Photo: Egmont Serieforlaget AS

(No, wait. That makes me think of all the creepy Munchkins. Forget that!)

Even though I've been visiting European Disney publishers and comics festivals for 25 years now, I still can never quite get used to how popular Donald Duck is there. Carl Barks' great stories alone can't explain it. The Disney name on the cover can't explain it. See if this is a possible explanation: after World War II (I'm sure you heard about it—it was in all the papers), the very first form of inexpensive mass entertainment to appear across the devastated continent of Europe was *Donald Duck* comics. From 1947 to 1950, Egmont began publishing these great American comics throughout middle and northern Europe, country by country, and other publishers took care of other areas of that continent. As a result, these characters became tantamount to national heroes in Europe! In the ensuing years and decades it became a tradition for the whole family to read the weekly *Donald Duck* comics, a tradition passed on through generations of faithful readers. (And the fact that the main feature in those *Donald Duck* comics was usually a story by Carl Barks didn't hurt one little bit!)

While Americans will always be ready to drop their interest in what is old for what is new and hot (regardless of its poor quality), Europeans are more interested in lasting quality, and show a loyalty to what has traditional value. Anyway, that's one way in which I try to explain the European popularity of Donald Duck and Carl Barks to my American friends.

Also during these visits, I met some people who became dearer friends to me than almost anyone I know in America. While I was still at my first stop in the Copenhagen offices, Nancy Dejgaard introduced me to the visiting editor-in-chief of the Norway branch, Svein Erik Søland—I already knew that name well! It was Svein Erik Søland whose ideas and suggestions were always being passed on to me by Nancy. Svein Erik was a powerhouse of new ideas, and I have always suspected that he had something to do with Nancy hiring this inexperienced American cartoonist who drew Donald Duck like Robert Crumb would. Not only that, but Svein Erik was just a really nice guy! In future volumes I'll outline how he influenced certain key later Duck stories in my timeline.

My first European trip and meeting with Svein Erik took place in early 1991. Later in 1991 came another major event in my life. Major life events were coming at me fast in this period, but this was perhaps the biggest event of my new Duck cartoonist career: "The Life and Times of Scrooge McDuck."

Watch for it—next volume! •

Rosa's earliest cover art for the first two chapters of "The Life and Times of Scrooge McDuck" (supplement to Danish *Anders And & Co.* 1992-33). See our next volume for a full-page version of this rare piece.

I Like Ike!

By Don Rosa

In previous volumes of the *Don Rosa Library* you've already seen mention of the name of Ray Foushee, my friend since high school (if not since birth), fellow comic collector and collaborator on my early comic stories. This archival feature presents some early screwball humor that Ray preserved so that you (and *I*) can still enjoy it here.

In the fall of 1970, I left Louisville to spend my second year of engineering college in a dormitory far from home. As Ray was the only other comic fan and collector I knew, I was not ready to lose communication with him. I had already grown accustomed to the pleasure of telling him about old comic books bought at flea markets, or new comics bought at the newsstand, and other comics news. In 1970 the only way to keep up this communication was for me to hand-write a message on a sheet of paper, fold it and place it into an envelope, write Ray's street address on the envelope (an address with no "@" in it!), glue something called a "postage stamp" on the envelope, and put this entire contraption into a "mailbox" for a "mailman" to deliver to Ray by hand, so that he could read my thoughts two or three days later! Can you imagine?! It's true! I swear it!

This is how humans communicated over distances in 1970. But I soon put my own Rosa twist on the idea—I drew a caricature of Ray on the envelope rather than writing his name. Soon I also drew a caricature of myself in place of the return address. Then I began drawing a gag on the envelope, perhaps referring to something that had happened during the past week. Soon I began making the postage stamp, Ray's home address and my return address label into part of the drawing!

Within a few months I was making each envelope into an elaborate gag scene, or into a parody of a magazine cover or such, with Ray's address and the Eisenhower postage stamp virtually unrecognizable as part of the drawing—and yet, as you can now see, the letters were still *all* delivered! Here we offer a selection of some of the approximately thirty-five envelopes I sent to Ray during my 1970-71 year at college.

All Illustrations with this article © and courtesy Don Rosa

Here is a grouping of the earlier, simpler envelopes. One shows Ray looking insane, labeled "It's a mad, mad, mad mad Ray": a reference to my favorite movie, in re-release at the time. Another shows Ray in a prison uniform (for reasons we don't recall) and sports a new return-address label that I just had printed. The next two show Ray with sore-looking eyes—he had just gotten his first contact lenses, which in those days were of rigid glass and painful to get used to—and Ray in his summer job as a painter. Another shows a scene from the then-current Apollo 14 moon mission, but is especially interesting in my use of the new Eisenhower postage stamp in a political poster reading "Elect Van Pooch," copying a Carl Barks gimmick! Yet another shows my increasing creativity in the placement of the postage stamp. Finally, an envelope addressed as if I were a preschool child.

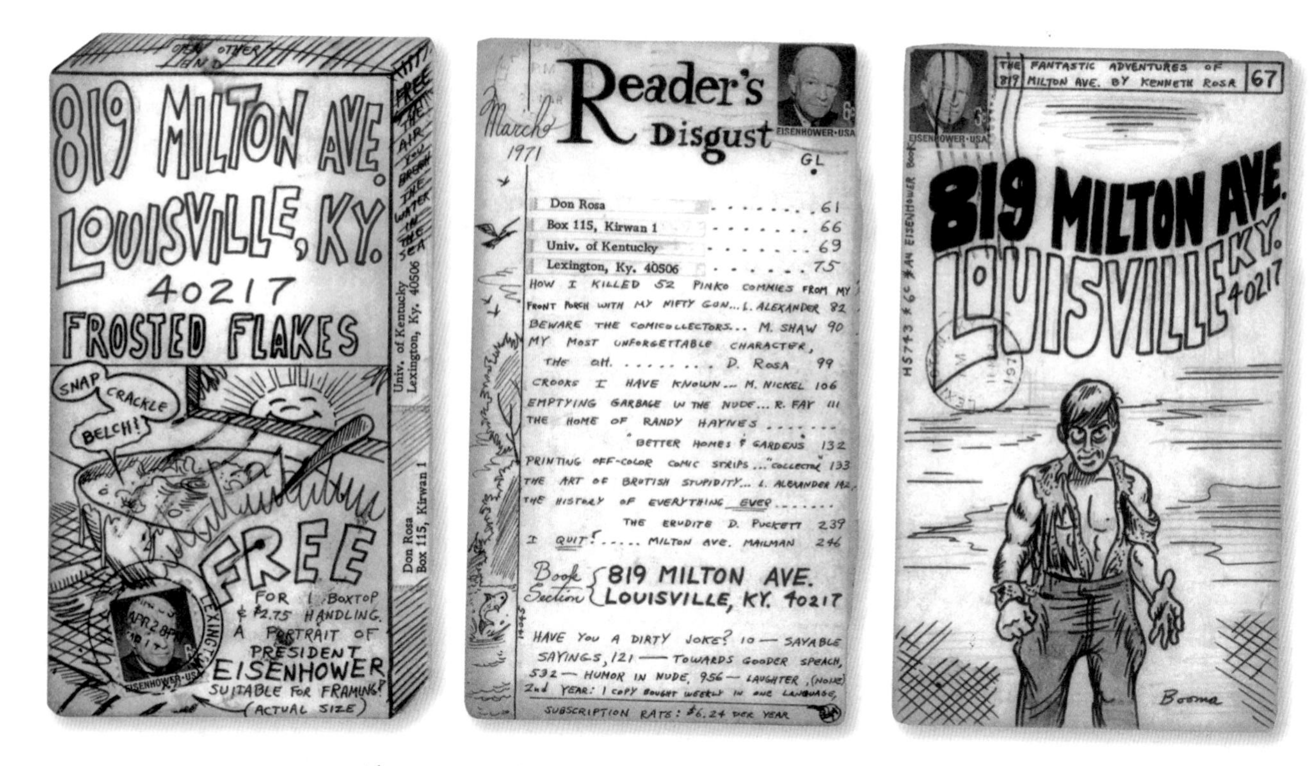

Above are parodies of a generic cereal box, a *Reader's Digest* cover, and one of the then-current type of paperback book that reprinted pulp adventure stories of the 1930s.

Below is one of my favorites, using six one-cent stamps rather than the usual six-cent stamp. The oversized six-cent stamp in the corner is a *fake* one clipped off the front of the booklet in which the stamps were sold; and yet the fake stamp was the only one the post office cancelled!

Since I was about to move back home for the summer, above was an attempt to use up the rest of my soon-to-be-useless address labels.

And then the final two envelopes, the climax of the grand postal experiment! First I warned the postman that the next envelope would be a test for him, followed a week later by a final envelope with *no* destination address. But the experiment failed—that envelope was *not* delivered to 819 Milton Ave. However, we can still include that envelope here forty years later, since the post office returned it to my college dormitory address, and the dorm forwarded it to my home address. Take a bow for the good old postal service. •

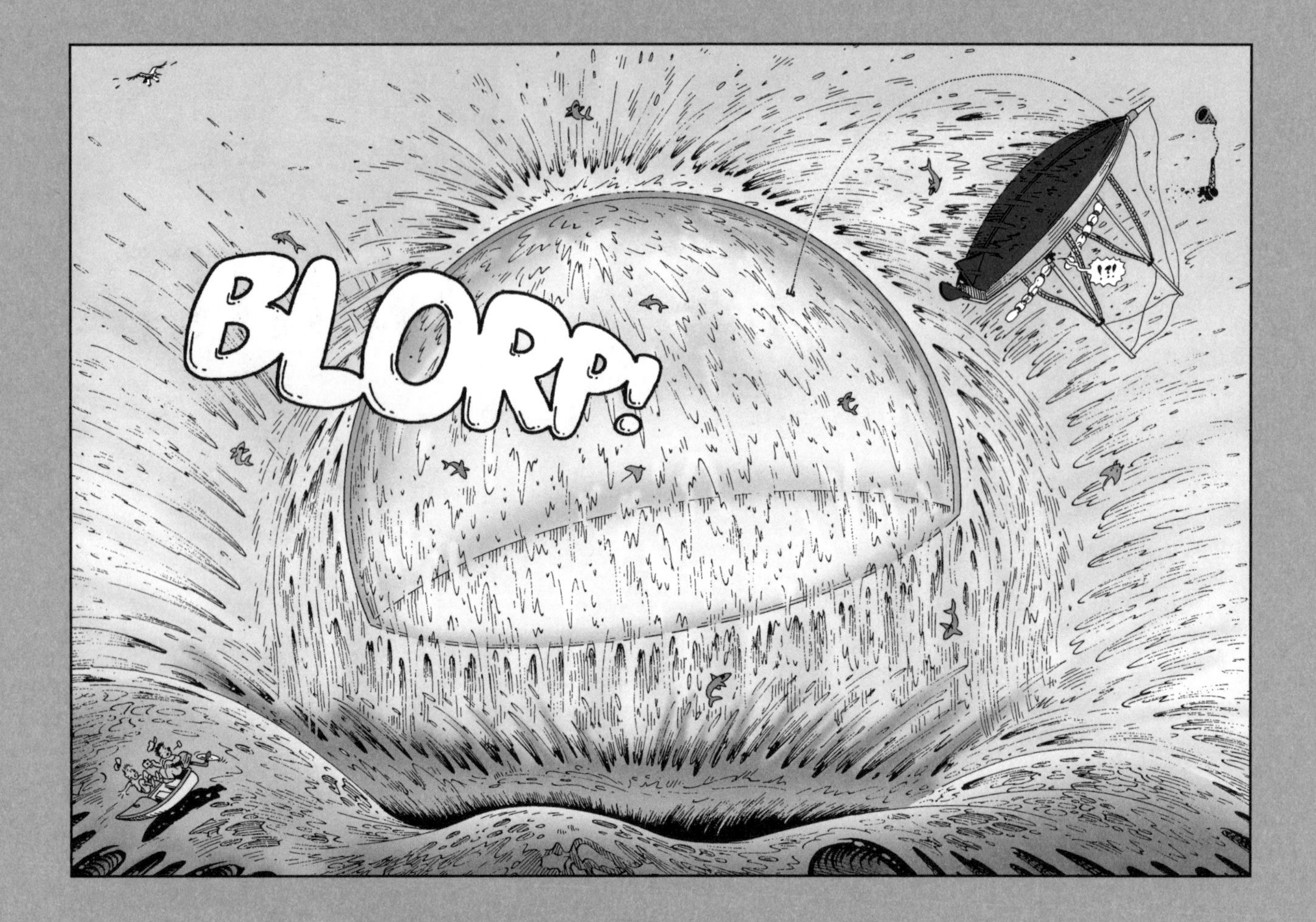

About the Editors

DAVID GERSTEIN is an animation and comics researcher, writer, and editor working extensively with the Walt Disney Company and its licensees. His published work includes *Mickey and the Gang: Classic Stories in Verse* (Gemstone 2005); *Walt Disney Treasures – Disney Comics: 75 Years of Innovation* (Gemstone 2006); and *The Floyd Gottfredson Library of Walt Disney's Mickey Mouse* (Fantagraphics, 2011-present). David has also worked with Disney in efforts to locate lost Oswald the Lucky Rabbit cartoons and to preserve the *Mickey Mouse* newspaper strip.

GARY GROTH has been publishing Don Rosa since 1970. Oh, and he also co-founded Fantagraphics Books in 1976. Fantagraphics is still going strong and he's still publishing Don Rosa. Life can't get any better than that.